Close Encounters of the Fungal Kind

Also by Richard Fortey

The Hidden Landscape: A Journey into the Geological Past

*Life: An Unauthorised Biography. A Natural History
of the First Four Billion Years of Life on Earth*

Trilobite! Eyewitness to Evolution

Fossils: The Key to the Past

The Earth: An Intimate History

*Dry Store Room No. 1: The Secret Life
of the Natural History Museum*

*Survivors: The Animals and Plants
that Time Has Left Behind*

*The Wood for the Trees: The Long View
of Nature from a Small Wood*

A Curious Boy: The Making of a Scientist

Richard Fortey

Close Encounters of the Fungal Kind

In pursuit of remarkable mushrooms

WILLIAM COLLINS

William Collins
An imprint of HarperCollins*Publishers*
1 London Bridge Street
London SE1 9GF

WilliamCollinsBooks.com

HarperCollins*Publishers*
Macken House
39/40 Mayor Street Upper
Dublin 1, D01 C9W8

First published in Great Britain in 2024 by William Collins

1

A catalogue record for this book is available from the British Library

ISBN 978-0-00-863968-6

Typeset in Dante MT Pro by
Palimpsest Book Production Ltd, Falkirk, Stirlingshire

Printed and Bound in the UK using 100% Renewable Electricity
at CPI Group (UK) Ltd

This book contains FSC™ certified paper and other controlled sources
to ensure responsible forest management.

For more information visit: www.harpercollins.co.uk/green

For my grandchildren,
Herbie, Sophia and Luke

Contents

1.	Borgo Val di Taro	1
2.	Mushrooms and toadstools	18
3.	The rotting log	37
4.	Smells	49
5.	Vampires	64
6.	Shiners	74
7.	Collaborators	81
8.	Puffers and friends	109
9.	Names names names	136
10.	Stinkers	149
11.	Parasites	159
12.	Morels and allies	172
13.	Things on sticks	183

14. Mea culpa   198

15. Eaters   205

16. Fielders   216

17. Survivors   228

18. Dung stories   247

19. Rotters   263

20. Mind blowers   281

21. Feeders   289

22. Puzzles   302

23. Perfetto!   313

     Acknowledgements   321

     Index   325

1.

Borgo Val di Taro

Trattoria Vecchio Borgo is a small, unpretentious restaurant on a narrow side street in a little Italian town in the hilly part of Emilia-Romagna. There are hundreds of restaurants in this region of Italy built to the same design – raised decking outside overshadowed by a plastic awning with scalloped edges that provides shade during the summer months, and inside a modest number of tables set for dinner. Impeccably white tablecloths are laid over red-and-white chequered sheets. The walls are decorated with a simple yellow wash, and display cheerful photographs of the chef and his friends taken over the years. They all smile at the camera, holding baskets.

The young owner, Mery, welcomes us with a warm smile and immediately brings us cold water in a flagon. It is as well we reserved our table in advance; the whole place is booked up during the festival. Mery's husband Cristiano is effusive in his welcome. He is a bald, extrovert and humorous man in early middle age with the robust proportions that are always encouraging in a chef. His gestures are generous and he is not above landing a decorous kiss on the ladies. He brings out a sample of his raw pasta to show us, which is some subspecies of spaghetti, laid out like skeins of wool on a platter. He makes it every day, rising at six to ensure the best results, and using no eggs, as the authentic recipe demands. We order it as *primi piatti* with a star ingredient to add glamour to its simple wholesomeness: fresh *porcini*. The best baby button mushrooms cannot be improved by adding other flavours. Onions, Cristiano tells us, kill the taste completely; herbs are only distracting. A glass of white wine from Umbria is all that is needed to accompany the dish.

The spaghetti arrives in a white china bowl with a wide rim, and it is delicious. I have never quite understood the concept of *al dente*, but this serving demonstrates what it means. The pasta offers a mere hint of resistance to the teeth. The *porcini* come finely cubed and generously heaped onto the pasta. There was some secret involved in their very light cooking, which I believe may have involved steeping them in hot water. Whatever, this is the apotheosis of the edible fungus, tasting simultaneously delicate and forthright, and with a texture that retains a certain crunchiness that does not compromise a lush aftertaste.

It is understandable that so many Italians are obsessed by *porcini*. Cristiano shows us a tray of the mushrooms he obtained for the kitchen earlier that day: a deep trug full of brown-capped beauties, many as big as a fist, with white stems inflated below like satisfied bellies. As we finish our meal, the mushroom collectors arrive – they are older and more weathered versions of the same faces that are pinned to the wall in the photographs. For years, these close friends have been devoted to finding special fungi in the thick woods that cover the hills around the town of Borgo Val di Taro. *Porcini* are central to their life and livelihood.

Every year Borgo Val di Taro holds a *porcini* festival, and this modest town becomes mushroom mayhem. In September 2023, brass bands play, streets and piazzas are lined with stalls, and the popular restaurants have to turn away hungry customers. The whole place is a hub of mushroom worship. For the rest of the year it is ordinary enough. Medieval ramparts built of local sandstone above the Taro river still survive on parts of its periphery and testify to its antiquity, but the old church does not boast any quattrocento masterpieces. In the old part of town narrow streets are lined with flat-fronted, four-storey dwellings, and include a few grander houses belonging to wealthier families; their sandstone walls are concealed by rendering tinted yellow or sienna, peeling off in places; in Italy this decay makes an atmospheric virtue out of slight dilapidation. The streets are closely paved with square red porphyry setts from Trentino, attractively arranged in fan design.

The suburbs comprise wider streets lined with prosperous villas, as in other towns in this part of Italy. In summer, the Taro is small and quiet, but the coarse gravel spreads that border the flow testify to violent winter storms draining rapidly off the surrounding hills. This is hard to imagine in the dry heat of the *porcini* festival. Now the Via Nazionale that runs through the middle of the old town is lined with stalls offering all manner of local produce besides fungi – great white wheels of cheese as large as car tyres, and a gallery of salamis, cured meats and sticky cakes; but in the wide Piazza Manara, *porcini* dominate everything. Great baskets of the precious delicacy are arranged by quantity and quality. Stallholders vie with one another for the best display. Choice specimens carefully arranged in shallow boxes retail at sixty euros, offering a range of cap colours from pale tan to rich umber. The soil has been brushed from each fungus to ensure mycological perfection.

Neighbouring stalls offer dried *porcini*: not the miserable little packets on sale in English delicatessens, but great drifts of finely sliced examples dried carefully in the sun to allow them to be stored safely and used over the next year. Many connoisseurs prefer to employ the dried fungi in cooking for their enhanced intensity of flavour. A few euros will buy a handful. The dried fungi are graded in quality from *ottimo* downwards; it looks as if larger specimens are the cheaper choice. Close examination reveals that there are tiny holes in some of the dried items – these will have been where the occasional fly larva feasted on the soft flesh, but the drying process will have reduced any uninvited guests to dust. The smallest and most flawless 'button' *porcini* are preserved in fat jars under olive oil – the plump shape of the jars mirrors the rotund form of the stems of these babies. They are mostly found in the smarter shops, and they are expensive. It is impossible to guess how many kilograms of the famous fungi are on display along the Via Nazionale – several hundred, perhaps? It is certainly a profusion of *porcini*, a plethora, an extravagance, a bounteous celebration. I have never seen its like before.

The area around Borgo Val di Taro is uniquely productive.

The low ground near the river has been terraced to make fields for livestock, retained by grey drystone walls constructed from roughly shaped sandstone blocks. Fungi appear on the higher wooded slopes that extend far into the hills beyond the town. In the morning, the peaks are concealed in mist, which gradually disperses as the sun gathers strength, but for a while the distant prospect resembles the landscapes beloved of Chinese artists, where much is hinted at but little revealed. The forests are mostly deciduous trees: oaks of several kinds, beech and sweet chestnut.

According to Cristiano, the ground beneath chestnut trees yields the best *porcini*. The local hunters are skilled at spotting their prey tucked into the leaf litter even though the brown caps match the colour of fallen leaves rather well. The forest floor is almost clear of the brambles that often bedevil walkers in our own woodlands. Instead, bright-red mountain cranberries flourish in small clearings. The *porcini* may grow in groups, but never far from the trees with which they have an intimate mycorrhizal relationship. Few of the trees are veterans, as the forest is carefully managed; a disease is affecting the sweet chestnuts which is ameliorated by coppicing, but this apparently does not reduce the fungal yield. *Porcini* look at their most appealing when they erupt from a mossy bank, young and firm. I wince at the overused word 'iconic', but it must apply to the shape of the young *porcini* being exploited time and again in everything from wooden nutcrackers (olive wood, with screw-down technology) to pepper pots and pincushions.

The townsfolk believe that the high humidity accompanying the morning mistiness – ultimately derived from breezes from the seas to the west – together with a warm climate in summer following snow in winter combine to produce perfect conditions for fungal fruiting. The nutrient-rich forest floor must contain a vast interlocking mat of fungal mycelium, just awaiting the right moment in summer and autumn to create an eruption of multifarious mushrooms and toadstools: the *porcini* are but one of a cornucopia of fungal riches.

Under the portico in the main square in Borgo Val di Taro an exhibition of some of these riches has been assembled by the regional fungus *gruppo*, featuring specimens tucked into mossy cushions to approximate their occurrence in the field – and to stop them drying out. In Italy, many regions have such dedicated fungus groups, some of them remarkably scholarly, and all happy to explain fungi to the tyro. Borgo Val di Taro lies close to the junction of Emilia-Romagna, Liguria and Tuscany, and has its own club of devotees. The local expert is a young woman who patiently explains to bystanders the differences between *porcini* and the usual cultivated mushroom, staple of the supermarket. Many Britons know and eat only the latter.

She demonstrates that the most striking distinction lies on the under-surface of the cap: the supermarket mushroom has gills (chocolate-coloured on the demonstration specimen) while the mature *porcini* bear what looks like a yellowish sponge in the same position. A close look reveals that the 'sponge' is actually comprised of hundreds of fine tubes about a millimetre across terminating in closely packed pores. This structure is what distinguishes *porcini* (*Boletus*) from mushrooms (*Agaricus*). Both tubes and gills are the whole purpose of the fungus – this is where the minute spores are produced that propagate the species. The difference in conformation of the spore 'factories' is so fundamental that *porcini* and mushrooms are placed in entirely different biological families. *Porcini* belong within the genus *Boletus*, and these only superficially resemble regular mushrooms in having soft flesh making up a cap and a stem – they are otherwise fundamentally distinct. Our young demonstrator gestures at the table in front of her to show that there are many and various kinds of these pore-bearing fungi, and emphasises that they should collectively be called 'boletes' – something I shall do throughout this book. One reason for the distinctive taste of *porcini* is that they are quite a different kettle of fish (to mix metaphors disgracefully) from the mushroom on sale in every supermarket.

Next, the expert gets down to detail, the real nitty-gritty, and most people stay to hear more. She explains that there are actually four different species of *Boletus* that are lumped together as *porcini*. You cannot tell them apart when cooked, and even the fresh specimens demand very close inspection. In all of them the pores begin white and darken to yellow as the spores mature. The commonest species is what the French call the Cep, *Boletus edulis*, which can grow under many different trees. I know it well. The Latin species name leaves no doubt about its edibility. It has a pale brown, convex, smooth cap, and when very fresh this is usually edged with a thin white line. The stem is lighter-coloured, often inflated below, and the upper part carries on its surface a network of narrow, raised white ridges. It is sometimes helpful to tilt the stem towards the light to see them. Bronze Bolete, *Boletus aereus*, is often darker, sometimes nearly black, and with brown tones on the stem as well, and in Britain is usually found under oaks; it is rather rare. Pine Bolete, *Boletus pinophilus*, is very similar, but often more slender, with red-brown cap tones, and prefers to live with pines. Finally, there is the Summer Bolete, *Boletus reticulatus*, which took me a very long time to be sure of its identity, because it really is very like the Cep in many features. It *does* appear early in the fungus season, and now I know it from its subtly furry cap texture. I could not understand all of the Italian of our guide, but the fact that she was stroking the cap of the mushroom as one might a cat suggests that she was noticing the same thing (the stem is also flushed pale brown). I must add that when you cut into the flesh of all these *porcini*, there is a pleasant, nutty smell, and there is no colour change; the flesh of many boletes turns quickly blue or green when damaged, and several have unpleasant odours.

This list of minutiae will give some idea of the subtleties of fungus identification in the field. Birders will know the comparable difficulties in identifying small warblers, but at least the fungi stay put and don't hop off into thick cover. For those who might say 'pooh, how can you be certain?', there is now the tool of molecular sequencing – an appropriate segment of DNA extracted from the fungus reveals how one sample relates to others. Samples of the same species will cluster together. All the *porcini* boletes are known to be 'true' species, as determined by the latest technology. It is impressive that pioneer mycologists more than a century ago had such a critical feel for these different species – fungi that even today cause lesser mortals to scratch their heads.

After the talk I ask our demonstrator about the Bitter Bolete (*Tylopilus felleus*). She does not see this species in northern Italy. Perhaps it is as well, because this is one bolete that can easily be confused with *Boletus edulis*. It is a similar colour and likes to grow in comparable places. One cap of the Bitter Bolete among a batch of *porcini* can ruin the taste of a whole dish. When it is mature, the unpleasant pretender can be recognised easily by its pink pores, but while it is of the petite dimensions preferred by gourmets, the pores are white like those of its delicious cousins. At this stage its only good distinguishing feature is a strong, raised *brownish* network on the stem. It is optional to nibble (and then spit out) the tiniest piece from the cap, when its extremely bitter taste gives it away at once. Fortunately, this pretender is usually rare, but one year I found it in abundance in a particular patch of mixed woodland in Oxfordshire. I can think of no better example to demonstrate the necessity of knowing how to recognise individual species by closely examining their every feature, with a good book to hand.

In southern Britain the numbers of *porcini* vary greatly from year to year. In Borgotaro they are reliable. In a dry year like 2023 they were still to be found at higher altitudes, tracking cooler and moister conditions. Even so, there are fluctuations; the oldest inhabitants still remember the *annus mirabilis* of 1952, when the *porcini* themselves made miniature mountains. They have been exploited for centuries in the same area. The local museum holds an unparalleled collection relating to the history of *porcini*, including an account of a document dated 1606 describing a mycological present sent by a Borgo nobleman, Flaminio Platoni, to

Ranuccio I of the grand Farnese dynasty in Parma, where the fungi were used to great effect by a famous chef called Caro Nascia.

By the nineteenth century, it was reported that almost all local families were involved with picking, pickling or drying. There was even a special word for the slicing process for the latter – *sfogliatura*. Pellegrino Artusi (1820–1911) in his book *Science in the Kitchen and the Art of Eating Well* described the subsequent routine: 'For two or three days keep them continuously exposed to the sun, then put them in stands and keep them in ventilated air and also again in the sun until they are completely dry.' In this condition Borgotaro *porcini* were finding their way as far as the USA to satisfy homesick Italians who had been forced by poverty to settle far away. My own drying technique does not rely on the unpredictable English sunshine, but uses the slow warmth of underfloor heating to the same end. Thin slices cannot be put into dry jars until they have the same texture as vegetable crisps. I notice one difference: the Italians do not remove the tubes of mature specimens, as I do, because I find their texture too greasy. Unlike mushroom gills, the tubes can be easily removed with a firm sideways push of the thumb.

The *porcini* boletes are widespread; they can be found throughout Europe, and further afield into North America and Asia. Everywhere they grow they acquire a different common name. In Britain they are Penny Buns, which is a nice description of the colour, feel and shape of the cap, although it is many years since buns cost a penny. Cep is also widely used, but it really should be spelled as it is in France: 'Cèpe'. In Germany it is Steinpilz; in Norway it is

Karl Johan's Sopp; in Sweden Stensopp; in Russian Belyy Grib. I suspect that there will be further special words for this special fungus in Basque and Armenian. This linguistic babel proves the value of the scientific name, as that is everywhere the same: *Boletus edulis*. I will use both English common names (capitalised hereafter) and scientific names in this book. My Russian friends tell me that they inhale the rich smell from their jars of dried Ceps when the long winters make them feel depressed. My Swedish friends tell me they have a word for the bitter 'fake Boletus' (*Tylopilus felleus*) – Gallsopp. I could not think of a better one.

The Borgotaro area has been awarded a unique fungal equivalent of *L'Appellation d'origine contrôlée*. The productive region was granted Protected Geographical Indication (PGI) status in 1996, a distinction of which the town is very proud. The noticeboards around the civic buildings tell you about it wherever there is an opportunity. Fungi from Borgotaro are as characteristic as Parmesan cheese from Parma. Quite apart from the *porcini*, these hills are famous for the variety and abundance of innumerable other fungi. Europe's leading mycology professor in the twentieth century, Meinhard Moser (1924–2002), regularly came here from Innsbruck to advance his research and made a particular study of the many uncommon boletes that grow near the famous comestibles. Moser wrote the first technical fungus identification handbook I ever owned (published in 1960). When I stayed in the rural Trentino family home of my friend, the distinguished mycologist Marco Floriani, not so far away from Borgotaro, I was told, proudly, 'Professor Moser slept in that bed', as if it had been Queen Elizabeth I.

A few other species of delicious fungi are on show on the festival stalls. Dark, warty balls the size of hens' eggs are recherché Black Truffles (*Tuber melanosporum*), of which more below. Then the mushroom Italians call *ovolo* is the most beautiful money can buy. It is golden, and its cap shines in the sunlight like a huge cabochon gem. Several stalls offer it for sale, but it is evidently a rare find compared with boletes. The *ovolo* is reported to be delicious, but I have never eaten it. The mushroom arises out of a white 'egg' – an enclosing bag of tissue – and smaller examples just pushing out from their nursery have the feel of a jack-in-the-box frozen in motion. When it is mature, the gills and stem are yellow, and on the stem there hangs a conspicuous, white collar-like ring (*annulus*), while the pale 'egg' from which it arose remains as a cleft cup (*volva*) at the base. This is *Amanita caesarea*, Caesar's Mushroom, and it was a favourite food of the Emperor Claudius (d. AD 54). According to the historian Tacitus, Claudius was murdered by means of poisonous fungi administered by his wife, Agrippina, which would make him the most mycologically embroiled of all despots.*

Given the elite status of the *ovolo* in the kitchen, it is ironic that the most poisonous toadstool we know is another *Amanita*, the Death Cap (*Amanita phalloides*), which also arises from an 'egg' and has a ring on the stem. I have never been fortunate enough to find a Caesar's Mushroom, but I have had many close encounters with the Death Cap, albeit never on a plate. It is a handsome toadstool, very similar in

---

* There are other diagnoses. He may have died from a natural seizure of some kind, according to modern medical opinion.

proportions to Caesar's, although some think it 'sinister', because of its deserved reputation. If as little as half a cap is consumed it kills slowly, painfully and inexorably. Many books describe the details, the worst aspect of which is that there are periodic remissions of symptoms, false hope dawns, before the agonies of poisoning return even more horribly.

The account in my *Larousse Gastronomique* (of all things) is very comprehensive and spares the reader no grisly details. I do not feel compelled to repeat them, though I have to emphasise that the lethal fungus does have to be ingested to do its work. Touching it won't kill you. The cap colour is a distinctive yellowish green, often with an odd streaky look, while the gills and ring are white, and the stem carries weak greenish bands, so only the 'bag' at its base is a shared feature with the *ovolo*. If there is a lot of rain the cap can fade to yellow, and it might pose more of a danger in this state, although it is never orange or golden. In Britain, there are some years when the Death Cap is quite common – so numerous in beech woodland on chalk near my home that my wife Jackie and I christened one locality 'Death Cap Valley'. I confess that en masse these lethal toadstools are a rather beautiful sight. Sadly, the *ovolo* is yet to be found in Britain, but since the climate is warming this is no longer as unlikely as it once was. The Isle of Wight would be a plausible landing point, where a number of rare and southerly *Amanita* species have already been recorded and there are plenty of beech trees. 'The island' was also the site of a fatal Death Cap poisoning in 2008, when the toadstools were picked in Ventnor Botanical Garden, apparently mistaken for a mushroom variety that was eaten in Thailand. The family at first blamed the sausages.

Finding Ceps in Britain is much more hit and miss than in Borgotaro. In some years they can be found with no trouble; in others they just do not show up, or when they do appear they have been discovered by slugs and flies long before you stumble across them. Occasionally, they are just perfect. A group of three Ceps I discovered in Oxfordshire growing from a mossy bank could not be surpassed. No slug had defaced them. The moss made them seem as if they were presented on green baize as a gift. They were young and firm, almost as if made from a kind of ceramic. The caps were uniformly the colour of lightly finished toast except where they faded to white at their very edge, the stems satisfyingly convex with a suggestion of Palaeolithic fertility figurines. The sunny autumn day was as near flawless as could be, with a few beech leaves turning colour and preparing to fall, but most still hanging on to await the first frost. A sunbeam picked out the boletes to add the final blessing. It seemed almost sacrilege to pick these porcinesque paragons. But I did. The correct way is to twist them gently out of the ground, doing minimal damage to the network of fungal mycelium from which they arise. They were then placed reverentially into a flat-bottomed fungus basket woven from willow, with something of the care that ensured the survival of Moses on the Nile.

When I started to recognise and collect *Boletus* in the last century, I was one of very few people scouting in the woods. It was not something that British people did. A good friend living in the New Forest would alert me when the Ceps were about, and in some years they were abundant. We did not give a thought to over-picking. Then we started to notice that others had been there before us. The Ceps had been cut off close to the ground, leaving pale little discs of sliced stems behind as evidence. We had to search longer and harder. It was clear that something had changed. We surmised that fresh Ceps were becoming part of the gourmet restaurant's bill of fare, providing a niche for commercial fungus hunters: they wanted to find a Borgo Val di Taro in Britain. Then, in the twenty-first century more people from the Czech Republic or Poland came to work in the United Kingdom, and in these countries Cep hunting is a national pastime. Poles go mad for their *Borowiki*. No doubt they wondered why the English seemed relatively indifferent to their woodland treasures. Around London, mushroom hunting was their weekend treat. The problem was that so many fungi were turned upside down to see if they had the pores beneath the cap diagnostic of the boletes. I have encountered woods where almost every milkcap or brittlegill has been turned over, gills upward, innocent victims of *porcini* mania. In this state their spore production is halted, and the reproduction of the species is compromised. This is distressing. A flower lover might feel a similar sense of dismay if she visited a favourite orchid meadow to find all the wildflowers trampled. Even worse, we heard tales of squads of ignorant 'pickers' going to the New Forest and collecting *everything* to take to an expert to sort out the profitable mushrooms from the rest, and the bycatch – innocent fungi all – summarily jettisoned.

Protection from this kind of fungal mayhem is difficult to enforce. We do not have many ancient, unfertilised open forests left in the United Kingdom, unlike the extensive tracts that cover central Europe and the spine of Italy. Forests that are easily accessible from cities are particularly vulnerable. Many of them are Sites of Special Scientific Interest (SSSI) and it is now illegal to pick there. Epping Forest, north-east of London, led the way; Burnham Beeches to the west of the capital followed, as did Nottingham Forest in the Midlands, and now the New Forest down south is protected, even though the number of successful prosecutions for illegal picking are hardly worth counting.

Now here is a paradox. In Borgotaro bolete picking has continued for centuries and still the baskets return brim full of bounty. The local hunters have special rights, but for out-of-town enthusiasts it is possible to purchase daily tickets for a few euros that entitle the visitors to harvest fungi in the hills. At the height of the fungus season cars queue to get to the booth that issues the appropriate permits. Each picker is limited to three kilograms of boletes per day. This would be a truly wondrous yield from a day in my own Chiltern Hills, west of London. Yet we know that the harvest in Italy shows no apparent sign of diminishing, even though the abundance of fungi fluctuates from year to year. Picking has not reduced, let alone exterminated the *porcini*.

I am reminded of a story I used to read to my children, *The Magic Porridge Pot*, in which a cauldron full of food would magically refill itself no matter how much was taken from it. In real life there is no such thing as a free lunch. However, it cannot be claimed that picking boletes for the table is driving them to extinction in these Italian forests. One plausible reason: the *porcini* itself is only the reproductive part of the fungus; the body of the fungus is the mycelium – that extensive and dense network of living fungal threads within the forest soil associated with tree roots of chestnut or beech. This web does not die with the plucking of the Cep. It can live for many years, even moving to adjacent trees. The fungi are nurtured by millions of minute threads scavenging the soil for minerals and other nutrients, and succoured in turn by the photosynthetic work of the trees themselves. For the fungi of Borgo Val di Taro, it is almost a magic porridge pot.

Near the end of our stay in Borgotaro we passed through the ancient gate of the town named Portello, where fungi were traded in past centuries. A series of steep sandstone steps lead through an arch towards the Via Nazionale. Laboriously climbing towards us, a local man with slightly wild hair and wearing a leather jerkin was carrying a woven willow basket over each arm, laden with *porcini*. He must have returned from the hills on the other side of the river, no doubt en route to replenish some of the heaps that had sold during the festival. This was a timeless moment. A similar man in similar garb carrying the same deep rectangular baskets could have taken those steps at the time the Farnese dynasty were still omniscient in Parma. Even the *porcini* were unchanged.

2.

Mushrooms and toadstools

This is a book about fungi, a biological kingdom of equal status to the kingdoms of animals and plants, but one that has never attracted blockbuster television treatments accompanied by a full symphony orchestra. Many naturalists know little of the secrets of moulds, mushrooms, truffles and toadstools, and the membership of mycological fan clubs is a tiny fraction of those dedicated to birds (which we now know are just flying dinosaurs). I spent my professional life as a palaeontologist in the Natural History Museum in London, focusing on ancient, extinct animals like trilobites, but fungi have been my source of pleasure and perplexity for more than sixty years. Many people find them alien and threatening: the way so many toadstools appear so quickly and disappear with equal dispatch; their strange forms and colours; their reputation as poisoners. A Red Cage Fungus (*Clathrus ruber*) appearing on a flowerbed like a scarlet buckyball weirdly emerging from an egg can still astonish even the most blasé fungus lover. I find the strangeness of fungi is exactly what is exciting about them. The reference in my title to the movie *Close Encounters of the Third Kind* acknowledges this otherworldliness, and honours a third, great kingdom of life.

Calculations of how many species of fungi exist in the wild are always changing – and inexorably increasing. A well-argued 2022 estimate of three million species is double that made by the redoubtable British mycologist David Hawksworth in 1991, and it is not difficult to find still larger numbers. It is less controversial that only about 150,000 species have been named scientifically, so what remains to be discovered must be vastly more than what we know now. I have already spent several thousand words describing something of the natural history of just one or two boletes, which points up the impossibility of attempting to be comprehensive. Instead, I will focus on a selection of the larger fungi (macrofungi), the kind that might be spotted on a country walk. I delve later into a handful of microfungi that have particularly caught my attention. I make no pretence of a systematic trawl through the myriad different architectures that fungi have invented. I focus on just a few of those species that have made me think or wonder – my own Close Encounters – on a lifetime's journey through a vast kingdom. Some science needs to be introduced, particularly where DNA sequencing has cast new light on old problems, but it is the unique charm of the mushrooms themselves that is centre stage. For those who are interested in field identifications, there is now a range of wonderful illustrated guides.* For those who get 'hooked', such books (and related online resources) take them further, but the sheer number of species can be intimidating, even to an experienced collector. The enumeration of species can become an obsession, rather like that of an extreme 'twitcher' preoccupied with adding to the list rather than the beauty of the bird. My intention is to explain the role that fungi play in nature, to illuminate some of their extraordinary adaptations, to celebrate fungal heroes and villains, and to recall special moments in woods and fields.

The distinction between mushrooms and toadstools is not at all scientific, but it could be described as traditional. Both are agarics – that is, fleshy fungi that release their spores from gills on the underside of the cap. Mushrooms are those agarics that can be welcomed on to the table – the edible favourites. Toadstools are agarics that cannot be eaten, in some cases because they are toxic or even deadly, but in many more cases because they do not taste good, or are too small to bother with. The distinction has nothing to do with scientific classification. On this criterion there can be mushrooms and toadstools in the same genus, with the frying pan as the terminological referee. To many readers the word 'mushroom' might well be synonymous with the cultivated

---

* Geoffrey Kibby has recently completed his heroic, self-illustrated four-volume account of British mushrooms and toadstools, and it would be hard to beat Thomas Laessoe and Jens Petersen's *Fungi of Temperate Europe* (2019), with some 2,800 fungi described with photographs. Beginners still find Roger Phillips's pioneering *Mushrooms* (1981) very useful. The 2005 New Naturalist *Fungi* volume by Brian Spooner and Peter Roberts makes the scientific background thoroughly accessible.

variety (*Agaricus bisporus*) that occupies so much shelf space in the supermarket, possibly allowing the Field Mushroom (*Agaricus campestris*) as an honoured guest. The use of 'mushroom' more broadly for all edible species and 'toadstool' for the rest may be arbitrary, but it is a useful flag in the field; I do not guarantee perfect consistency. The mushroom family Agaricaceae is capable of a more formal definition, but then (for scientific reasons we will come across) will include things that do not look like mushrooms. The word originally derives from an ancient Greek root, so it could be said that agarics have a long pedigree. I met an Irishman in our woods using the word 'garrets' – same word, local variation. The boletes introduced at the beginning of this book have densely packed tubes where the agarics have their gills, and on many restaurant menus they, too, would be advertised as 'wild mushrooms'. *Boletus* is another name that has come through from the classical era. I rather relish these antique roots (or should that be mycelia?).

Agarics and boletes present variations on a cap-and-stem construction that provides the best means of distributing minute spores to perpetuate their kind. Imagine if a primitive mushroom were like an open umbrella. This would allow the spore-bearing surface to be raised above the ground to reach the breeze. The underside of the umbrella would make a protected area for spore generation equal in span to the upper surface. By adding fine gills (*lamellae*) radially under the umbrella, the area of fertile, spore-bearing surfaces is multiplied under the same 'cap' – the mycologist Nicholas Money has estimated a twenty-fold increase. It is hardly surprising that this efficient system has evolved more than once. Another way of doing the same thing would be to create numerous tiny, spore-bearing tubes under the coverall: the *Boletus* option. This has also been repeatedly evolved. It might be said that the shape of a mushroom is almost a logical deduction.

Many other fungal designs will be encountered in this book, all of them dedicated to the same end – to cast their millions of spores upon the four winds. They can be brackets or puffballs, or 'corals' or crusts of any colour and texture, or inconspicuous spheres, or brightly coloured waxy cups. The most general description for this culmination of the life cycle is 'fruit body' – the sexual reproductive phase. The technical term for this is *sporocarp*, but I am attempting to keep such scientific labels to a minimum in general. However, I do add a few such terms in brackets for accuracy where it is appropriate. 'Fruit body' is a good description of what is, after all, the fruition of a life cycle. In some fungi it can last no more than a few hours. When it rains, tiny inkcaps (*Coprinopsis*) appear on my lawn shortly after dawn and are gone before the sun is high in the sky. Conversely, some hard brackets last for years; tough *Ganoderma* with an upper surface as hard as a tortoise shell appears at the base of living and dead trees, each season adding a new spore-bearing layer underneath. They are both accurately described as fruit bodies; their different life strategies are dedicated to furthering the same reproductive imperative.

Mushrooms and toadstools are the natural culmination of the food and energy accumulated by the mycelium – the hidden workhorse of every species. Fungi do not grow in the same way as plants that conjure their substance from sunlight and air. Fungi take advantage of the creative work of plants, either by consuming and recycling plant material (*saprotrophs*), or by entering into mutually beneficial partnerships with them. The basic building blocks of fungi are not blocks at all but tiny threads (*hyphae*) that are often less than a hundredth of a millimetre wide. These threads conduct nutrients and chemicals to where they are needed for growth. They actively seek out food most appropriate to the fungus, questing through wood or litter. Under the microscope, hyphae all look superficially rather similar, but they carry the instructions to make a Pin Mould or a Parasol Mushroom. Fruit bodies are constructed of hyphae, woven into tissues that can make a stout stem, or a colourful cap. They intertwine to buttress a gill, or spin precise cups or spheres to harbour spore production. They can even insinuate themselves between the tiny cells of trees and herbs, as ubiquitous as they are unseen.

Hyphae work together to construct mycelium, the fungal network that scavenges nutrients from the soil, and only appears when a mushroom is plucked carefully from the leaf litter as dangling white threads – apparently so feeble, yet so potent. Mycelium infiltrates soil as memory infuses consciousness. There are estimates of its abundance that leave you giddy: that if unravelled the mycelium associated with a single tree would stretch to the moon. When I was writing about the history of life, I always struggled to describe the meaning of four billion years of geological time. It was never satisfactory, because our minds are not geared to appreciate such numbers. It is equally difficult to imagine the living soil so minutely penetrated and enmeshed by living threads. On occasion, a damp log can look almost covered in a fog or shroud of pale fuzz where mycelium is most active, allowing us a brief image of its ubiquity. Merlin Sheldrake has done a brilliant service in explaining the networks generated by mycelium in his 2022 book *Entangled Life*, which rejoices in the interconnectedness of mycelial systems, and how collaboration governs success as mycelium fuses or spreads according to opportunities for nourishment. Possibly the most unusual aspect of the life of mycelium is what it means for the concept of a fungus *individual*. The fungal network fans out as it grows, but older parts can and do die out where nourishment is no longer available. Hence physically separate parts of the mycelium can take on a separate existence, and, migrating over time, may become widely removed from one another; but they are still the same individual (*genet*). Modern DNA identification techniques based on molecular sequencing offer proof of this identity. One fungus individual can be dispersed, but united in history. A split personality is the norm.

When I was young I enjoyed a series of dramatically illustrated books entitled 'Ripley's Believe it or Not!' They featured lurid stories of the strange-but-true variety somewhat allied to the *Guinness World Records* books. I would harangue my parents with some gem from Ripley, such as 'Did you know the venom from a bite of the Australian Fierce Snake can kill ten thousand mice?' The best example of strange-but-true was yet to come, but how I would have relished announcing to my elders that the largest organism on Earth was a mushroom! No example better exemplifies the potential immortality of mycelium. In the forests of Oregon in north-west USA a single individual of the parasitic Honey Fungus *Armillaria ostoyae* spread from tree to tree to cover an area exceeding nine hundred hectares. Genome evidence proved it was indeed one organism. Deducing the weight of the mycelium was bound to be approximate, but there is general agreement that taken together it would outweigh a blue whale. It was the greatest! The fruit bodies would contribute an additional weight at the right time – clusters of yellow-capped, slightly scaly mushrooms, with pale gills and a rather tough stem carrying a ring near the top. As an inverse corollary, it could be argued that this is the organism with the *lowest* fertility in the world, because each of the hundreds (if not thousands) of mushrooms it includes sheds millions (if not billions) of spores, and this happens over very many years – more than two thousand if the original report is to be credited. If just one spore from each mushroom had germinated successfully and grown onwards, there would be no trees left anywhere on our planet.

A germinating spore releases a tiny hyphal thread that must 'taste' the environment to see if suitable nutrients are available. A saprotrophic species, for example, must land in appropriately moist leaf litter. The vast majority of spores will not survive the hit-or-miss of dispersal. When a spore *does* germinate in a favourable site, its hyphae must then assert themselves if there are species already established in the same area. It is tempting to invoke 'nature red in tooth and spore'. And if *that* hurdle is passed the hyphae will branch and coalesce to set the mycelium off on its outward quest for nourishment.

Whether it is on a Petri dish in a laboratory or litter on the forest floor, the feeding threads will radiate outwards from the starting point, drawing a mycelium circle that in some agarics may take years to become yards across. When the circle is large enough and the conditions of temperature, rainfall and day length are just right, and a compatible mycelial partner is nearby, the network will organise to produce 'buds' (*primordia*) that will develop into fruit bodies. For large agarics the whole process rarely happens overnight, as is sometimes assumed, but once a mushroom starts to expand its stem (*stipe*) to lift the cap upwards it really does become the ideal subject for time-lapse photography. As the stem extends the cap opens out like an umbrella in a rainstorm: it is a synchronised performance. Since fungi are otherwise hard to photograph in motion, there are countless bravura performances available on the Internet of agarics arising in their reproductive glory. It is as if flaunting a hundred different kinds of parasols is the whole story rather than just the climax of countless questing explorations by tiny hyphal threads. The opening of the cap heralds the ripening and release of the spores in their millions – or rather, billions. A study on the Cultivated Mushroom suggested that more than 1.3 billion spores are released when a single fruit body matures. We are back to the problem of the age of the Earth: four mushrooms yield more spores than the years that have elapsed in the history of life. It is kind-of relevant but also kind-of absurd: nobody can really grasp what it means. Time outwits us, just as the fecundity of a single mushroom is a quantity beyond the grasp of a creature for whom three score and ten is both a lifespan and a calibration of reality.

When mushrooms develop they tend to fruit at the same time around the periphery of the mycelial web, producing a fairy ring. It is, perhaps, a prosaic explanation compared with the charming idea of wood sprites dancing in circles, but the rings are marvellous in their own way as a demonstration of the hidden life of agarics. Some saprotrophs like the Clouded Funnel (*Clitocybe nebularis*) are very often discovered in clearly marked circles in deep leaf litter. Rings of mushrooms can be found in grass as well as in woodland. In an open part of the New Forest I discovered one splendid example produced by a scarce species, Spotted Blewit (*Lepista panaeolus*), that was probably a hundred feet across, with several dozen fine mushrooms on display; it must have been decades in the making. The most obvious rings are produced in short turf by the common Fairy Ring Mushroom (or Champignon) (*Marasmius oreades*) – a modestly sized pale-buff agaric with a relatively long, thin and very tough stem, pale, widely spaced gills, and a smell of bitter almonds. This mushroom drives the keepers of bowling greens to distraction because it often kills a circle of grass as it advances, and paradoxically enriches the soil ahead, so its progress is marked by a brown circle outlined in deep viridian. Bowling greens are supposed to look like flawless carpets. Mowing machines and rabbits help to keep turf short and favour ring growth. Unlike rabbits, fairy rings cannot be discouraged from growing by the shaking of fists and the utterance of curses. The Fairy Ring Mushroom is an acceptable edible species – but only its cap – and once a fairy ring is identified the fruit bodies can be followed around the circle.

However, there is a poisonous toadstool that often grows in the same habitat, also in rings, also often off-white – the Fool's Funnel (*Clitocybe rivulosa*). On one occasion I discovered the two different fungi with overlapping rings, so a careless picker might have made a serious mistake. The Fool's

Funnel has much more crowded gills and a shorter, softer stem, and the cap can be depressed in the centre, where the *Marasmius* often has a convex 'knob' in the middle. Trusting the differences does require a measure of self-confidence. Fairy rings also demonstrate how some parts of the mycelial web may die. Semicircles and arcs are commonly found in both grassland and woodland. You have to sketch in the rest of the ring in your imagination.

Mushroom or toadstool, after collection their identification follows a protocol that soon becomes second nature. The cap colour is the first thing to notice, but by no means the most important. Is it slimy or dry? The colour of the gills is at least as significant: white, black, brown, pinkish, in every shade. Fungi with nearly identical caps can have very different gills (their spores are usually the same colour), and vary greatly in stature. How are the gills attached to the stem? Do they run down it, or turn up towards it – or maybe they do not quite reach it? Does the stem have a ring upon it like a short skirt or a bracelet – or lack such a feature altogether? Does the flesh change colour if it is bruised, and is it tender or tough, or exude a bitter juice? Is there an odour? Is there a bulb or a bag at the base of the stem, and does it root down into the ground? A beginner can be surprised to see an experienced mycologist holding a tiny toadstool up to the light and sniffing it as if it were a fine glass of wine. It could be said that the identification of a mushroom employs every human sense except hearing, but that has not stopped me wishing that a particularly obscure species could tell me its name.

★   ★   ★

Fungi are so numerous and so diverse that there has to be some preliminary understanding of how the great kingdom is subdivided, if only to stop the reader becoming overwhelmed. Without a map nobody could find a way through the innumerable species out there. The question is: what map? There is now a vast quantity of data from molecular studies that have thrown up all manner of new insights into classification. Many such discoveries concern how families of fungi are constituted, and these tend to be of greatest interest to a dedicated specialist rather than a dilettante fungus lover like myself. Nonetheless, the essentials are important. We need a vocabulary as well as a map before we can make progress. Nineteenth-century mycologists had good microscopes and made many discoveries. Some of these pioneers were superb artists. Beatrix Potter was enamoured of fungi before she developed the animal characters that immortalised her. Potter's fungal drawings are as exquisite as they are accurate; it is possible to make confident identifications from them even today. She mastered the microscope and observed spores in the process of germination. If the scientific establishment in the late nineteenth century had been more generous to the female sex, she might have been known for mycology rather than storytelling. Even more extraordinary were the brothers Tulasne, who must wait a while for an introduction. Before the beginning of the twentieth century, the broad patterns of fungal life had been delineated by a series of remarkable and prescient observers – more than I can do justice to. We have to begin there.

The larger fungi that are the focus of this book were soon

divided into two great groups based on their reproductive structures observed at high magnification. All mushrooms and toadstools, boletes, puffballs and bracket fungi on trees are Basidiomycetes. The name is derived from the unifying feature of all these multifarious fungi – their spores are born on the apices of a special, sausage-shaped cell, the basidium. A section through a gill of a mushroom shows both sides lined with these cells, which are supported by hyphae forming a layer at the centre of the gill. The gills are there to support a fertile covering (*hymenium*) of basidia that are the factories for a vast output of spore production. Each basidium usually bears four spores like jewels on the edge of a crown. When they are mature, a special mechanism launches them into the space between the gills to be carried off in an air current. Professor Terence Ingold, who studied spore release in detail, described the basidium as 'a spore gun of precise range'. You may prefer Nicholas Money's comparison with Wile E. Coyote, the cartoon character who travels briefly horizontally into space before succumbing to the pull of gravity.

All this happens at a scale measured in thousandths of a millimetre (micron μm). The basidium of the Field Mushroom (*Agaricus campestris*) is about twenty microns long, and the spores it carries are about seven microns in length. Very few agarics have spores longer than 15 microns, and some are no larger than rod-like bacteria. In fungi with tubes rather than gills – boletes and many bracket fungi – the basidia line the sides of the tiny cylinders on the underside of the cap. There are some crust fungi and 'corals' that have neither gills nor tubes, and in these the basidia simply

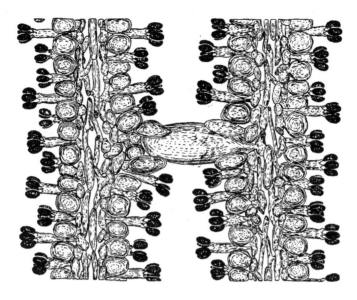

Basidia, each bearing four spores, lining the gills of Hairsfoor Inkcap
(*Coprinopis lagopus*) as portrayed a century ago by
Arthur Henry Reginald Buller.

cover the fertile surfaces. The club-like corals are often little
more than candelabras covered with spores waiting to be
released. I shall refer to all these kinds of fungi simply as
'basidios' hereafter.

The second great group of larger fungi is termed
Ascomycetes, including morels and other cup fungi, wood-
warts, Candlesnuff and many thousands of smaller and less
conspicuous fungi. Their sexual spores develop in enclosed
structures called asci rather than being released directly
into the atmosphere, as in basidios. Asci are developed in
a palisade – the fertile surface (*hymenium*) can line the inside
of an open cup or disc, or be enclosed inside small flasks
or spheres. Asci are generally elongate, sac-like and almost
invariably include eight spores, which are much more

varied in form, and often larger than, those carried on basidia. They can be thin threads or fat, spiky balls, or divided into compartments, black, brown or colourless, according to species.

When they are mature the spores are forcibly ejected from the asci, and puffed up into the air currents – hence their informal name 'spore shooters' (as opposed to 'spore droppers' – basidios). I have watched the process under the microscope, and it can be sudden and surprising. In nature, cup fungi will exhale a visible, hazy puff of spores into a passing breeze. The different ways asci release their spores is important in their scientific classification – some asci have neat 'lids' that open like hatches, others have double walls that change on maturity. I shall refer to this great clan simply as 'ascos' here, in line with 'basidios' – the 'mycete' parts of the formal names just indicate that they are fungi. I find two other informal terms useful in describing ascos, although neither is strictly employed scientifically today. 'Discos' are ascomycetes like cup fungi (*Peziza*) and morels (*Morchella*) where the hymenium is openly visible – as in the interior lining of a bowl-like fruit body, or the top surface of a tack-like one – and 'pyrenos' are those in which the hymenium is concealed inside a flask-like structure, usually blackened with melanic pigments (*pyro* indicates 'burned'). Modern studies have revealed that these former categories have arisen several times from different ancestors – they remain useful here only as descriptive shorthand.

The division between ascos and basidios is an ancient one. Convincing fossils of ascos have been found remarkably well preserved in a Scottish silica deposit known as the Rhynie Chert, accompanied by other microfungi. This rock is of Devonian age (*c.* 410 million years old), taking us back close to the origin of terrestrial plants. The separation of basidios and ascos from a common ancestor is likely to have happened even further back in time. Some botanists suspect that fungi accompanied plants from water on to land, building towards the mutually beneficial

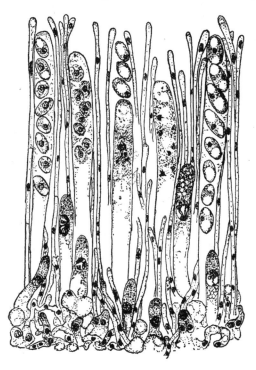

A section of the spore-bearing surface lining the cup (apothecium) of the asco *Neottiella rutilans* showing the sac-like asci with eight spores, interspersed with long narrow sterile cells (paraphyses).

collaboration between the two kingdoms that persists in their partnerships today. It is conceivable that plants would have failed to colonise the land without their fungal partners scavenging vital elements such as phosphorus. Not surprisingly, fossils of fungi are very rare, as they decay so quickly, but a perfectly recognisable inkcap has been discovered inside a specimen of Miocene amber (c. 16 million years ago). Spores are commoner, but often hard to match with those of living species. The earliest known basidio fossils are their distinctive feeding threads (*hyphae*) from beautifully preserved material contemporaneous with early coal deposits and about 330 million years old. For much of geological time, speculation has to take the place of facts.

I must briefly visit another, controversial Devonian fossil, *Prototaxites*, that has been claimed as an asco and has attracted sensational headlines of the 'When Fungi Ruled the World!' variety. The 'thing' forms columnar structures that are mostly rather small, but can attain a height of more than eight metres, making it by far the largest terrestrial organism in the earlier part of the Devonian period, so the hype is not without foundation. Although *Prototaxites* was discovered in Canada in 1843, it long resisted definitive interpretation, but the fungus version seems to be carrying the day. The early land plants that lived alongside *Prototaxites* were low herbs, so it would indeed have towered above its photosynthesising neighbours, and surely must have lived for many years to achieve such a size, even though it is constructed only of tiny interwoven 'hyphal' strands. Surreal reconstructions of its living landscape show looming, pointed pillars overshadowing their lowly plant companions drenched in atmospheric ancient twilight. Some ascus-like structures have been found associated with the fossil, so the claim that it was a giant asco achieved wide currency, even though such long-lived, Brobdingnagian fungi are unknown among living members of this group.

Recalling that nearly all fungi rely on feeding on, or part-nering with, photosynthesising plants, I find the size difference between plants and alleged fungus really prob-lematic. If *Prototaxites* were feeding upon dead plant material it would be strange enough, but if it were a parasite that would be even stranger. There are no cat fleas bigger than the cat. If a mutually beneficial association had already been established, that is not so different from the relationship

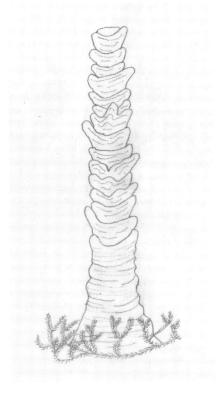

Sketch by my colleague Paul Kenrick of the giant enigmatic Devonian *Prototaxites*, which has been claimed as a fungus. Note the small size of the herbs among which it grew.

between *porcini* and chestnut trees in Borgo Val di Taro – but it does not make sense for the fungus to be bigger than the tree. I have only once had a close encounter with a fungus outsizing its partner. That was in western Newfoundland, where on very poor soil, and in the face of almost continuous strong winds, diminutive willow trees grew – you might say crawled – close to the ground, and on calm days in the fall their associated boletes actually 'overtopped' them. Special circumstances sometimes produce paradoxical results, but even in this case the fungus was nothing like eight times the height of its host. French mycologists seem to me to have put forward the most sensible explanation of *Prototaxites*. They claim it is comparable in structure to a lichen – that is, it is a collaboration between an asco fungus and a photosynthesising partner (possibly a blue-green 'alga') forming a living 'skin' that could grow through the seasons. Extant lichens can live for centuries, and their collaborative partnership makes them the toughest organisms on Earth. *Prototaxites* was not reliant on the plants it grew among and led its own strange life. Maybe this was 'when giant *lichens* ruled the Earth'. These are not part of my story here.

3.

The rotting log

In the small piece of beech woodland that we purchased in the Chilterns, some things have just been left to rot. A wild cherry tree – more than sixty feet tall – snapped in a gale and came to rest among the bluebells. I have been watching its slow disintegration for more than ten years. This tree had grown in competition with beech trees in our fragment of forest, which for all its undisturbed appearance has been managed by human hands for nearly a thousand years for useful timber; its official classification is 'ancient, semi-natural woodland'. The beeches had been cultivated for the nineteenth-century furniture trade, and long before that had supplied London with firewood, until the discovery of useful coal and the construction of canals to take it around Britain; log fires then became redundant. Beech trees continued to provide wood for the tough backs of bristle scrubbing brushes until the middle of the twentieth century, when plastic ousted natural materials. Since then, these trees have grown as they pleased, vying for the clear light above the hills. Their trunks rise nearly straight, just gently bowed this way and that to provide a pleasing distraction from monotony. Our wild cherry trees grew alongside the beech, so that their trunks became fine stands of unbranched timber, reaching for their share of the heavens, where in April they burst into extravagant white blossom for just a few weeks, when petals rain down from above like gentle snowflakes.

Cherry wood is brittle, and a winter gale proved too much for our tree; the upper fifty feet split off messily and crashed down on to the beech leaves that make up the litter on the ground. Its photosynthetic work was over. From now on the tree was a victim in the kingdom of the fungi. I could examine it closely where it lay, checking the stages of its decomposition. The thinner twigs and higher branches had broken in the fall, and would not last long. The trunk proved a more serious proposition, but its long-term destination was decay into obliteration. How are the mighty fallen? In ways unseen by human eyes, the tree's demise stimulated the mycological underworld into action. At the microscopic scale a new phase in the cycle of life was beginning, as the resources that the tree had sequestered for sixty years or more became available for exploitation. Millions of cellular 'mouths' could be fed. Mycelium would be quickening into active life that had been in a state of dormancy or suspended animation within the tissues of the tree itself for many years, or hanging on in clefts and crannies. Who knows how many different fungal species were lurking, biding their time? Sugars sequestered in the sapwood – the fruits of the tree's photosynthesis – now provide nutrients for hundreds of millions of single-celled yeast fungi, the foot soldiers in the advance guard of decomposition. The internal plumbing of the tree that connects trunk with twig now supplies elaborate conduits for fungal colonisation; bark that once kept unwanted organisms away from the vulnerable tissues of the tree now serves to seal in the decomposers as they set to work.

The bark of wild cherry is rather particular, forming a shiny casing around each branch and trunk. It has a bronzed and polished look to it. It never seeks to break lengthways, but can be ripped cross-wise; it is extremely tough but also flexible. When beech bark gets weathered it can be picked off in pieces and broken like a biscuit, but cherry bark is obdurate. It outlasts the wood that it protects; I have found thin cylinders of bark left behind on the woodland floor once the wood within has completely rotted away. This bark is evidently stuffed full of chemicals to deter invaders. Which is fine for the fungi consuming the wood within, but becomes more of a problem when the fungus is ready to produce its fruiting body to propagate and spread its spores. The fallen cherry had been processed by hidden mycelium for some months before blatant evidence of fungal activity became visible from the outside of one of the fallen branches.

Cherry bark has transverse 'blisters' at intervals along its length that provide zones of weakness. From several of these I observed very white fungal matter, a kind of mycelial cushion, I suppose, made from many thousands of hyphal strands and oozing out from the interior of the branch. Within a few days, the cushions had extended beyond their exit point and started to form circular patches several centimetres across on the branch, growing on *top* of the shiny bark barrier, like a prisoner prospering after a release from confinement. Several patches were visible, most of them forming on the underside of the branch in question. Their white surfaces started to develop a kind of corrugation, a wrinkling, and as they grew the central parts, which seemed to be thicker, turned a darker creamy colour. Within a few days the wrinkles had grown into 'teeth', readily visible to the naked eye. Under a lens, these 'teeth' resemble nothing more than an untamed Alpine landscape, but they are, of course, the apotheosis of the fungal life cycle, for on their surface the spore-producing cells – the basidia – had already started to release the countless colourless, sausage-shaped spores that would potentially spread the fungus through the wood and beyond. This was how our cherry succoured the Toothed Crust (*Basidioradulum radula*) to be an early coloniser of its dead wood; it was a trailblazing saprotroph.

In late spring a strange white knob appeared on the flank of the felled trunk: it looked almost as if someone had hammered it in there, but it was the other way round – the knob had pushed its way out of the tree. It grew larger every day. Perhaps it was more like a bag being blown up slowly by some sprite living inside the log. It seemed almost too large to emanate from a fallen trunk, but it kept on growing. As it did it turned distinctly yellow and seemed to separate into a stem and the beginnings of a cap, but one with a curiously inflated margin, like puffy lips. Finally, it started to flatten out and turned into something like a regular bracket fungus, but kept its soft texture all the while. Some milky drops exuded from its growing edge. The bracket was Chicken of the Woods

(*Laetiporus sulphureus*), sometimes called the Sulphur Polypore, but there was no hint of the tar smell of the Sulphur Knight (*Tricholoma sulphureum*). Shallow pores appeared beneath the growing cap, and this is where the spores would be discharged. It was quite a specimen.

Chicken of the Woods is rather a desirable edible fungus, but only if it is young and soft and can be cut with a knife – when it is almost like cutting through Cheddar cheese. It seems to like cherry wood, and sometimes piles up bracket upon bracket if it is really happy, but it will also readily grow from the dead wood of many other trees. It is even found on yew, which is notoriously poisonous and hosts few fungi. I have found it on a yew tree in a dark corner of an ancient churchyard where its yellow flesh shone with a supernatural brilliance, and one not altogether benign. It is alleged that some people are allergic to this fungus and have vomited violently not long after ingesting it. The launch of a book by a well-known 'mushroom guru' was marred when the gourmet dish he had prepared from this 'Chicken' as a special and appropriate treat made several of his guests quite ill. Maybe they were just allergic to the flesh of *Laetiporus* (after all, some people cannot eat any mushrooms at all). But there are other possibilities. Perhaps one of the fruit bodies had been harvested from a specimen growing on yew, which had absorbed some of the toxins from the tree? If this were the case, we should be as careful to identify the host correctly as to get the mushroom right.

Another possibility is that there are more species of *Laetiporus* than we think: could it be that the yew 'Chicken' is a different and more dangerous species than the cherry

'Chicken'? One is good to eat, the other bad. More and more 'cryptic' species are being recognised, as the ties between fungus and host are discovered to be closer than was once thought. The precautionary principle might suggest we should take no chances and eschew the Chicken of the Woods, or at the very least test our sensitivity to it before embarking on a plateful. Despite its soft texture, this particular Chicken endures for months, becoming a white ghost of its former self. The flesh turns corky and dense. We left our example to see what happened to it. Two specialist species of beetle were able to eat it, but this particular spawn of our cherry did not prove a popular item on the menu in the forest in its old age. An obstinately persistent white lump lay on the woodland floor for months.

As winter approached, one of the small branches developed frills. Along its length a series of dozens of thin little shelves or brackets were lined up – a few of them doubled up to resemble some weird new kind of leaf – and arranged themselves as if deliberately to please the eye. The part of each bracket closer to the branch was a pleasing yellow orange, while the distal edge was nearly white and crimped like a petticoat. My first thought was that they were rather delicate examples of the common Hairy Curtain Crust (*Stereum hirsutum*) that can be well nigh ubiquitous on lying beech logs in the early stages of decay. A close look dispelled that idea at once. They were not really brackets after all. Each frill was carried on a short stem, so it could better be described as a fan. The branch had become a fan dance! Then again the underside of the fan was gently veined and wrinkled, and paler than the top of the cap. This would be the spore-bearing surface. The texture of the whole was rather soft, unlike the rubbery 'feel' of the Curtain Crusts. This was something really interesting.

I found it identified in a big book on *The Fungi of Switzerland*. We had the Crimped Gill (*Plicaturopsis crispa*) on cherry in our own wood! In Switzerland it had been found on several types of broadleaved trees, though no mention was made of cherry. Could this be a new substrate for this charming little fungus? There seemed to be very few records of it from the United Kingdom in 2016, so it was possible that it was becoming commoner than it once was. Subsequently, this has indeed proved to be the case; in just a few years finds in the Chiltern Hills are numerous enough to no longer cause forayers to whistle through their teeth. I have found it several times on cherry, so perhaps it has an advantage over some other species on this particular substratum. It even seems possible that it is one of those species moving northwards as global warming continues. Fungi see the world in such an intimate way that a few degrees change in winter might give one species the edge over another. On the other hand, the merest whiff of some pollutant could push the balance the other way, and this fungus would then become rare again. Or maybe warming provoked a northward shift of some *other* fungus that previously occupied the niche favoured by the Crimped Gill today . . . A vacancy opened up, and was filled with alacrity. We know so little of the trajectory of our natural environments, and even less about the predilections of the organisms that populate them. All I know is I am gratified that the Crimped Gill chose our wood.

By the next year, as its supporting branches decayed away, the broken trunk of the cherry tree had sunk enough to lie on the ground. It did not take long for wood mice to discover a safe haven beneath it, and even these little mammals would carry spores on their fur, taking them to a nice moist place for germination. The Toothed Crust was still present, but other fungus players must have established their mycelium within the trunk by now, as tiny fissures in the protective bark allowed access for spores wafting in from elsewhere. The mycelium progressed through the log, unseen until it was ready to turn hypha into mushroom. After another year or so, the Common Bonnet (*Mycena galericulata*) displayed slender, grey-brown toadstools from the severed end and again from a knothole some feet away from it – presumably all part of the same mycelial individual. This toadstool is one of the commonest species on broadleaved wood so it was no surprise when it turned up, but its features had to be checked because there are so many different bonnets. The large size (for a bonnet), slender, tough stipe darkening in colour towards the base, white, rather wide-spaced gills that turn upwards towards the stem, and the typical smell – all those checked out, but a subtler test remained. On the Common Bonnet where the gills meet the underside of the cap they are interconnected by tiny veins, and you have to mangle a specimen to see this. Now all features agreed. The Sulphur Polypore returned another year, though not in such splendour, and was then seen no more.

As the trunk lay on the ground, different fungi moved in. Several years passed before they became manifest, but I suspect that the fungi had been at work long before, sequestered inside the wood, reprocessing cellulose into food. These fungi are shy; they mostly shun the light. Their place is on the damp undersides of logs and sticks. To see them the log has to be lifted and turned briefly towards the light. It is another world down there. As soon as light floods in, the inhabitants of the underworld scatter off into shelter: shiny black ground beetles lead the charge, scuttling on their six legs to get back into the soil; orange centipedes almost match them for speed, and surely surpass them for flexibility, whereas millipedes curl and twist in embarrassment at being exposed; spiders often choose to remain immobile. Woodlice amble at their own even pace on their numerous appendages, as if powered by some minute internal engine, their antennae attuned to finding a new safe haven.

Nibbled pits of wild cherry testify that mice have been through, storing food against hard times. There is a pallid worm or two turning slowly in the damp. Smaller invertebrates contribute to the impression that this world is full of hidden life: springtails hop like fleas and apparently vanish; a tiny snail carries a whorled spire; and tinier things still with thin legs ambling unhurriedly are very likely mites. It is busy down in the dark. The fungus fruit body marks out a conspicuous area on the underside of the log. It is a thick white patch the size of a small saucer attached to the log's surface. Its most conspicuous feature (downward-facing surface in situ) is an almost regular mesh of small pores just a few millimetres deep and less across it; towards the edge of the fruit body the pores are stretched into somewhat meandering slits. The whole thing is a spore manufactory, and it is quite tough – much tougher than a conventional toadstool – so it can persist for weeks producing more and more spores. The fertile surface lies around the inside of the pores where thousands upon thousands of basidia churn out the colourless spores that could in principle found another mycelium in another log. We have to replace the log into its original position to envision that the orientation of the pores is now vertical, so that spores, once released, would drop down into that febrile world of darkness beneath. Each spore is only about ten thousandths of a millimetre long, so that the narrow confines under the log would not be the barrier to spore dispersal one might think. We can be sure that some of the tiny mites eat the spores, as under a lens they can be seen laboriously climbing over the fertile surface like weird little mountaineers. Anything scurrying or crawling past the poroid surface would be dusted with spores, dropped from above, to carry them anywhere else that chance would favour.

The fungus in question is called *Antrodia albida*. It does not have a common name. That is not unusual for the lurkers under logs. A stream of walkers could pass through the woods and not know the white patch was there, just getting on with the job of breaking down wood and feeding mites. It is passed by unnoticed and unnamed. Of the several hundred species of fungus that have adopted this inconspicuous way of life hardly any have a non-technical name, and some of the technical ones, like *Szczepkamyces*, are hardly encouraging. This does not reflect their importance in nature, because these 'rotters' are the unseen heroes of decomposition, working in the dark to reduce wood to humus, molecule by molecule. However, a later arrival on our cherry log is one of the few that *does* have an informal name – the Common Mazegill, *Datronia mollis*. It often grows on the flanks of logs, with much of its fruit body hugging the sides and the top just turning outwards to produce an inconspicuous shelf with a characteristic black 'crust'. The 'gills' are not really the same as the gills on a mushroom, although the spores are born there. They are more like the pores of other wood-rotting fungi transformed into greyish maze-like contortions, and often on steep surfaces converting further into flattened spines or even cascading curtains looking like miniature frozen waterfalls.

Those who regularly solve crosswords will doubtless spot that the name *Datronia* is an anagram of *Antrodia*, and back in 1879 the species in question was indeed called *Antrodia mollis*. Later work made it clear that this fungus was not really closely related to other *Antrodia* species, hence necessitating the coining of a new name to make a home for *mollis*, one that neatly made a nod towards the old one. This seems rather satisfactory, but it would be remiss of me not to mention that even more recent work in 2020, inevitably based on molecular evidence, has moved *mollis* once again to yet another genus, *Podofomes*, and were I compelled to be up-to-the minute, I should be writing about *Podofomes mollis*. None of which makes the slightest difference to the quiet work of these wood rotters, turning my cherry log back to soil, except to add that their biological distinctions (reflected in their separate names) mean that *Antrodia* and *Datronia* (= *Podofomes*) choose to do it in two different ways.

I have not yet seen the end of our wind-felled cherry log – it is still a work in progress – but I have seen what remains of an earlier fall. A ragged cylinder of cherry bark is all that outlines the ghost of a log left lying long ago. It was there when we bought our woodland, so we know its almost total decay has taken more than fifteen years, though we do not know how many more years we have to add. The substance of the tree is now present only as a few small piles of red-brown, cubic-cracked remnants held inside a bark cradle, so we do know that one of the 'brown rotters' has been at work – it could even have been *Antrodia*. At this stage it hardly seems possible that there is anything left to feed a fungus, but when I rootle around in the crumbling wood there are the unmistakable white threads of fungal mycelium catching on my fingers, still hungry, still questing, until the last syllable of recorded time.

4.

Smells

Fungi, being nature's chemical factories, can be as fragrant as a parfumier's parlour or as stinky as sewer gas. Since the time of the pioneering mycologists in the nineteenth century it has been known that distinctive smells provide an important clue to identifying species of fungi. I have often wished that I had the olfactory equipment of a hound, for a dog's dictionary of smells is vastly superior to our own. A canine nose could probably sniff out by smell alone a dozen times as many mushroom species as we can, picking up differences so subtle that a mere hominid would be humbled. We know that a truffle hound can be trained to pick up the evanescent scent of these precious subterranean fungi. I have seen this at work, as the olfactory detective runs over the forest floor, nose down, turning its head this way and that, tail wagging furiously, just waiting to pick up the faintest whiff of fungal gold in order to please its master. However, *Homo sapiens* has trouble with smells. Even the 'mushroom smell' that is so typical of Cultivated and Field Mushrooms is hard to define. The smell reaches sensors in our nose when volatile compounds are released from the mushroom, and then disperse into the atmosphere. At least 150 such special chemicals have been detected emanating from fungi – an airborne cocktail differing from species to species. The chemistry of scent molecules is complicated, although many include eight carbon atoms; their nomenclature is intimidating and need not detain us here; but I cannot resist mentioning that the typical smell of the Cultivated Mushroom is probably down to the molecules 1-octen-3-ol and 1-octen-3-one, the latter in smaller quantity but with more powerful effect, and both derived from fatty acids. Doubtless, a bloodhound could be trained to track them down. Odours are an indispensable prompt for the insects that are obliged to feed on fungi, or lay their eggs on fruit bodies to develop into hungry maggots. With their hypersensitive antennae, many insect species must be able to pick out a favourite food among the rich chaos of smells that hovers over the autumnal woods and fields. They home in on one particular chemical signal, much as a connoisseur might recognise a Château Lafite 1982 among a plethora of inferior red wines.

Most of us humans are not so refined. Our categories are fuzzier. Is it sweet or sour? Pleasant or nasty? Like clean laundry or old socks? We usually have to refer smells to other smells. Almost everyone – there may be mycophobes who would disagree – would describe the 'mushroom smell' as wholesome or pleasant, and certainly there is nothing to make the nose wrinkle or the eyes water. But these adjectives don't really help to run down the essentials of the odour.

We have to compare a new fragrance with smells we already know, the bad ones and the good ones: honey or vinegar; burned sugar or rotting meat. Is it a vile stench, or an olfactory blessing? Incense or insult? We are obliged to refer to a short list of familiar smells that we can pinpoint with certainty.

I have led fungus walks for many years, and how to deal with smells continues to be a testing part of the experience because of the idiosyncrasies of people's olfactory tuning. A handful of species present little difficulty. The Sulphur Knight (*Tricholoma sulphureum*) is a common toadstool in deciduous woods in the autumn, often fruiting in small troops. It is yellow in all parts – even the widely spaced gills – although the spores are not yellow but white. It has a very strong odour of coal tar, the same smell that emanates from major road repairs as new tarmac is laid down over old before being squashed into place by a steamroller. It is an unmistakable strong pong, and my group all concur with me if I ask them to recall the highway repair scenario. Even Mr Contrarian, who likes to disagree on principle, will agree with the crowd for once. No other toadstool has exactly the same odour, and the diagnosis is supported by its sulphur yellow colour and helpful Latin name. It is hardly necessary to add that it is inedible.

Relatively few mushrooms come up in spring, and several are very good to eat. Some evidence suggests that global warming may be adding species to the list. The all-white St George's Mushroom (*Calocybe gambosa*) often appears within a day or two of St George's Day on 23 April. It is happiest in old grassland rather than woodland, and frequently grows in fairy rings, which can be several metres across. I often find it on roadside verges if they have been mowed, but not too closely. From a distance it can look somewhat like a Field Mushroom. In the hand it is very different. It is an altogether chunkier species with firm flesh and crowded, sinuate gills, which are white and stay white, unlike the pink gills, eventually turning to purple-black, of the Field Mushroom and its relatives. There is no ring on the stem, which can usually be seen on such *Agaricus* species. St George's is an unrelated mushroom that just happens to be white (or slightly yellowish) and favours meadows. What gives it away at once is its intense smell, especially if the flesh is rubbed. My old books always say that the odour resembles 'new meal' – technically, it is described as 'farinaceous', which of course also refers to flour. Very few people visit millers these days, so the old description is sadly redundant. I once made a special trip to an 'artisan miller' on the River Thames to check it out. The odour can be rather strong and is certainly not so pleasant as the smell of newly baked bread – some books suggest old, soggy bread is a better match. My fungus beginners usually nod vigorously when the 'floury' smell is pointed out to them while a good young specimen is passed around.

Unlike the sulphurous smell of the Knight, the 'floury' smell is quite widespread. Life would be simpler if all the 'floury' fungi were in a single genus, but instead the capacity to produce this particular smell must have evolved on several occasions. The prolific nineteenth-century mycologist M.C. Cooke was sent a gift of St George's Mushrooms 'but the odour was so powerful and oppressive that the house was soon filled with it, and we were compelled to transfer the mushrooms to an outhouse until the hour of sacrifice arrived'. Nonetheless, when the St George's Mushroom is cooked the more unpleasant notes in the smell diminish markedly, and with its compact, almost crunchy texture it has become a favourite with collectors for the pot. The inhabitants of the Basque country particularly seek it out. St George's does stay loyal to sites it likes, so those in the know can look forward to late April. My wife Jackie and I struggled to find the perfect complement to its pronounced flavour, and finally came up with a happy marriage. St George's can stand up to asparagus, and the two combine well in a risotto. It is one of the mushroom dishes on our calendar.

A possible rival for intensity of farinaceous smell is another edible white mushroom, but this time an autumnal one, and it is called the Miller (*Clitopilus prunulus*), which does not allow much room for doubt about its effect on the nose. It, too, is white, and seems to have a particular liking for the sides of woodland paths. However, it is much more delicate than the St George's Mushroom, and its cap is often lobed and sometimes a little funnel-shaped. It has a very distinctive 'feel' to it. Again, my older books have a good phrase: 'the feel of a kid glove'. It has a kind of luxurious smoothness, not as slippery as satin, nor yet as tacky as leather. This sort of feature is hard to convey without having the mushroom in front of you; mushroom people become aware of very subtle distinctions. The Miller differs rather obviously from St George's because its gills (and indeed its spores) are pink, not white, and the soft, thin gills curve to run down along the stem (decurrent). Some people find its mealy taste over-whelming.

Clitopilus prunulus was one of those fungi that everybody thought they knew well – one of those reliable, easy-to-identify mushrooms that could be found on a traipse through the woods most years. I thought it was one of the few mushrooms that would never spring a surprise. But I was wrong. In late 2008, while doing my usual autumnal pottering around beech woodland in the Chilterns, where there were scattered examples of the Miller among the litter, I noticed that these specimens looked unusually robust, perhaps a little convex, and that some were distinctly greyish on top. Even though it seemed such an old friend, I thought I had better confirm my identification under the microscope at home. There is a regular routine to this: I cut off a tiny scrap of the gill edge with a scalpel and put it on a slide, add a drop of water and 'squidge' it gently down with a cover slip. The traditional way of doing this is a tap with the rubberised end of a pencil. The effect is to splay out the cells along the gill edge, and dislodge spores. It is quick and effective.

What I saw surprised me: all along the gill edge was a line of minute cylindrical cells – almost making a palisade. These were infertile cells called cystidia – they don't produce spores, although plenty of spores were being produced along the *sides* of the gills. I knew that *Clitopilus prunulus* had a fertile gill edge, so it seemed that what I had before me was a different species of the Miller! This was a greyish, more robust form, which displayed a different gill edge. At this point the amateur scientist writes to the Jodrell Mycological

Laboratory at Kew to get help, and help duly came from a learned guru of agarics, Alick Henrici. This strange species had been named already, but only as recently as 1999, by two Dutch mycologists, as *Clitopilus cystidiatus*. It was then a new species. I believe that my discovery, made walking insouciantly through the woods in South Oxfordshire, was the first time it had been seen in the United Kingdom. Surely this is one of the great rewards of knowing about fungi: you can make discoveries on your doorstep. You don't have to go up an uncharted tributary of the Amazon to find something new.

I am obliged for 'health and safety' reasons to mention another meal-smelling toadstool at this point. The Livid Pinkgill (*Entoloma sinuatum*) is very rare in my experience; I have only seen it a couple of times in my life. This toadstool is very poisonous and might be confused with the St George's Mushroom by a novice, since it is also vernal, pale-coloured and robust. I have seen it growing in grassy glades with hawthorn. The only place I have seen the species in quantity is on the island of Sardinia, so maybe it is more prolific in warmer climates. It belongs to a different group of agarics from the St George's and provides another example of how the fungi throw up 'lookalikes' to discombobulate the unwary. However, the spores are pink (as are the gills when mature), so a spore print will readily identify it and provide a clear distinction from the white-spored St George's. Under a microscope the spores of Livid Pinkgill are also coarsely angular rather than elliptical.

My beginners group gets into more trouble with the False Death Cap, *Amanita citrina*, a toadstool seen from late summer onwards. Like the Sulphur Knight it is a common toadstool of woodlands – indeed, I have seen the two species growing together. The False Death Cap is an elegant example with a pale lemon-yellow to white cap, and a relatively more impressive, much longer stem than either the Field Mushroom or St George's Mushroom – in fact the stem is usually longer than the cap diameter, so the latter is held well above the forest floor to spread its spores. In dark, autumnal beech woodland, before the leaves have fallen, the caps sometimes shine as if illuminated by some mystical spotlight from above the litter. When carefully dug from the ground the base of the stem is a perfectly rounded sphere with a sharp upper edge. So one can see where the mushroom arose from an original egg-like ball as its stem elongated: then as the cap expanded, a veil covering the white, free gills split away to leave a ring hanging on the stem. It is a lovely creature, but as its name implies it somewhat resembles the Death Cap. Though it is not deadly, it is far commoner than its lethal relative. And its smell? Our group hums and haws as an example is passed around. 'It definitely reminds me of *something*,' says one young woman helpfully. 'It's certainly distinctive and not particularly unpleasant,' volunteers another. 'Smells like a mushroom to me,' says Mr Contrarian. I have my surprising answer ready: 'Have you ever smelled that curious odour when you cut potatoes?' This leads to general assent – 'Yes, that is exactly right, new potatoes, we should have known that all along.' It seems everyone (except Mr Contrarian) could recognise the smell of the False Death Cap once they had been told what it was. It is a particularly useful character for this one species of the Death Cap family, especially since the Death Cap itself can occasionally 'wash out' in the rain to a paler colour. However, the smell could only be *precisely* diagnosed with reference to another smell.

Poking up from the leaf litter small, graceful 'bonnets' (*Mycena*) invariably abound in woods during the autumn. They, too, have their own smells, but some of the species are so small that the sight of a mycologist apparently trying to stuff a tiny mushroom up her nose is enough to astound any passer-by. Lilac Bonnet (*Mycena pura*) is one of the commonest species on most forays; with an obtuse pale-purplish cap atop a slender, polished stem, and pale gills, it can form troops under the right conditions. Of course, it has a characteristic smell, best appreciated by slightly bruising the flesh and then sniffing. This time, one of our group gets the distinctive odour quite quickly: radishes. Another finds it to be more like cucumber. Mr Contrarian says it smells like mushroom to him. There is an overall consensus that this small toadstool is of a radishy/cucumbery persuasion and that its smell is consistently present. Since this pretty little toadstool has some of the same poison as Fly Agaric in its tissues, the smell could be taken as a warning: don't eat me. This radishy smell is quite common among toad-stools of several different kinds, and as far as I know is always a warning that its possessor should not go near a frying pan. I have never gone so far as to take radishes into the woods to try out the comparative odour test on the spot. It is enough to attract stares for sniffing small mushrooms let alone waving around a bunch of radishes at the same time. I have my limits.

One odour that nobody gets wrong is aniseed – the

powerful aroma of Pernod. The Aniseed Funnel (*Clitocybe odora*) is an attractive blue-green colour, can be up to a foot across, and has sloping (decurrent) pale gills, often exaggerated by a funnel-like cap. It is possible to find it by smell alone as you walk through the woods. There is another, much less conspicuous *Clitocybe* (*C. fragrans*, Fragrant Funnel) that smells almost as strong and usually appears in mossy ground late in the year. Aniseed Funnel is a common species and one I am always glad to see to prove to beginners that not all fungi are hard to identify. Unlike the smells described above, very few fungi have developed the capacity to synthesise anethole, which is the chemical responsible for the aniseed odour. There are a couple of anise smellers, however, growing on trees, *Lentinellus cochleatus* and the bracket *Trametes suaveolens*, neither of them common, so the Aniseed Funnel is not unique; the appropriate biochemical toolkit can be geared into action by more than one fungus.

Perhaps more recherché is the smell of coumarin – new-mown hay, or, if you prefer the stronger version, fenugreek. It is a widespread chemical in nature: in our own wood Sweet Woodruff is a prolific herb that develops a lovely fragrance as it dries, reminiscent of sweet vernal grass. This carrier of the coumarin chemical was formerly used to sweeten bed linen, and it must have been rather wonderful to climb in under sheets smelling of new-mown hay. Coumarin is a relatively simple organic compound, and at least one fungus synthesises it as a metabolite. This is a tiny puffball (*Phleogena faginea*) that grows gregariously on sticks and wood, with short stems supporting a spherical bag of spores, only about three millimetres across. It hardly looks like a regular fungus, but under the microscope its affinities are indisputable. I was delighted to see it once on a cold November day in Suffolk; despite its small size the spicy smell was quite evident. That discovery would not have been made had I not been on a foray with more than a dozen experienced fungus fanciers. One of them had seen the Fenugreek Stalkball before, and that had the extraordinary effect of sharpening his senses for recognising it the next time. It is still not a common sight. Several mushrooms smell of curry as they dry on a window ledge, one unsurprisingly called the Curry Milkcap (*Lactarius camphoratus*). This is a small red-brown mushroom found in conifer forests, and like all milkcaps it exudes white latex where the flesh is damaged. The smell of the dried fruit body is surprisingly strong: one specimen drying out in the sun can infuse a whole room. It has a relative growing under birch trees that smells of coconut. A good nose is a useful addition to sharp eyes in the search for a full basket of different fungi.

Relatively few fungi have really offensive odours. The phalloids – the stinkhorn and its allies – are mycology's masters of disgusting smells and deserve more attention below. Most brittlegills (*Russula*) offer little to offend the nose, but one group of species, centred on the Stinking Brittlegill (*R. foetens*), smells distinctly of Camembert cheese, or, if you prefer, old socks. In some summers these smelly species are common under the oaks along the Sandlings Walk in Suffolk, and forayers are free to haggle over socks or Camembert to their heart's content. The conclusion is usually no better than that one person's cheese is another person's socks. Whether the smell of kippers is unpleasant or pleasant is a matter of individual taste, but the small, warm-brown toadstool Cucumber Cap (*Macrocystidia cucumis*) smells very strongly of smoked fish to me, even though both its common and Latin names mention cucumber. Smells, as I have emphasised, are personal.

However, few would quibble with the smell of *Gymnopus brassicolens* (Cabbage Parachute) as belonging to rotting cabbage, and it has two close relatives that smell even more offensive. This modestly sized, pale-brownish toadstool with a dark, minutely bristly stipe is found in woodland litter, and its nasty and peculiar smell is welcome to the forayer as a way of distinguishing it from several similar species that only smell of garlic! Fungi are chemical magicians, and most of those chemicals are complex organic molecules exhibiting the endless versatility of carbon to make friends with oxygen, hydrogen and nitrogen. There are a few smells that seem to be simpler – more inorganic chemistry than organic. A tiny amount of cyanide – no more than that in a bay leaf – can be picked up from the common and perfectly edible Fairy Ring Mushroom if the fruit bodies are put in a tin for half an hour before sniffing. An unpleasant smell of gas emanates from the gills of the common discovery Stinking Dapperling, *Lepiota cristata*, which looks like a very diminutive copy of the pleasant-smelling Parasol Mushroom. Among the bonnets there are species that smell of chlorine or nitric acid. One of these is a small, trooping greyish toadstool with a conical cap (*M. leptocephala*) that often comes up in great numbers in coniferous woods: when crushed, its flesh exudes a strong smell of bleach. Nobody is tempted to ask: 'Can you eat it?'

So far as I know, people have not succeeded in making perfume out of fungi, although one company in Boston seems to be trying. By contrast, flowering plants are synonymous with pleasant aromas – roses, lavender, gardenia, jasmine and so on – which form the basis of the vast fragrance industry. Even the most fervent Italian enthusiast for *porcini* might draw the line at finding their lover doused in essence of *Boletus edulis*. Nonetheless, a handful of fungi do have sweetish smells. A common relative of the Sulphur Knight with similar stature, but having an unremarkable green-tinted, greyish cap colour and white gills, is rather disparagingly known as the Soapy Knight (*Tricholoma saponaceum*). It has a pleasant, if slightly sickly-sweet aroma. In the nineteenth century it was originally described as smelling 'like harlots'. Presumably the author, Elias Magnus Fries, considered that his fellow mycologists would readily recognise the comparison. Modern books tactfully refer to 'cheap soap'.

Some fungi smell of honey. I knew something was going wrong when I could not detect the sweet smell of a pretty red waxcap mushroom called *Hygrocybe reidii*. The textbooks gave 'odour of honey' as an important discriminatory feature of the species to separate it from many other kinds of small, red waxcaps growing in nutrient-poor grasslands. I could not smell a thing. This olfactory failure was the beginning of a slow decline. Over the last decade I have been progressively losing my sense of smell. Sweet smells were lost first, and then one by one others faded away. It was not just mushrooms – no more roses for me, nor savouring the subtle notes of white wine. No more summer evenings enjoying the honeysuckle. I could not even detect the wholesome aroma of a fresh Field Mushroom. Some of the fibrecaps (*Inocybe*) smell of ripe pears, and I could no longer discriminate those from similar-looking species that had a spermatic (semen) odour. For a while I could still pick up the famous 'new meal' smell of St George's Mushroom, and the strong aniseed fragrance of *Clitocybe odora* and the young Horse Mushroom (*Agaricus arvensis*) cut through the decline in my nasal function, but I had to face up to the fact that I was losing one of the most important senses to have in the field. I was no longer master of my own nose. The condition is called anosmia, which is rather like describing losing a leg as 'apodia'. It does not help much. It is apparently not uncommon in the senior years, and I remembered that my mother had suffered the same loss before she died.

Nonetheless, something had to be done. Nowadays, on a teaching foray the first thing I do is ask among the group who has a well-developed sense of smell and appoint them as the 'Official Nose'. Those in possession of a distinguished-looking anterior appendage tend to get first look, though I soon learned that good sniffers don't necessarily have huge noses. Young females are often the most sensitive. I pass the first fruit body to the Official Nose and ask him/her to confirm (or not) that the specimen in question smells of potatoes/bitter almonds/old socks. The specimen then continues its journey round the other noses to have its aromatic volatiles sampled by the assembled nostrils. Usually, this works very well, though I once chose a Nose who obviously enjoyed disagreeing with the accepted word on pongs. If I said *sotto voce* that this small mushroom smells of radishes it would be countered by 'No, I think it is more like kohl-rabi.' 'Camembert cheese?' 'No, much more like Epoisses, in my opinion.' Then it was a relief to discover the Sulphur Knight with its uncontroversial, if penetrating hum to restore faith in the leadership.

5.

Vampires

The ugliest fungus I know fruits in the Australian rain-forest. About seventy miles south of Sydney, in the state of New South Wales, a steep scarp composed of resistant rocks faces the sea. By Australian standards this slope is decidedly wet, as the area catches all the mist and rain that blows in from the ocean. The car journey from Sydney passes through territory that can be matched over much of that vast continent, dominated by a huge variety of the eucalypts that seem to fit so well into the landscape. Sickle-shaped, glaucous leaves dangle in the sunshine. Some species are flowering, displaying their clustered powder puffs of white stamens. We pass through pleasant towns, with houses fronted by English roses laid out in neat gardens. Beyond Robinson the ground becomes more barren, the mallee trees more stunted, and the topography is flat for miles.

The Jamberoo Mountain Road comes as a shock, as it plunges steeply down the escarpment at the edge of the plateau. Almost at once the vegetation changes dramatically.

Eucalypts are much less prominent, and partly replaced by stately trees of great girth and height mostly with smaller, dark-green leaves, making a canopy that is very effective at screening out the light compared with the open airiness that accompanies forests of gum trees and their allies. To reach my sister-in-law's house in the rainforest, we have to turn off onto an unmetalled road that winds its way for several kilometres through the stately trees. Small streams, tumbling through rocks, bound down the slope and are guided into culverts beneath the track. During downpours these rills could turn into torrents; signs of former 'wash outs' remain by the trackside. It is easy to spot where the chainsaw has been at work dismembering trees that have fallen across the road. This is hardly the place to build a house.

The New South Wales subtropical rainforest is a special habitat. It is biologically rich. The trees that tower above us belong to many species but, as is typical of rainforests, their leaves all tend to look similar – small and glossy with little points at the end, known as drip tips, that take away the excess moisture when the rain comes down. You can only identify these tree species when the flowers or fruit fall to Earth from high above. A scattering of very tall eucalypts have adapted to the same habitat. These forests once abounded in 'red cedar', a fine wood for construction that was almost exterminated in the nineteenth century, when it was known as 'red gold'. Despite its common name it was no conifer. Lilly Pilly is one of the tall trees blessed with a name minted in the rhyming doublets that Australians love so much. The name of another, abundant tree species – coachwood – speaks for itself. Tree ferns make verdant fountains in the understory. Snakes lurk in hidden gullies. Leeches also lie in wait, and when they sense the body heat of a passing walker they loop towards them with intent. They hang around the lekking grounds of bowerbirds. They inveigle themselves into crevices in flesh, between the toes, behind the knees, using their subtle wiles to anaesthetise the victim, whose blood they choose to suck until a bloody stain reveals their subterfuge. It strains the naturalist to welcome them into the inventory of biodiversity, but they have their place, as do huntsman spiders, the size of a small plate, that can make a visit to the dunny exciting if they decide to take up residence behind the door (as they usually do).

Caroline Lawrence is waiting to greet us at the end of the exciting drive. Her house is perched on the steep scarp slope and has a balcony commanding a magnificent view over the crowns of the forest trees below towards the plain beyond. Everything is luxuriant. A bird-feeding station is visited by gorgeous green and scarlet king parrots. There is even a bat hanging off one of the light fittings. Everything seems to be hanging off something else, even the house off the cliff. We are taken to a studio added by the sculptor who built the main house, which has an old sofa with skinks living under the cushions and a colony of microbats established in the door panel. This is serious habitat.

Jackie and I have arrived in March, which is when the mushroom season often reaches its zenith down under. Caroline has become a convert to the joys of mushrooms and is determined to walk me through a selection of her special species. Damp logs lie scattered under the shade of the thick canopy. Plucking a leech from my leg before it can get a hold, I marvel at a clump of delicate, gently pointed small toadstools that I take to be bonnets but are coloured intensely blue. I am used to subtle shades of olive or brown among the bonnets, but this was a revelation, a blue of such intensity it looked as if it were somehow illuminated from within. Nor were they alone. Nearby, among the litter, another remarkably blue toadstool lurked, but this time a darker, intense Prussian blue, and the gills were decidedly pink. This had to be one of the pinkgills (*Entoloma*), but I did know of one or two uncommon European blue pinkgills, so it was not entirely unfamiliar.

As we ambled along a crude path through the forest, there were toadstools on every side. Little white bracket fungi clustered in tiers on damp logs and had coarse hexagonal pores on their lower surfaces where I would have expected to see densely packed short tubes; these proved to be bonnets in disguise (*Favolaschia* species*). They were distant relatives of some of the commonest fungi in our own woods, but their gills had changed into a beautifully regular but delicate pattern resembling honeycomb. On another rather rotten stump I saw what seemed to be the familiar Coral Tooth Fungus (*Hericium coralloides*), a star find on any foray in the New Forest, resembling a dense cascade of white icicles dripping off the edge of a weathered and crumbling log, each 'tooth' lined with basidia shedding millions of spores. The stroll was revealing a tantalising mixture of the familiar and the unfamiliar. Some finds were brilliant antipodean

---

* A species of *Favolaschia* is now well established in England, yet another example of fungi moving around the planet.

cousins of their pallid English relatives, others apparently had spanned the Earth almost unchanged, like the country rose gardens we had seen by the road in Bowra, which would not have looked out of place in Haslemere.

Then came the ugliest fungus.

We were off the path, picking our way carefully between logs and fallen blocks of weathered rock partly covered by moss and litter. It was an invitation to twist an ankle, or fall into a dark and hidden hole. Caroline had several scars to prove it. In front of us, arising from the ground was what presented as a slightly glistening turd, all greeny-brown and fully life-size. For a few seconds we were lost for words apart from an involuntary 'ugh!' or something similar. When a kind of ghastly fascination took over, it was clear that the upper part of the 'thing' was densely pockmarked while the lower part was smoother and was some kind of stem (or stipe). This was obviously a fungus fruit body, and the stipe evidently emerged from the ground from something hidden below. It seemed a reasonable guess that this weird mycological monster was up to no good, so the next obligation was to investigate what happened if we followed that stipe down into the ground. This involved some removal of rocks and not a little scrabbling at the subsoil, and below the surface the stipe became almost white, more like a dead man's finger, with a texture to match. It continued for quite a length – actually, rather more than a finger length. Then it seemed to turn a corner into something segmented, almost white, and as long as a chipolata sausage, something that parted rather easily from the soil. In one of those moments that on the stage would be called a *coup de théâtre*, we recognised a 'face' on one end of the segmented sausage. It was a huge caterpillar!

At this moment everything fell into place. I was taken back to the New Forest a decade earlier, when I had been shown some much smaller, bright scarlet cylinders arising from the soil; they were the fruit bodies of parasites of buried caterpillars – the Scarlet Caterpillar Club, *Cordyceps militaris*. Our find must have been a much scaled-up, and much uglier version of a similarly parasitic fungus. It was without doubt an asco – and the roughened surface of the fruit body was where the spores emerged from the mouths of numerous ranks of small flasks (*perithecia*). A search through reference books quite quickly came up with a name for a species that was first collected in Tasmania in the mid nineteenth century: *Cordyceps gunnii*. One wonders whether Mr Gunn (the discoverer) would have felt honoured to have his name donated for eternity to an ugly parasite. In a strange way just putting a name on the fungus diminished our initial revulsion at its weirdness and unsightliness. We could now visualise the spores of a vampire fungus germinating on the body of a healthy caterpillar, its mycelium feeding off the tissues of its host even as the head end continued to browse on decaying tree roots to sustain its lethal interloper. The caterpillar body amassed the fungal tissue. Then came the *coup de grâce* as the caterpillar finally *became* the entomo-pathogenic fungus, when the developing fruit body sought the air. At that point the spoils of its voracity were deployed in spores spreading its lethal infection to other hosts. We subsequently found another example that was indeed dusted with white spores. The favoured prey, the entomological equivalent of the bashful maiden in the *Dracula* movies, is the larva of a substantial insect known commonly as the Ghost Moth, the many species of which support a villains' gallery of specialised *Cordyceps* and its relatives. They are scattered over the world, but perhaps the sinister appearance of *gunnii* is the best match for its grisly lifestyle.

Modern molecular studies have 'split' the old genus *Cordyceps*, and so the name I should now use for the ugliness champion is *Drechmeria gunnii*, which I regret, as it removes it linguistically from its relatives with similarly lethal lifestyles. The most famous of these is tiny compared with the Australian mycological orc. *Ophiocordyceps unilateralis* is the fungus that infects carpenter ants in tropical forests and turns them into zombies. It is a *gunnii* story that finishes higher above ground level and with more dramatic bells and whistles. Even while this fungus continues its mycelial work in the body of the ant, the command centre in the ant's head compels the enslaved creature to climb a thin plant stalk, before it clamps its jaws into the stalk and dies in what is the best possible light and humidity for what happens next. At this stage it could be argued that this creature is a motile fungus rather than an insect in its death throes. A miniature, skinny version of the fruit body we observed off the Jamberoo Mountain Road now erupts from the 'neck' of the ant – always from the same place where the cuticle is thin – and in a few days is shedding spores in the thousands every hour, which are carried off in the air currents to find another ant.

The language we are compelled to use to describe this extraordinary life history inevitably seems to imbue the fungus with some strange kind of mycelial intelligence, an almost-human sense of purpose. Some narratives relate this undoubtedly remarkable story as if it had lessons to teach us all. What the ugliest fungus in the world and its many insect-devouring relatives tell us instead is that the Zombie Ant Fungus is one variation on an evolutionary theme rather than a parable of mycelial intelligence. If estimates derived from evolutionary trees are to be believed, the family of moths that includes the ghost moths comprises one of the most primitive groups of all the moths and butterflies (Lepidoptera), so it may be that fungi with *Cordyceps* habits evolved a very long time ago in harmony (if that is the word) with their hosts. This could even have been during the Cretaceous Period while dinosaurs were still alive and flourishing. That would allow more than seventy million years of natural selection to hone that sense of purpose, to fine tune that metaphor for intelligence. Relatives of *Cordyceps* may have been pursuing their lethal trade before, and alongside the appearance of modern mammals and birds and bees, and doubtless long before the first humans. What is *not* plausible is that *Cordyceps* could 'jump' hosts to infect our own species, which was the premise behind the gripping television series *The Last of Us*. If an organism has spent so many millions of years building itself into the intimate life cycles of arthropods, it cannot readily take on another role, as if it were just an actor changing clothes.

After we dug up *Drechmeria gunnii*, I recalled another occasion when I had seen similar objects. I had been to China in the 1980s at a time when the outrages of the Cultural Revolution were still fresh and bloody in the memories of my scientific colleagues in the university in Nanjing. Several of them had spent years picking potatoes while being scorned by Red Guards as useless intellectuals. Our party was taken on a walk through a street market, and that always includes a visit to a store holding traditional Chinese medicines. Among several unspeakable dried animals, there was a basket holding a dozen or so strangely hooked objects. One side of the 'hook' was a mummified caterpillar; it subtended a dark prong. It was some kind of *Cordyceps* – fungus and host sold together as a curative package. My hosts explained that it was a very potent drug in the Chinese pharmacopeia. As is the way of such things it had claims to be everything: a tonic, anti-inflammatory, anti-stroke and even anti-cancer. It was much in demand, and very expensive. It is scarcely surprising that a fungus with such a long history of interaction with animals should be fully charged with interesting bioactive compounds (one of these is unimaginatively called cordycepin).

With their known effects on nervous systems, it is also plausible that these chemicals might include psychotropic compounds, although zombification is one of the few things that is not claimed as one of the medicinal properties of this Cordyceps. The scientific name of the fungus is *Ophiocordyceps sinensis*, and it is native to the Himalayas, where it has been a famous herbal medicine for centuries. Sherpas negotiating high passes can spot with unerring accuracy the tell-tale fruit bodies growing from their subterranean moth caterpillars. As China became wealthier, demand for the miracle nostrum has . . . well . . . mushroomed. To many inhabitants of those harsh mountains, *yartsa gunbu* is a vital source of income, providing by far the best way to rise above subsistence level. The result is overpicking, and this leads to more frenetic searching in more out-of-the-way habitats, and a further diminution of the supply. In a mycological twist to the Tragedy of the Commons, the price then rises, making the search still more frenetic, the profits still more tempting. It is not difficult to imagine where this trade is heading, and the only organism that will benefit in the end is the ghost moth.

6.

Shiners

When darkness falls on the Jamberoo Mountain Road the bats and moths go to work in the rainforest. Those small marsupials that had not been hunted by feral cats and foxes come out to scrabble after beetles or dig in the ground for small truffles. The dark is most alive just now, and it is pleasant to sit outside in the cooling air listening to subtle scratching sounds or the coarse doubled-up call of the nocturnal owlet nightjar. The trees loom large overhead. It takes a while to get the rods in your 'night eyes' in working order. Any short walk along the path at night is an adventure, but nobody could anticipate that it would be a mycological one. The clearing around the house is lined in places with the carcasses of dead trees. From one of them a strange glow emanates. It shines from a series of substantial fungal brackets making tiers along one side of a large prostrate log. They are luminous fungi! They shine as if the daylight that had left the forest still lingered on in their glowing tissues. On close inspection the light they produce is very curious; it comes from within the body of the fungus as if powered by some weird internal electricity. It has a greenish tinge that gives it a spectral quality, as though the wood itself were holding out illuminated hands. I have never seen its equivalent in man-made light – it is a little similar to the muted nightlights left on for children who have a fear of the dark. I did not think to test whether I could read by light of the gentle radiance, but I could surely see it reflected off the faces of my companions. I need to look closer. This is a bracket that bears gills on the underside that run into the stem where it attaches it to the log. It is another ghost – the Ghost Fungus (*Omphalotus nidiformis*).

This is where I have to own up to a mistake in a close encounter of the fungal kind. I had noticed these fungal fans earlier in the day – in fact, they were hard to miss. In daylight they displayed pale caps above, with a slight purplish tint, a few of them somewhat funnel-shaped, and with thin white gills below, running into the stem. I had confidently identified them with a British species even though I was in another hemisphere and in a rainforest. After all (I reasoned), a few other old acquaintances had appeared in the same place. This clump appeared to be the well-known and much-studied Oyster Mushroom (*Pleurotus ostreatus*), one of the few mushrooms you can buy in supermarkets because it is equally familiar as a good edible species. My mushroom had the right colour, the right gills, the right habit and was growing in the right place. It even occurs on beech logs in our own piece of woodland in the Chiltern Hills, so you might say it was a familiar friend. But what a deceiver! If it had got as far as a frying pan, I would have been very unpopular with Caroline, because my misidentification would have had unpleasant consequences. The Ghost Fungus is poisonous (not lethal, but noxious) – and cramps and vomiting do not make a kindly gift. Its resemblance to the Oyster Mushroom is a fine example of convergent evolution. *Pleurotus* and *Omphalotus* do not even belong within the same mushroom group, but they do live under similar circumstances on dead logs. Comparable habits engender comparable form. If I had looked harder at the 'down under' species I would have noticed subtle differences in the edge of the gills, or perhaps in odour. But luminescence was the clincher.

I had seen another luminous species of *Omphalotus* on a field trip in Italy. This toadstool (*O. olearius*) was bright orange with very sloping gills and grew in clusters at the base of ancient olive trees, so it is far less like an Oyster Mushroom than the Ghost Fungus. In the daytime it was easily spotted from afar across the olive groves; it is found throughout the Mediterranean region. At night it glows like its Australian relative. A very similar fungus (*O. illudens*) from North America is known as the Jack o'Lantern – a name that certainly leaves no question that it, too, is luminous. These orange-coloured species are very rarely encountered in England and restricted to the warmer southern counties, where oak is the usual host. Some samples have been attributed to the Jack o'Lantern, but one collection is apparently the same as the European species. Whatever you call these attractive toadstools, they both shine at night and have a very deleterious effect on the digestive tract if eaten, inducing several days of vomiting and diarrhoea until the last fragment is flushed out of the system.

Fortunately, no fatalities have been reported. It may seem surprising that such a brilliantly coloured toadstool should find its way on to the menu, but the Jack o'Lantern is reported to be the most frequent cause of mushroom poisoning in the north-east United States. This can only be because inexperienced collectors believe that the brilliantly coloured fruit bodies are particularly succulent chanterelles (*Cantharellus cibarius*). The colour and sloping gills are admittedly somewhat similar, but everything else is different – the clustered habit on wood, the thin gills (as opposed to the chanterelle's vein-like folds) and the absence of a pleasant, apricot-like smell. Perhaps my own confusion was forgivable, after all, because all these luminous toadstools have, at one time or another, been called *Pleurotus*, long before it was recognised that Oysters and Jack o'Lanterns are not closely related on the evolutionary tree.

Growing mycelium can also be luminous, and while it is rapidly working, its influence can spread into the wood it is invading. The 'shining wood' that results has been noticed since classical times. John Ramsbottom recalled in *Mushrooms and Toadstools* that the great illustrator of fungi and minerals James Sowerby had noticed in 1797 luminous threads 'creeping among saw dust and bottles' in a wine cellar. The growing tips of the mycelium are particularly bioluminescent, presumably because that is where metabolic activity is liveliest. Ramsbottom tells the tale of troops on the Western Front during the First World War sticking bits of shining wood on to their rifles so that they did not bump into their fellows in the dark of the trenches. During the Second World War, in the Arnhem campaign in 1944, troops digging defences were startled to see shining, luminous patches that they took to be bodies concealed in the dark, but the strange lights proved to be emanating from infected tree roots.

In pre-scientific times it would be easy to imagine such a phenomenon triggering myths of survival beyond the grave in some strange underworld. The fantasy writer H.P. Lovecraft was fond of invoking weird colours not quite of this earth in his representations of submerged and alien worlds, and one wonders whether he knew all about the properties of shining wood. I used to entertain my children with stories about a kingdom of tunnels beneath London in which the very walls exuded light, far from the reach of the sun. Maybe this is not as impossible as I had imagined now that we know about minute, glowing mycological lamps. Many different fungi are able to produce this spectral light (about twenty-five British species), but not all individuals of the same species are necessarily able to perform the trick. The species responsible for many examples of luminescent mycelium is the Honey Fungus (*Armillaria mellea* and its relatives), the aggressive destroyer of so many of our familiar trees. This is one of very few fungi that can be recognised from its mycelium alone – or, more correctly, from its black, bootlace-like rhizomorphs, which include masses of hyphal strands. These 'laces' are both distinctive and enduring, and can be found looking like inky veins on lying logs long after the bark of its victim has decayed away. Having killed one host, Honey Fungus quests for another victim; the rhizomorphs lead the charge. A dismayed gardener may grieve the loss of a prized cherry tree only to see its neighbouring plum tree sickening and wilting; and if he could but see inside the earth the dark threads of death would be seen to migrate between his two trees. Even felling and burning the first infected tree is no remedy, because the Honey Fungus can prosper and spread on its remaining dead roots. As the growing tips of mycelium encounter a new feast, they glow with excitement.

There is a principle in biology that every feature of an organism is available for natural selection to work on, refining or modifying it for adaptive reasons, whether it be flower or feather, tooth or tail. A feature as unusual as luminescence should have a rather obvious function, but in fungi it is very difficult to see what that might be. Luminosity is a feature of many marine organisms, and there it can be employed for a purpose. Deep-sea angler fish have a shining lure on the tip of their 'fishing rod', which dangles in front of a ferocious mouth armed with a battery of needle-like teeth. The light attracts hungry crustaceans or small fry, which are swallowed in a microsecond by those dreadful jaws. No such purpose can be recognised in Honey Fungus, although it is thought that the biochemistry of the light source is similar in fungus and fish: a substance naturally produced by the organism (luciferin) is oxidised by an enzyme called luciferase in the presence of oxygen, and emission of light accompanies the reaction.

In the example of the Ghost Fungus and its allies, luminosity coincides with the release of countless spores from the gills and it has been suggested that the fungus might be attracting nocturnal insects that could be recruited into helping spread the spores around the rainforest. Fireflies use their luciferin to attract their mates in the same habitat, so signalling is not so implausible. This kind of scenario is very hard to confirm or falsify, because there is no critical test to prove it. Other species of otherwise similar-looking fungi (including the true Oyster Mushroom) are not usually luminous and grow successfully in the same forest, which might suggest that there is no particular advantage to glowing in the dark; and there is no conclusive evidence of flies being attracted to the Ghost in the way they are magnetically drawn to the putrid stench of a stinkhorn (p. 149). This theory cannot explain why mycelium should glow, as mycelium is *not* the site of spore production and release. We would be left with two puzzles rather than one. There is evidence that mycelium is most luminous when growing actively in a moist environment, and that absence of oxygen switches the light off. This leads to a 'neutral' hypothesis that might well conclude that the whole light show is simply an accident of metabolism – just a by-product of fungal attack on wood. This too leaves a queasy feeling. Why should all the species of *Omphalotus* around the world conserve the mechanism for making light if it were of no adaptive importance? However, some species of mushroom have strains that are not bioluminescent and apparently live satisfactory lives, which does indicate that the light show can be switched on or off without dramatic effect. The mystery of the Ghost Fungus remains, to add to the long list of puzzles that the fungus kingdom has set us.

7.

Collaborators

In October the beech woods in the Chilterns are transformed. The leaves are still green, but a cool edge to the breeze betokens change. Late autumn is in prospect, and a few freshly fallen leaves presage what will happen in November, but for now the sun sweeps past the elegant beech trunks to throw shafts of light that penetrate to the forest floor. Mushrooms and toadstools are everywhere. The sun reveals brilliant scarlet caps tucked into mossy banks. White caps shine, dark ones have their disguises unmasked. Under the trees pale funnels (*Clitocybe*) grow in obvious fairy rings, as if under instruction from a dancing master. White puffballs line the paths. You might think some biological klaxon had sounded instructing all the fungi lurking in the leaf litter to get into their reproductive finery before they miss the dance. Even if they cannot be seen, the air is thick with spores of a hundred different species carried on the lightest breeze through the wood and beyond, over the fields to the next cluster of trees. It is impossible to resist the impression that this day is a celebration of the fungal kind, when mycelium of all sorts gathers its resources to join others of their persuasion in fruiting with abandon.

In some favoured parts of the beech wood half a dozen different species of mushroom are within the compass of an arm's reach. In 2023 it rained a lot in September, and that was followed by a warm spell in early October, the heat and moisture combining to make the perfect conditions for the spore-dance. Only a few, precious weeks in the year are right for the hidden fungi to announce themselves to the world in their typical attire. They had been there all along, doing their hidden business as mycelium, their true identity concealed in superficially mundane similarity to others, like Clark Kent awaiting the moment to reveal his superpowers (and an appropriate change of costume). To a questing mycologist this is the time of plenty. After walking through the same woods in winter and high summer and failing to see so much as a small brown Scurfy Twiglet (*Tubaria furfuracea*), suddenly there is an embarrassment of riches. It is difficult to know where to turn. Several of the fungi are old friends of a good size and do not need to be disturbed to be identified. Where birch trees have grown among the beeches the scarlet Fly Agaric is invariably present and can be left to continue its business, and the Brown Birch Bolete (*Leccinum scabrum*) will surely be nearby. The Blackening Brittlegill (*Russula nigricans*) is often the most abundant of its kind and soon acquires a smoky grey tint that sets it apart from almost all other fungi under the beech trees, and if any doubt remains one example can be turned over to show the very widely spaced gills that distinguish it from all of its relatives. Many other species require closer examination.

This fungal bonanza is a mixture of saprotrophic and mycorrhizal mushrooms and toadstools. The former are breaking down the abundant lying branches and litter in the woodland; the latter are consummating their intimate relationship with the trees under which they are growing. Those bonnets so common on branches and twigs – even on single leaves – are all saprotrophs, as are many other wood recyclers now fruiting on standing trunks or other dead wood. Their location announces what they do in the ecosystem. Species growing on the ground do not identify their habits, and those dining off the leaf litter can be as abundant as mycorrhizal forms: the litter feeders will include all the toughshanks (*Gymnopus*), inkcaps (*Coprinopsis* and allies), funnels (*Clitocybe* and allies), brittlestems (*Psathyrella*), puffballs (*Lycoperdon*), stinkhorns (*Phallus*) and many more. They are the decomposers, guaranteeing the structure of the soil, the recycling of nutrients – I might say the basic health of the habitat. Some of them are mentioned elsewhere in this book. Here I need to focus on the other group, those that forge intimate relationships with the roots of many plants, including trees. These fungi are the mycorrhizal collaborators. They cannot survive without their partners, and the plants that they nurture are equally in debt to the fungi that accompany them though their lives.

Some of the most beautiful fungi are collaborators. This book began with the most famous of them – the Cep (*porcini*, Penny Bun, etc.). This is the most sought-after of the boletes – those mushrooms resembling agarics in size, shape and texture, but having tubes where a 'regular' mushroom has gills. Nearly all of the boletes are mycorrhizal, and some of them are confined to associations with particular trees. Several of them bruise deep blue when they are handled, and none of these should find their way into the pot. There are dozens of different kinds, and the species obliged to grow in association with oaks, birch, pine or larch are sometimes most easily identified by knowing your trees! Because they are partly fed by the resources of a mature tree, it is possible to find boletes early in the year before the main explosion of other fungi. In the deep sunken lanes that are typical of the Weald, in one unusually dry season I found plentiful examples of the handsome (if inedible) white-capped Rooting Bolete (*Caloboletus radicans*) long before any other mycorrhizal fungi had deigned to put in an appearance. My bolete-obsessive acquaintance goes foraying from July onwards, when most of us have not even thought of dusting off our baskets.

The harlequins of the toadstool world are the brittlegills (*Russula*). They can dominate some parts of the forest floor, and the cap can be any colour of the rainbow: blue, green, red, yellow, violet; even white or brown. I have mentioned that the Blackening Brittlegill (*Russula nigricans*) changes from white to black as it ages. While their size range is similar to that of the 'shop mushroom', a few are more delicate. Of all the common mycorrhizal fungi, brittlegills paint the woodland with its brightest colours. All of them have white stems with a curious texture: when broken between the fingers they snap suddenly. I liken them to sticks of old-fashioned blackboard chalk. This property is related to the microscopic structure of their tissues, which are made of myriad spherical cells very different from the fibre-like hyphae of typical agarics. The same property makes the gills snap and crumble if stroked – hence the common name. As so often, smell and taste (for the expert) are important identification tools: a tiny nibble is enough if kept on the tongue to see what happens, after which it can be spat out.

The red- and yellow-capped varieties often outnumber other species in my beech wood – the commonest scarlet species is probably the Beechwood Sickener (*Russula nobilis*), with a taste so hot and peppery that you do not have to wonder about its edibility. A number of generally similar, bright-red brittlegills are there to confuse fledgling mycologists, as they can be very hard to identify. The red coloration might be taken as a warning of taxonomic headaches to come. The Ochre Brittlegill (*Russula ochroleuca*) commonly provides the yellow tones in autumn woodland, and is not usually very hot tasting, and has a white stipe, but beginners sometimes confuse it with the wholly ochre-coloured Geranium Brittlegill (*Russula fellea*) with a taste from Hades. Some brittlegill species have confusingly mixed cap colours, mottled purple and green, and the gills and spores vary from white to egg yellow, and the fruit body can smell of Camembert, geraniums, newly baked bread or nothing at all. I am glad I have a friend with a very good sense of smell who can identify some of the more esoteric species; choosing from about two hundred British ones can be tricky. In France, fungus lovers eat those that smell pleasant and taste nutty, without too much regard to taxonomic detail. I would advise caution.

The milkcaps (*Lactarius*, *Lactifluus*) are related to the brittlegills and have similar flesh: they are strictly mycorrhizal. They have a feature that identifies them immediately. If the cap flesh or gills are broken, a milky fluid appears almost at once. This milk is not necessarily white – it might be orange, for example – and it may change colour on exposure to air, all of which is important in the identification of species. Most mycologists like milkcaps because there are not too many species to sift through, and they are chunky and well-formed, often with the margins of a concentrically zoned cap slightly rolled under when young. Their colours tend to be more subdued than many of the brittlegills, with various shades of orange-brown, or grey, or green, and, as always, white. With these fungi identification involves tasting the milk, which can be mild and pleasant, or fiercely peppery. The milk of the Fiery Milkcap *Lactarius pyrogalus* is once tasted, never forgotten. It is an attractive, pallid species with saffron-coloured decurrent gills that is common under hazel (*Corylus*) trees, to which it is bound in mycorrhizal partnership.

The first time I tested the milk I was simply following a field guide and wanted to make sure I had not made a mistake. White milk leaked prolifically from a damaged gill; I put a drop on my pinky and applied it to my tongue. For a few seconds I had an almost sweet sensation, then it was followed by the most intense combination of heat and pepper I have ever experienced, that seemed to expand beyond the tongue to occupy the whole of my head. Toothache is not dissimilar. Nor did it fade quickly; for at least half an hour I felt the afterburn. *Pyro* is Greek for 'fire' (as in pyromaniac) and *galus* is milk, so the specific name spells it out. Another common milkcap, associated with birch (*Lactarius torminosus*), is almost as fierce. It has an attractively zoned cap with pinkish tints and a very hairy margin. I have often found it around young birch trees forming a perfect circle of fruit bodies some distance from the trunk, clearly pointing out its mycorrhizal compass. A curious fact is that it is a popular edible species in Finland. Repeated blanching is supposed to leach out the fire without destroying the crunchy texture, then pickling preserves them, as we might pickle onions. I confess that I have used the taste test for these hot milkcaps to silence unreasonably voluble greenhorn mycologists if I am leading a party through the woods: but it is a ruse that can only be used once per foray. Milkcaps are often choosy about their arboreal partners, with most species of broadleaved trees having a few favoured associated fungi. There are lactarii for willows, alders and oaks. As with the brittlegills, conifers have a different suite of species again.

The Deathcap and most other Amanitas are not quite so choosy, but equally mycorrhizal. I have mentioned some of the common species elsewhere in this book. The scarlet Fly Agaric can be found with many trees, though it seems to like birch best. The Destroying Angel (*Amanita virosa*) is pure white, and for a long time I believed I had found the only example in Oxfordshire; inexperienced forayers often mistake the white form of the False Death Cap for this lethal beauty. I believed it was very rare until I looked in the birch woods around Ullapool in western Scotland, where I saw troops of these deceptively innocent-looking toadstools. It is one of many fungi that have distributions broadly related to latitude – or rather to the temperature, pollution levels, moisture and other factors that go with it. There are also many milkcaps and brittlegills that prefer glens and the flanks of Monroes to the Home Counties – and who can blame them?

Having both a ring on the stipe and emerging from a volva, *Amanita* is structurally the most complex of the mycorrhizal agarics, but other groups are equally important in the ecology. *Tricholoma* species (knights) are a regular find in many woodlands and embrace a collection of mostly robust fungi lacking both ring (there is one exception) and volva, and with white, sinuate gills. Brown, greyish, yellow and white colours predominate, and again there are species that prefer to partner with one tree or another among the thirty or so British species. Some have characteristic odours: I have mentioned Sulphur Knight (*T. sulphureum*) smelling of tar (p. 61) and Soapy Knight (*T. saponaceum*) of 'cheap soap', while others have pleasant odours of flowers or newly baked bread, as already noted. Some have scaly caps – that is what introduced the *Tricho-* (Greek for 'hair') into the generic name. Whether 'knight' is appropriate for the common name is debatable. Many of the more familiar species do have a cap that opens out into a shield shape, with a central boss, but it is hardly unique to these particular fungi.

Most varied and important of all the mycorrhizal agarics associated with trees are the webcaps (*Cortinarius*), including toadstools that have rust-coloured gills (and spores) at maturity, and range from robust, stately and handsome examples to classic little brown mushrooms (LBMs). The cortina that gives the genus its name and distinguishes it from all other agarics is a cobwebby connexion between the edge of the cap and the stipe, but it can be hard to see once the cap has expanded. It can be coloured in some species. The webcaps

An abundance of porcini at the mushroom festival in Borgo Val di Taro, 2023. Photo by Jackie Fortey

The Death Cap (*Amanita phalloides*), the deadliest toadstool of them all, arising from its volva. Photo by Andrew Padmore

The Yellow Stainer (*Agaricus xanthodermus*) is probably the commonest cause of poisoning; note the yellow bruising. Photo by Jackie Fortey

White mycelium – the unspectacular business end of the fungus. Photo by Jackie Fortey

Chicken of the Woods (*Laetiporus sulphureus*), a relatively soft bracket fungus.

A fairy ring produced in the grass by the Fairy Ring Champignon (*Marasmius oreades*). Author for scale.

Photo by Jackie Fortey

Crimped Gill (*Plicatura crispa*) on cherry in our wood.

Photo by Jackie Fortey

Luminous fungus (*Omphalotus nidiformis*), photograph taken by its own luminosity, in New South Wales, Australia. Photo by Joseph Neilson

Possibly the ugliest fungus I know, the Australian Cordyceps (*Drechmeria gunnii*) on the caterpillar it parasitises. Photo by Genevieve Gates

The ectomycorrhizal Orange Milkcap (*Lactarius aurantiacus*), with 'milk' droplets from damaged flesh. Photo by Penny Cullington

A Brittlegill (*Russula grisea*), one of the less colourful species of this ubiquitous mycorrhizal genus. Photo by Linda Seward

One of the hundreds of species of mycorrhizal webcaps (*Cortinarius sanguineus*). Photo by Jackie Fortey

Extraordinary Sandy Stiltball (*Battarrea phalloides*). Photo by Jackie Fortey

The elegant Weather Earthstar (*Geastrum corallinum*) opens its 'arms' under wet conditions…

…but curls them up under dry conditions.

Photo by Richard Fortey

A group of rare Earthstars (*Geastrum brittanicum*) arising from needle litter.

Bird's Nest Fungi (*Cyathus striatus*), some with 'eggs' containing the spores.

Rooting Shank (*Hymenopellis radicata*).

Courtesy of Linda Seward

Stinkhorn (*Phallus impudicus*) with flies aboard. Photo by Jackie Fortey

Red Cage Fungus (*Clathrus ruber*) freshly emerged from its 'egg'. Photo by Stuart Skeates

can be any shade from white to scarlet, golden yellow, or any conceivable gradation from pale brown to nearly black. Some have striking 'bulbs' at the base of the stipe. The colour of the young gills is an essential feature, often violet, yellow or brown. A coloured veil can be present. The cap and stipe are covered in gluten in other species. A sensitive nose will pick up different smells.

Although they may be vital to the life of a tree, the webcaps are a taxonomic jungle. Many mycologists have devoted their lives to 'sorting' them, and it is ongoing. Some are easy to recognise: *C. violaceus* with its dry violet cap, *C. sanguineus* with its bloody red one, *C. armillatus* with its orange bands obliquely painted on its elongate stipe. Many others leave the average mycologist scratching their head. Only one species has been regularly eaten, and many more are known to be very poisonous. I am fortunate to have accompanied the doyens of unpaid (but hardly amateur) British webcap expertise, Geoffrey Kibby and Mario Tortelli, on one of those magic autumn days when mushrooms and toadstools are everywhere. I had one particular site in Oxfordshire in mind for them, on the chalk under beech trees – which is known to be where webcaps are particularly happy. It was not disappointing. One species after another was identified with aplomb by my guides. Geoffrey, with his slender, aquiline nose, is sensitive to subtle smells in a way I have been unable to enjoy for many years. He reminds me of a rather fastidious, aristocratic canine as he pokes around the bushes. Mario is taller and more laconic, but equally knowledgeable, and a skilled photographer. There was one unexpected discovery. I had identified a particularly striking large golden-capped webcap as *Cortinarius elegantissimus* (it does not have a common name, though Most Elegant Webcap would be an obvious tag), but Mario was suspicious that it might be something else. Indeed it was, as the spores were completely different from those of the Most Elegant. *Cortinarius bergeronii* could be added to the British catalogue of more than three hundred webcap varieties.*

Exactly how many species of webcaps there are is now being attacked by sequence analysis of critical segments of their DNA. This may, to be optimistic, at last provide arbitration on the many taxonomic issues that earlier generations grappled with. A monograph published in 2022 devoted to these tricky toadstools was tellingly entitled *Taming the Beast.*† The trouble is that apart from a minority of distinctive species, others blend into one another, or have subtly different flesh reactions with chemicals that had previously proved useful in discrimination, like caustic potash or sulphuric acid. Even Geoffrey Kibby admits that formerly, before the new techniques were available, he only got about three-quarters of his identifications 'right'. What is clear is that the total number of species recognised is still increasing. The same is true for another mycorrhizal genus, *Inocybe* – the fibrecaps – with duller gills than the webcaps, and a cap that typically looks as if it had been thatched radially with fine straw. If anything, the discrimination of species is *more*

---

* Kibby and Tortelli published their splendid summary of British species in 2022: *The Genus Cortinarius in Britain*, Summerfield Books.

† Molecular evidence allowed the 'beast' to be divided into ten genera, which will eventually help identifications, but which are currently beyond the remit of the present writer.

difficult in this case, because many fibrecaps are small and uncharismatic LBMs, unloved save by a few dedicated enthusiasts. Then we have to add a host of even less conspicuous mycorrhizal fungi, some of them fruiting as no more than hard-to-see white patches on the forest floor. So many species, so much to learn. A cynic might ask: does it matter how many there are, apart from what the poet W.B. Yeats called 'the fascination of what's difficult'? It does matter, for surprising reasons.

Mycorrhiza is essential for healthy tree growth. If I dig anywhere under the canopy in our beech wood it does not take long to come across the growing tips of tree roots. They often have a slightly puffy appearance, resembling some finely branched corals; they have a solid feel that is unlike the rootlets of herbs. These tree roots display ectomycorrhiza (*ecto* – external). Each tree root is covered on the outside by a mantle of fungal mycelium, much as fingers might be encased by tight kid gloves. This is where the collaboration between tree and fungus is enacted. There are other kinds of mycorrhiza, particularly one termed endomycorrhiza (*endo-* internal), where the fungal interactions occur *within* the plant cells as finely plumose 'bushes' (arbuscular mycorrhiza); this is produced by microfungi very different from the mushrooms and toadstools that are the focus of my story. I will not give it the attention it deserves in nature. The mycelium producing the *ecto*mycorrhiza could belong to any one of the larger fungi that were compatible with that particular tree. In the case of our beech trees, it could be an appropriate brittlegill, milkcap, *Amanita*, bolete, webcap or fibrecap – or one of many more I have not listed.

There must be hefty competition to gain the benefits that follow when a tree root is colonised. This is a collaboration that will be fought for.

The technical term for the fungus-tree partnership is mutualism, a positive symbiosis where both partners benefit. A one-sentence description of the mycorrhizal relationship might be: the fungus partner supplies the tree with water and nutrients, while in return the tree provides the fungus with sugars (and fats) derived from its photosynthetic activities. Both parties share the benefits of sun and soil. The hyphal threads of the fungus scavenge through the ground and the litter. Since hyphae are usually only a few thousandths of a millimetre in diameter, an active network can consist of many thousands, even millions, of tiny, questing interconnected threads. Imagine it as a kind of pervasive mist passing through the soil. The statistics are as hard to grasp as the prodigious numbers of spores produced by a mushroom: a regular claim is that a gram of soil may contain a hundred metres of hyphae. To put it on another scale, in a hectare of forest soil there may be several tonnes of mycelium, much of it belonging to mycorrhizal basidios. This prodigious network allows trees to benefit from the soil on a scale that could never be attained by roots alone.

Although it has been known for many years that fungi obtain nutrients vital for the health of its host, the complex biochemistry of the processes involved has powered many a PhD thesis in more recent years. It is not just a question of picking up useful elements as if they were lying in packets on a supermarket shelf. The most important of these elements are nitrogen, phosphorus, sulphur and iron, all of which fulfil important roles in the growth of healthy plants. The enzyme tool kit of the mushroom is adapted to work on complex molecules in the soil, cutting them down into smaller units that can eventually be absorbed by the roots, charged with valuable gifts. Phosphorus is an essential component in basic biological processes at the cellular level. Sulphur is necessary for the formation of chlorophyll, and thus a sine qua non for photosynthesis, and nitrogen is needed to manufacture amino acids. Iron is not rare in nature – in fact, it is very common as iron hydroxide in many soils – but it cannot be absorbed directly by plants in this form. It has to be wrapped up inside an organic molecule to make a parcel that can successfully be delivered to the roots; fungi have perfected this gift-wrapping at the submicroscopic level. Without iron, photosynthesis cannot prosper and leaves become pallid and die. The fungus partner in turn needs sugars as the fuel that powers the growth of mycelium as new cell walls are required. The exchange of gifts between fungus and tree takes place where the cells of the two organisms are adjacent on the roots. The process might be compared with a customs post between two countries, where protocols have to be observed before passage between different territories can be permitted; the trade runs both ways, through gates, but fluctuates in intensity according to supply and demand. Some gates can only be passed through if a specially designed (molecular) key is applied. If trade ceases, the border can be shut down – or opened up elsewhere. The peaceful forest floor is the site of millions of these unacknowledged transactions, which must continue if the health of the habitat is to be maintained.

When a seedling beech appears in our wood, a pair of opposed, pale-green seed leaves shaped rather like small table tennis bats arise first. Then a shoot pokes out between them; this little shoot has the potential to develop into a new tree and produces the first leaves that look like those of its parent. This seedling would doubtless produce roots to match, tentatively exploring the ground. A mycorrhizal partner would be waiting for this moment. Perhaps a nearby mycelium would attempt to set up a link; or maybe potential candidates would lurk in what has been called the 'spore bank' – a stash of fungus spores that can endure within the leaf litter until an opportunity arises. With such a prosperous future in store it seems incontrovertible that competition to make a mycorrhiza with a newcomer would be intense. Equally, a seedling without a mycorrhizal chaperone would be doomed to fail. The odds are probably stacked in favour of fungal partners already on the patch, and these would most likely belong to the nearest mature beech tree. There is good evidence for this. Radioactive tracers have proved that nutrients derived from a nearby tree are transferred through the fungal web to the seedling: and since such seedlings are within a few metres of where the beech nuts drop to the ground there is most likely a genetic relationship between the seedling and the nearby tree. Around a fine old tree there may be many such seedlings that might be helped through their formative years.

You could – if you wished – describe this as the 'mother tree' looking after its 'offspring'. When the old tree eventually dies the 'offspring' finally have their chance in the sun, having been nursed in this way through their adolescence. Although the possibility has been mooted since 2009, one book, Suzanne Simard's 2021 *Finding the Mother Tree*, took this idea to its apogee, revealing a further agenda in its subtitle – *Uncovering the Wisdom and Intelligence of the Forest.* The woodland trees are quite like us! This idea had already been popularised in a bestselling 2019 book by a German forester, Peter Wohlleben (*The Hidden Life of Trees: What They Feel, How They Communicate*). There was no ducking the comparison with human emotions in this book – trees 'screamed' as they were being felled, according to his account. The forest was a collection of families. At the same time, the sphere of influence of the mycorrhizal network was growing. It could spread from tree to tree. A whole woodland could be interlinked by a connecting web of mycelium.

Communication channels through this network could pass nutrients to where they might be needed. Information could travel the same way; if nasty beetles arrived in one part of the wood, trees further down the line could be informed so that they could prime their chemical defences. The 'wood wide web' was a brilliant phrase to encapsulate what was supposed to be going on beneath the forest floor, a mycological metaphor for the interconnectedness of an ecosystem. It had both timeliness and novelty. Mycologists who for years had been promoting the importance of fungi in nature were now at the popular centre of the action – at last, they were all the rage. It is small wonder that awareness of the wood wide web grew apace, like vigorous and penetrative mycelium. At a time when everyone was being urged to plant trees – for the good of the planet, for the benefits to mental health – 'tree hugging', at one time viewed with some suspicion as a hippie eccentricity, became a way of showing sympathy with that ubiquitous web. Animations that are easily accessible on the all-too-human worldwide web portrayed trees with glowing roots sending their beneficence from one neighbour to another. There was something definitely comforting about this model of what goes on in our woodlands. It quickly gained traction.

Scientists should always be on the alert for anthropomorphism – attributing human characteristics to biological processes – and one of the obvious features of the wood wide web was that it was shot through with notions of 'just like us'. Trees showed their wisdom and intelligence, they had feelings and metaphorically 'spoke' to one another. This was more than just a tool to make difficult concepts explicable, it was seductive to investigators, too. The collaboration between unrelated organisms that undoubtedly happens in the mycorrhizal 'trading station' had been extended to the scale of whole forests, a kind of salve to Tennyson's view of 'nature red in tooth and claw'. Yet there were reasons to be cautious. Rigorous scientific experimental work on wood decay proved that fungi were actively antagonistic to one another at that scale, and in no way collaborative. Although short-distance transfer of nutrients via the mycelium of mycorrhizal fungi had been established experimentally, the longer range had not been fully investigated.

By 2023, some of the scientists who had originally been involved in the wood wide web were urging caution, and a summary in the scientific journal *Nature Ecology & Evolution* led by Judith Karst laid out the story of how the citation of research had been biased towards www-positive results and was not sufficiently critical. Experiments still needed to be done. The undoubted attractiveness of the idea had led to a lack of rigour. Writing for a lay audience of wood owners in *Smallwoods* the same year, Professor Katie Field said, 'Anthropomorphic language can serve as a valuable tool in scientific communication [but] it is crucial to exercise caution and ensure that it does not lead to an oversimplification that compromises accuracy and depth of scientific understanding.' This is certainly sober language compared with that of the 'mother tree'. None of these caveats undermine the importance of mycorrhiza in healthy woodland, but it may not play such an interconnected role, or operate on the scale assumed by the wood wide web hypothesis. It says much for the integrity of the scientists that they have raised their own doubts.

As a mere field mycologist, I have to recall what I said about the huge species richness of mycorrhizal fungi, particularly among the agarics. The most prolific genera are linked to living with tree roots: hundreds of species of webcaps (*Cortinarius*) and fibrecaps (*Inocybe*), dozens of brittle-gills and milkcaps, tens of boletes and knights, and Amanitas, and many more. They are all dependent upon securing that place cuddled up to tree roots where a life of collaboration can begin, a life that can last longer than that of most saprotrophic fungi. There is no doubt that establishing and keeping that posting is competitive. There are different survival strategies among these fungi once they are established; for example, molecular evidence has revealed that some species are much commoner on roots than they are as fruit bodies. It is perfectly possible that the vast number of these mycorrhizal species reflects a matching number of techniques for getting ahead of their rivals, or maybe adapting to very particular niches.

In other branches of biology the kind of enrichment that has happened in the webcaps is known as a 'species flock'. These are often associated with active speciation, for which competition is an important driver. This does provide a cogent reason for wanting to know as much as possible about these special collaborative mushrooms; all those names *do* matter. If the wood wide web has anything to recommend it, there must be a change in life strategy from an aggressive mode to a collaborative one once a billet has been safely secured on the roots of beech or birch. All those brittlegills and webcaps and their numerous compatriots are seeking an angle. Perhaps their spores can endure in the soil awaiting their chance. Maybe their mycelium secretes special chemicals that repel rivals. Could this explain why there are so many species on the autumnal forest floor? On the other hand some toadstools – like the Fly Agaric and the Deceiver (*Laccaria laccata*) – seem to have wider tolerance of different host species, so competition and specialisation cannot be the whole story.

One very odd fungus seems to behave differently. *Cenococcum geophilum* has been known since 1820, but was named by Elias Magnus Fries in 1827. This species is very common in woods of all kinds where its dark hyphal threads can form links with both conifers and broadleaved trees, so it is unusually catholic in its tastes. The same species is also unusually widespread, having a virtually global distribution. A most peculiar feature of this fungus is that its fruit body remains undiscovered. It appears to lack the culmination of the fungal lifestyle. Molecular studies reveal that it is an asco rather than a basidio, and that it is distantly related to a well-known saprotroph (*Glonium*) whose very dark fruit bodies look like scabs on wood. What *Cenococcum* produces for its survival are black, grain-like concentrated capsules of mycelium (*sclerotia*) that endure in the surface of the forest soil. Being safely enclosed in a wrapping of the black pigment melanin, these capsules protect the fungus so well that they are known to spring back to life after years (some claim centuries) in the soil whenever a new opportunity arises. Since *Cenococcum* is also host tolerant, it can move from tree to tree – perhaps even from oak to pine and back again – and might even be a possible candidate for moving a single web of mycelium through a stretch of woodland. Whether this develops a channel for sharing resources is another question. If only it could connect one woodland to another across a continent then its reach would be limitless, but who would dare suggest a wwwww (world-wide wood wide web)?

In our woodland in late summer small excavations near the trunks of beech trees are marked by little piles of soil and leaf litter that reveal where some creature has been digging. It must have been after something. Closer examination reveals the characteristic rootlets of beech trees exposed in the sides of the excavation, showing the plump, slightly pinkish appearance of a fungal covering. So whatever was being unearthed must have something to do with roots. Using a child's toy rake, a nearby patch of litter and old beech nuts can be readily cleared away to reveal the top of the soil layer. Then raking becomes more difficult as the earth is quite flinty, with lots of pebbles that get in the way, but here are the branching roots. What cannot be seen are the yards of fungal hyphae, finer than cobwebs, that must permeate the soil in every direction, feeding nutrients towards the root tips. Then a 'pebble' is scratched out of the ground that looks different. It is a finely warty, orange-brown sphere, not much bigger than a glass marble. Within a few minutes three more items of a similar size and colour emerge from beneath the soil layer. This must have been what the diggers were after: truffles, or more precisely False Truffles (*Elaphomyces muricatus*).

Subterranean fruit bodies: a find with all the thrill of the esoteric. These small brown balls belong to another class of collaborators that never see the light of day. Truffles are as obligatorily mutualist as any brittlegill, but their life is conducted in secret. One of my finds even shows fine mycor-rhizal 'hairs' on the outside of the sphere. When cut with a sharp knife this small truffle reveals a thick, two-layered skin surrounding a marbled interior where the spores are maturing. It looks a little like an earthball (*Scleroderma*), but the resemblance is misleading, for the earthballs are basidios whereas *Elaphomyces* is an asco – the marbled interior is where the asci grow and mature and release their black spores. The puzzle remains about the identity of the animal that made the holes in the ground that showed me where to dig. *Elaphomyces* are also known as 'deer truffles' and it might be presumed that deer find them by smell and eat them. There are indeed deer in my woodland, but I have only seen them browsing; perhaps secretive, small muntjac deer might be able to dig under cover of darkness. Badgers pass through the wood, and have an acutely developed sense of smell (they even sniff out subterranean bee nests) and they are good diggers. The ubiquitous grey squirrels may be interested. The case remains open.

Truffle is a catch-all term for many fungi that develop subterranean fruit bodies. The truffles of gastronomy are species of just one genus among many. Most are ascos, but basidios have also evolved into truffles. The more they are studied, the more it is evident that 'being a truffle' is just another life option for fungi, and, such is the endlessly creative ingenuity of the mycosphere, a life below ground has evolved independently many times. This might seem extraordinary: after all, it is like volunteering to bury yourself alive! There are good reasons for this self-interment. Truffles provide many more applicants for the post of ectomycorrhizal partner – adding to what is already a very long list, and in my view increasing competition still further. Developing below ground has several advantages; buried fruit bodies are less prone to suffer from the water loss that often curtails the reproductive lives of their surface cousins, and their favoured potato-like shape is an economical way of packing the greatest number of spores into the smallest possible volume. They do, however, face an obvious problem: how to spread their spores in the absence of any possibility of reaching a breeze. Their cunning ruse is to smell delicious. Wild pigs cannot resist them, and their snouts are the right shape to grub them up. Human beings drool at the first mention of the White Truffle of Italy or the Black Truffle of France. In Australia, subterranean fungi have become the principal food of marsupial mammals like potoroos, and I have seen their diggings that prove it. Whatever-it-is in my wood falls for a similar temptation. The spores pass through the intestinal tract of the guzzler to be spread around the woods; and wild pigs do produce a lot of manure. Rainwater helps the spores to find their roots of choice. The life cycle is renewed.

The Black Truffle, Truffe du Périgord (*Tuber melanosporum*) is the most commercially important species of *Tuber*, the genus that includes the gastronome's objects of desire. It is particularly well known from southern France, but it is not uncommon in Italy and Spain – wherever the Mediterranean climate coincides with a limestone soil and its oak or hazel partners. It was once the basis of a major industry to supply the tables of Paris; in the late nineteenth century up to 1,500 tonnes a year of the precious *Tuber* were sent from the Midi northwards, often on specially commissioned trains. Since these truffles are black, they must have looked like shipments of coal; but what a cloud of fragrance must have trailed behind! Covered with polygonal warts, and dark, with a mottled interior, they deliver more than they promise from their appearance. The *sanglier* or wild boar that the penetrating odour evolved to attract still live among the upland scrubby oaks, in spite of the removal of their special foodstuff. By the late twentieth century the truffle yield had declined greatly to about 20 tonnes. Truffles had moved from the quotidian to the recherché. The market price has risen accordingly.

Much is now known about the conditions necessary for the collaboration between truffle and its partner to prosper. The best truffle fruiting happens in association with middle-aged trees in open situations: dense forest is disappointing; young trees have to wait. Although they will never be farmed like mushrooms, seedling trees *can* be inoculated with mycelium to give them the right partner from the start. Then the nascent trees have to be planted in the correct terrain, but the first crop cannot be harvested until the trees are at least fifteen years old. Truffle farming demands a leisurely state of mind. Climate change is likely to allow the Black Truffle to prosper further north from its traditional range. There is at least one secret site in southern England where inoculated hazel trees are apparently happily living in company with Black Truffle, but it will take fifteen years to know whether the experiment has been successful. If it is, it should be most profitable.

Trained pigs and dogs are still employed to find Black Truffles. These olfactory sleuths smell them out even deep underground. Twenty years ago I joined some trufflers with their dogs in Sardinia. I found it less appealing than I had imagined. The small dogs seemed to be kept dangerously thin, to ensure that they were hungry for the meagre rewards they received from sniffing out the sites where the hidden booty lay concealed. They looked like undernourished strays. The hunters were taciturn, and reluctant to locate a treasure tree in our presence, as if they thought we might sneak back after dark to try to find one for ourselves.

A more appealing version of their trade is to be found in the charming film *The Truffle Hunters* (2020), which follows the fortunes of elderly Italian fungus seekers, wild of hair and beard, as they tramp through the woods of the Piedmont in search of their fortune. A splendid variety of dogs are their indispensable helpmeets, each one devoted to its master, several of them equally wild of hair, and probably regarded as more important than the wife (if the wife had not already left her obsessive spouse). The hunters are focused upon a truffle even more sought after than the Black Truffle: the White Truffle, *Tuber magnatum*, the truffle of Alba, which is almost confined to a relatively small area with oaks in Piedmont in northern Italy (it is also known in part of Croatia). As might be guessed from its common name, the fruit body is almost white and smooth; it is often lobed and irregular. These truffles are both rare and hard to find, so the market price is always high. It is debatable whether or not Beluga caviar is the more expensive, but £5,000 for a kilogram of Alba truffle would not be unusual. The odour is extraordinarily intense – the taste is similar – a distillation of everything that is *umami*, a promise of mouthwatering deliciousness, ripe and many-layered. It is also most penetrating, infusing the atmosphere with its succulence. The chemicals producing its unique perfume are volatile, so the truffle should be eaten as soon after discovery as possible – and very thinly sliced to dress scrambled eggs to make them little short of divine.

Some might say that the fragrance of White Truffle is almost *too* pungent, insistent, balancing on that delicate point between ripeness and decay. I have had only one close encounter with the famous delicacy in all its glory. In London I was presented with a tiny piece as a gift. I had to take it home wrapped in gauze in a small cardboard box. At that time my commuter train had rather small compartments, holding perhaps a dozen passengers. I had my precious gift in my small briefcase, and it wasn't long before the confined space of the carriage was infused with *umami*. Several of my fellow commuters were giving me covert glances. They had clearly identified me as the source of the smell, and I inferred that they thought I must be suffering from some rare variety of body odour. By the time we arrived at Maidenhead station, two of the passengers had alighted and pointedly moved to the next compartment. I was torn between bluffing it out or confessing. The next station was where I got out. As I moved to let myself out of the carriage I uttered a strangled explanation: 'It wasn't me. It was the truffle!' I did not linger to assess the reaction.

The British native is the Summer Truffle (*Tuber aestivum*). Although still a pleasant addition to an omelette, it is no match for the Périgord or White for intensity of flavour. It looks like a more coarsely warted version of *Tuber melanosporum*, usually of a size that can be comfortably held in the palm of the hand, and in my experience its companions are beech or hazel, although other trees have been mentioned. It was once more widely appreciated than it is now. John Ramsbottom described how large estates in the nineteenth century employed specialist truffle hunters (and their dogs) to keep the table supplied. In *Mushrooms and Toadstools*, he records meeting the last professional British truffler, Alfred Collins, who died in 1953, the same year in which Ramsbottom's New Naturalist book was published. Collins lived in Jubilee Cottage, Winterslow, near Salisbury, where chalk and beech combine to make ideal conditions for underground fungi. Lilian Moody (Alfred's daughter) recalled her truffling father in *The Countryman* in 1995. Alfred was the last in a long family line of Collins trufflers, having been taught the skills by his father Eli. He trained his terriers so well that they allegedly jumped over prone rabbits rather than lose the trail of the fungus. 'When the dogs located a truffle they started scratching the ground above it', where-upon Alfred employed a special digging spike to retrieve the delicacy. The spike was bequeathed to the Salisbury Museum, where I hope and expect it is still curated. His daughter recalled: 'On a good day Alfred would gather 25lb of truf-fles.' He supplied fresh truffles by post, each package carrying his own postmark to ensure authenticity.

I have crossed paths with Summer Truffles several times. In Savernake Forest, to the east of Marlborough, there are many fine beech trees with clear stretches of leaf litter uncluttered with brambles beneath. I had read that truffles could be located by looking for swarms of trufflivorous (to coin a word) flies that dance above the site of the fruit bodies. Whether by luck or judgement, I did spot numbers of tiny, dancing flies and did indeed find a black Summer Truffle not too far below the surface. This was a long time ago; it was my first subterranean fungus. Many years later a stranger arrived at my door in Henley-on-Thames carrying a plastic box. He had been told that I knew about such things. While cutting a new drainage channel near a hazel in his garden, he had come across these curious, dark concretions in the trench. They were evidently Summer Truffles. I said how interesting they were, but that they would need micro-scopical examination to confirm their identity if he wouldn't mind. That evening, we enjoyed a very good omelette.

The doyenne of British scientific truffle hunters is Caroline

Hobart. When a fungus foray starts its stately progression through the woods, Caroline quickly identifies a likely tree and settles down on a small rug, leaving the crowd to forge onwards. She often stays put for most of the day. The superficial layer of fallen leaves is brushed aside and then Caroline gets to work with a small rake with flexible teeth (I believe it is a children's toy). Once she reaches the root zone, the rake is the right size to pick out even small truffles, which may be no bigger than a pea. None of her finds are of culinary interest, but they are all vital to the health of the tree under which she is sitting.

During the course of a day's work she might easily find half a dozen different species of truffle. On one occasion she pointed out a small, slightly knobbly, pale example that when cut exuded a white, milky juice. This was no asco – in fact, it was a basidio related to the milkcaps I mentioned at the top of this chapter, which release an identical 'milk' if any part of the fruit body is damaged. It was another case of a mushroom adopting the underground life and getting closer to the roots that would guarantee its survival. Jackie found a further example in our own wood. We have got used to staring closely at the ground without worrying what passing walkers will think. Although we are dominated by beech, one part of the wood has an understorey of hazel. Near the largest of these trees Jackie noticed one of those scrapes where digging had taken place during the night (animal unknown), and at the bottom of the scrape was a small, brown, spherical object. I recall that she believed it was some kind of animal excretum, but it was very sharp-eyed of her to spot it. I recognised it as a truffle. Furthermore, it was a truffle with an unpleasant smell – quite the reverse of yummy *umami*. Clearly, not all truffles were there to attract the same animals, and it looked as if this one had been left behind in disgust by whoever dug the hole. I presume the fetid smell was the lure to attract some carrion lover like a crow – or maybe it is true that pigs will eat anything.

In any event, it was a case for Caroline Hobart's unrivalled memory, and the specimen was duly posted to her in Sheffield. She was pleased to report that my wife's little truffle was *Melanogaster ambiguus*, which is much too rarely encountered to have acquired a common name, though you might guess that the Latin translates as 'black stomach' – and its interior is indeed coloured dark by its spores. It is another basidio-turned-truffle. This species, however, shares a common ancestor with *porcini*, with which this book began. It is a bolete that has taken the route underground, doubtless to vie with its terrestrial relatives for space on the roots. In 2020 it was one of many fungi having their molecular sequences determined to reveal their evolutionary origin. It is hard to resist the temptation to anthropomorphise! Spore dropper or spore shooter, every fungus wants to win the race to be the ectomycorrhizal champion. The race took them into the soil, and drove their desire to make the most attractive chemical perfumes. This language would rightly make the purist wince, but maybe can be pardoned for once to explain how the most expensive foodstuff in the world came to be hiding under an oak tree.

8.

Puffers and friends

I have had a long relationship with the Sandy Stiltball (*Battarrea phalloides*). It is one of Britain's scarcest toadstools, and also one of the oddest. It looks as if it is cobbled together from several different kinds of fungus. The fruit body arises from an 'egg' as if it were going to develop into some kind of stinkhorn, or possibly something like the Death Cap. But then a dry, brown and rather shaggy stem a foot high appears, which is unlike that of either stinkhorn or toadstool – it looks almost like a wooden stick. Then, to crown it all, there is a small puffball perched on top as a cap. It's a crazy, mixed-up mushroom! A closer look reveals that the cap is actually a mass of cinnamon-coloured spores, making an imperfect umbrella a few centimetres across. The fruit body arises from a cup-like volva hidden in the ground. I had wanted to see this fungus in the flesh ever since reading about it as a young-ster in John Ramsbottom's *Mushrooms and Toadstools*. Its exotic features are made even more glamorous by its rarity and unpredictable appearance: here skulking under a hedge bank, there tucked inside a hollow tree. It is a Will o' the Wisp of the fungus world, challenging searchers to find it, only to pop up some place where it was least expected.

More than thirty years ago I first learned where *Battarrea* could be seen in all its eccentricity. I have had a long association with the easternmost county of Suffolk, and particularly the stretch of country adjacent to the coast between the small towns of Aldeburgh and Southwold. The Suffolk Wildlife Trust advertised what was claimed to be the smallest nature reserve in Britain – a single hedge bank by the road adjacent to Blyford Church – from which emerged many examples of the elusive fungus. East Anglian churches are nearly always set on slightly higher ground, as much of the landscape was once dominated by marshland. The older churches are constructed almost entirely of flint, because it is the only building stone available locally, although the arches and coigns are predominantly made from imported limestone blocks (many of which came from France after the Norman Conquest), as flint is practically useless when it comes to making corners. Blyford Church is a typical example of its kind. Most of the churchyards in East Anglia have never been fertilised, and the graves have been left alone to rot away over the centuries. This kind of neglect is good for the fungal tribe.

Blyford Church was once surrounded by elms, but Dutch elm disease had removed the larger trees, the dead remains of which could be seen poking out in places from the hedge bank. When I went there, six examples of the Sandy Stiltball appeared along a few metres of the bank, poking out beyond the grass. I had to blink several times to ensure that they were real. They really did look like an amalgam of toadstool and puffball. A few more old dry, brown stems remained from the previous year's crop. These fungi were evidently remarkably persistent. The drivers of passing cars looked curiously at this odd fellow apparently staring intently into an ordinary hedge bank; there was nothing unusual about this site apart from the fungi. Very sandy soil was evident: this part of Britain is also geologically the youngest, and unconsolidated sediments underlie much of it. Because sand drains readily, the site was also very dry, which is not usually favourable for fungi. Since *Battarrea* is a saprotroph, it was a reasonable supposition that it was feeding on the wood of the dead elm. There was plenty still to go.

I returned to Blyford Church over the following years, and the Sandy Stiltball repaid me by showing up, but gradually the numbers of fruit bodies decreased, and then they were seen no more. I assumed that my relationship to *Battarrea* had come to an end; but I was wrong.

In the summer of 1998 I was back home in Oxfordshire and walking on one very wet day along an ancient footpath near Henley known as Pack and Prime Lane, in the Chiltern Hills. Allegedly the name of the track was derived from a time when a traveller was advised to pack a pistol and prime it to protect himself from footpads and ne'er-do-wells. A dangerous soaking was more likely on that day, and a generously proportioned oak tree offered shelter, and invited me to notice a Sandy Stiltball emerging from a low bank just behind the tree. I could hardly believe my eyes, for it had never been recorded in Oxfordshire before. The specimen was collected to send as a voucher to Kew Gardens' mycological repository. I must have presented a curious sight rushing back home cradling my booty sheltered inside my coat while water cascaded down my back and my hair was plastered to my head. The written account of the discovery noted that there was nothing sandy about the locality, though it *was* a dry bank like the other places the Stiltball favours.

When the COVID pandemic began to recede we were allowed once more to make short journeys in the area around Henley. Just over the Buckinghamshire border the small village of Hambleden is the perfect brick-and-flint cluster of cottages arranged around a chalk stream and a fine parish church, all set in an unspoiled valley flanked by beech wood-land. It has been used in countless period television dramas wherein Miss Marple or Lord Peter Wimsey nails the verger as the culprit. The old churchyard had the 'feel' of some-where that should yield mushrooms. I was as surprised as delighted in finding the Sandy Stiltball there, in a corner right under a yew tree: three fine specimens in tip-top condition. The members of the Bucks Group of mycologists were alerted, some of whom came to worship the rarity. It could have been that the dense canopy of the yew made the soil very dry beneath the tree, but there was no sand near this locality either. I was starting to prefer the common name used in North America – Scaly Stalked Puffball – one that did not explicitly tie it to sand. Whichever name is preferable, I doubt whether anyone could challenge me for the Most *Battarrea* in Britain Medal, although it is unlikely that there would be many other contenders for the title.

In the 1990s I also saw the Sandy Stiltball (or whatever) halfway around the world. When I was looking for trilobites in the Great Basin in western USA, there it was by the side of the highway, emerging from the ground in the semi-desert. Much of this area comprises vast valleys where a few choosy cattle browse the sparse vegetation to produce what may be the best steaks in the world. By this stage I was quite insouciant about the strange fungus. It is not uncommonly found in semi-arid regions in North America, and particularly where I was now working. My discovery did suggest the reason for the most important adaptations of this fungal curiosity. It is specifically adapted to dry conditions wherever they occur. It keeps itself all wrapped up in a cosy subterranean 'egg' until ready to emerge. When the stem expands it is dry and hollow, and the spore mass on top expends no energy on making a fleshy cap. Implausible though it may seem, Suffolk and Nevada can be similar, especially where the former has porous, sandy ground. It is rather remarkable that the original descriptions came from British material, a country where it is so rare. The botanical savant Thomas Woodward found it near Bungay in Suffolk in 1783 and by 1785 it had received the name *Lycoperdon phalloides*, acknowledging its odd mix of puffball (*Lycoperdon*) and stinkhorn (*Phallus*) characteristics. The genus name *Battarrea* appeared later, in 1801. Whether subsequent examples are collected from the USA or Africa, the reference material typifying the species remains that from Suffolk, England.

It does seem extraordinary that the same fungus can be found on either side of the Atlantic Ocean and across half a continent. When I cautiously picked my way through the cholla scrub in Nevada, all the plants – the fragrant sagebrush, tough creosote bushes and fearsome cacti – were completely different from those I knew in Britain; only the Stiltball was familiar. It was the biogeographic joker in the pack. To my surprise a few other fungi were tucked under the scrubby vegetation, for even semi-deserts have dead roots underground that can feed mycelium after rainfall. One fungus rising from the ground looked like a white 'button mushroom' the size of my fist that had refused to open up, presumably remaining closed to save what moisture it could while it completed its life cycle. I could not identify it then, but the spores inside had evidently ripened, without the fruit body turning into a regular toadstool. I could find no evidence of gills when I broke one specimen open, but the spores had apparently been produced on a slightly spongy internal tissue. It had a stout, rather tough white stem. When it matured it effectively became just a bag of spores on a stalk.

Judging by the white cap and very dark colour of the spore mass, I had wondered if it could even be related to our familiar *Agaricus* mushroom of field and commerce. It was assuredly another fungus springing a surprise and it was not until I had my books to hand again that I found a possible name for it: *Agaricus deserticola*; its relationship to the typical mushroom of the supermarket shelves had been confirmed by DNA analysis in 2004. The Great Basin had presented me with examples of what are termed secotioid fungi, in which the usual method of spore dispersal from the gills has been abandoned in favour of a kind of arrested development, with spore production internalised. This adaptation is all about saving water to help survival in arid environments by 'boxing in' the mechanics of propagation, and is yet another astonishing example of the inventiveness of the fungal kingdom. It could have been mistaken for a puffball.

One more mushroom remained to surprise me in the Nevada scrub. The American mycologist David Arora described it thus: 'To the feverish, sun-fried, dust-encrusted fungophile driving deliriously across the monotonous mushroom-meagre desert while dreaming of cool coastal pine forests bulging with boletes and flower-filled mountain meadows overflowing with *Agaricus*, it is likely to be mistaken for a miraculous mirage or wistful hallucination.' What it does look like is a foot-high, slender, ghostly pale drumstick emerging from dry ground, often in small groups. It has a white, rather scaly cap in the shape of an unfurled umbrella and a long, distinctly spindly stem with a bulbous base – but the cap never opens. No mirage this, but another specialist for desert life: Desert Shaggy Mane, *Podaxis pistillaris*. It, too, has traded in a conventional lifestyle as a toadstool in favour of keeping its cap closed up until its whole spore mass is ripe for dispersal.

Nonetheless, there was something about the shape of this Shaggy Mane that reminded me of another toadstool. This fungus had what birdwatchers call the 'jizz' – the overall *gestalt* – of another, familiar mushroom, the Shaggy Inkcap (*Coprinus comatus*). Not only the scales on the surface of the cap, and its deep spindle shape, but even the dark colour of the spores resembled a fungus that commonly grows from buried wood in England, where the climate is as wet as the Great Basin is dry. Its other common name is Lawyer's Wig, which is not a bad description of how it looks when it freshly appears on lawns and in flowerbeds in England, though it is not long before the cap dissolves into a wet, inky mass of spores. It looks as if the strange fungus poking out of the ground in the desert must be another specialist version of a familiar one, and molecular evidence has recently confirmed that inkcap relationship of *Podaxis*. It is evident that several different mushrooms evolved similar solutions to living and reproducing in very dry places where mushrooms seem to have no place by rights – an example of evolution on parallel paths if ever there was one.

Like the Sandy Stiltball, the Desert Shaggy Mane has an extraordinarily wide geographical distribution. I was to meet it again when trilobites took me to the remote outback in Queensland, Australia, where the last thing you expect to see in the dry plains is any kind of fungus. It appeared among the scrubby mallee gums in a vast area of semi-desert visited by dingoes and kangaroos but hardly a human. Old men among the Aboriginal tribes are reported to have used the spore mass to darken their white hairs – a strange parallel to the long use of inkcap 'ink' as a pigment in England. Most surprising of all was to find it on the dry side of the Hawaiian island of Maui, growing from volcanic debris; I discovered it while researching my book *The Earth: An Intimate History*, when fungi were the last thing on my mind. Hardly any other terrestrial organisms have such a spread, which poses interesting questions. The endemic floras of arid Australia, Maui and the Great Basin have absolutely nothing in common, so how does a fungus break all the rules of biogeography? It seems implausible that *Podaxis* was spread by human agency, even though there are well-documented examples of fungi being moved across much of the world, like the Devil's Fingers (p. 155) from New Zealand to Britain. The remote areas in which the Desert Shaggy Mane grows seems to make this unlikely; very few people go off-road in either the Great Basin or the Australian outback.

Yet it also stretches the imagination to think of wind-borne spores travelling the immense distances involved. Most fungi shed the majority of their spores quite close to their fruit bodies; only a very special breeze would take them thousands of kilometres. Could the species have spread by way of a series of arid 'stepping stones' – Maui being the Pacific link in the chain? The remote Hawaiian Islands are, however, an overflowing cornucopia of introduced species, most of them disastrous for the native organisms, so if it were to have been introduced anywhere this might be the place. *Podaxis* was first noticed by Carl Linnaeus in 1771, and possibly first recognised scientifically in Australia in the early twentieth century, so there is time for an alien introduction, although it is as likely that it had simply escaped attention 'down under'. The Desert Shaggy Mane looked so well adapted to both its outback and Nevada homes that it is hard to believe it could be other than native to both. I have not yet had the opportunity to see it in its reported South African home but I can almost visualise the habitat in my mind's eye.

Stiltball, Desert Mushroom and Desert Shaggy Mane would once have been classified within a great group of fungi termed Gasteromycetes ('stomach fungi'), which included basidios that develop mature spores within an enclosed 'bag' of various shapes and sizes – and hence differed from the gill-bearing agarics that release their spores directly into the air. Puffballs, earthballs, earthstars and even stinkhorns were once all placed in this great group. It would have been tempting to call them 'gasteros' here; but that does not work any more. It is now clear that not all these 'stomach fungi' are closely related – they have a number of separate origins from different ancestors and can no longer be lumped together. It was as if brown bears and koala bears had once been placed in the same category because of their general bearishness, when now we know that the larger bear is a placental mammal and the smaller a marsupial, and so they do not belong in the same taxonomic drawer. Classifications reflect knowledge. They change with advances in understanding, and time and again the relatively recent availability of cheap DNA sequencing has placed many previous assumptions about fungi under the molecular microscope.

All of which is a preamble to stating that the three peculiar fungi that grow in arid climates we have visited in this chapter are all agarics. They belong in the *same* group as Field Mushrooms, waxcaps and Death Caps, for all their bizarre attributes. They have similarities at the molecular level that place this beyond question. It is an extraordinary thought that any kind of puffball might have evolved from a conventional mushroom – they look so different. Even though nature is full of dramatic evolutionary gymnastics, this one could look like a somersault too far. So consider this scenario. On several occasions in the long history of the fungi, the kind of strategy used by *Podaxis* to ripen its spores 'under cover' may have led to specialised fruit bodies that were in no hurry to spread them. The outer hyphal layers of this modified mushroom became the longer-term cover (*peridium*, often in two layers) for a 'bag' of spores, to be released at leisure. Some kind of mouth (*ostiole*) developed at the apex of the fruit body to allow the spores to escape when they were ready to do so. By this point you have a typical puffball.

The most important evolutionary step was permitting the spores to mature from basidia retained inside the 'bag' in a tissue (*gleba*) woven from mycelium. Young puffballs are often firm inside and the solid interior is white. As the spores begin to ripen the interior tissue becomes soft and yellowish. Eventually all that remains are mature brown spores, often accompanied by the spongy mycelial 'struts' (*capillitium*) that allowed the interior to develop, the whole still enveloped in a membrane (the inner layer of the 'skin'), which is by now quite soft and pliable. The puffball is ready to puff. The touch of a raindrop may be enough to release a cloud of tens of thousands of spores from the apex, but a mature puffball can endure for weeks, or even months, so turning into a repository for reproduction for a greatly extended season compared with a conventional mushroom. The puffball can cope better with drought than its gilled contemporaries. It is still quite a step to evolve a specialised puffball from an 'unopened' mushroom like *Podaxis*, not least that this modified mushroom does not 'puff' – it simply decays into a mass of black spores – but it does provide a model to explain how and why natural selection might work to push the design of the fruit body in the puffball direction.

The puff of brown 'smoke' that comes from quickly squeezing a mature Common Puffball (*Lycoperdon perlatum*) remains the best way to demonstrate the reality of spores to a group of fledgling mycologists. It often elicits a delighted gasp. Within a few seconds the cloud has dispersed into the air, and this is a good time to explain how those spores are still everywhere about us no matter how invisible they are, carried on the whim of the breeze to find exactly the right place to germinate. Even in the middle of winter in a damp wood slightly sad-looking, deflated specimens of the Stump Puffball (*Apioperdon pyriforme*) clustered on rotting wood can still be persuaded to perform, if a little half-heartedly.

The Giant Puffball (*Calvatia gigantea*) is probably the world's most conspicuous fungus. Huge, bloated, white and shining, and often much larger than a football, it emerges singly or in clusters in fields or on the margins of woodland among straggly nettles. It gets noticed. I have more than once spied one from a passing car and stopped to collect it, ignoring the terrified protests from my family. Local newspapers have been known to feature a monster specimen in a photograph in conjunction with a small child for scale. I have seen it growing in graveyards and in the central reservation of a motorway (the one I didn't pick). It does not last long in its pristine whiteness, gradually yellowing, losing its outer skin and becoming much less conspicuous. Eventually, it adopts the umber brown colour of the mature spores and then it hangs around for months in fields and hedge banks, supported by its mycelial skeleton, as light as a soufflé. Passers-by might give it a desultory kick, and then a cloud of spores will be released in wisps of diffuse smoke. This puffball does not have a special 'mouth' to release the spores, nor a clearly defined stem, which makes it rather different from the majority of its tribe. Most of the walkers who notice the brown ball will make no connection between this strange object and the white globes of its heyday.

The Giant Puffball is a sphere of superlatives. Consider the number of spores in one good-sized fruit body: there are estimates that such a specimen might yield 7,000,000,000,000 – seven trillion – spores (I have never counted them myself). Each spore is round and slightly spiky and about five thousandths of a millimetre across. So upon this micro-dust depends the future of the species. To put it in context, our galaxy the Milky Way has about a hundred billion stars, so a single puffball is seventy times as prolific. By the same token this puffball must have one of the lowest fertility success rates of anything on Earth, since there is (to put it generously) no more than a trillionth chance of any given spore producing a new mycelium and puffball. My coral specialist friend tells me that some reef corals release unfathomably large numbers of tiny larvae during a brief spawning episode, though these are many times larger than a spore – but the stratagem is comparable, since the job of the larva is to find exactly the right spot to develop in an endless ocean: safety in vast numbers. I believe that the Giant Puffball may be commoner than it once was, as it seems to tolerate nitrogenous conditions that are becoming more prevalent. As the edges of artificially fertilised meadows become full of nettles, the Giant Puffball can still find a home. It can only be eaten when it is very young, while the interior is still as white as a cheap supermarket loaf. If sliced and fried in butter till it is golden on both sides, it makes an excellent companion for scrambled eggs. If the inside has started to go a little yellowish the taste will already have a nasty acidic edge.

In fields with short grass in late summer a common sight is what look like scaled-down Giants – Grey or Brown Puffballs (*Bovista*). They are particularly found on golf courses, where they must infuriate players who mistake them for golf balls in a prime position to make it on to the green. At the same stage they can look like button mushrooms from afar and there have been occasions when I have sprinted across a fairway, basket in hand, only to be disappointed. As it matures, *Bovista* loses the white outer layer of its covering and the tough inner layer darkens to lead-grey or brownish according to the species. When fully mature this puffball becomes almost feather light and blows about in the wind, the spores escaping through a ragged hole in its surface. I have found it stranded in the middle of a road. It becomes the fungal equivalent of tumbleweed – those dried-up herbs of several species that bowl along southern American highways in the wind, which helps to distribute their seeds. Nature seems to be full of such similes.

The pestle-shaped Common Puffball is also edible when it is young and white inside, but I think it is hardly worth the trouble. Like all the true puffballs it is a saprotroph, and can be found on the ground by roadsides or in woodland, and in all weathers, so it is not fussy. It also has a worldwide distribution, which must surely testify to the efficiency of puffing into the wind, as well as its adaptability. Unlike the Giant Puffball, it has a stout stem that remains a stem and is not part of the fertile head. When it is young the top of the puffball is covered with little pyramidal warts of two sizes; these have a beautiful regular, but scattered arrangement. They can easily be brushed off the surface. As the puffball ages the warts leave behind a polygonal pattern as the fruit body changes from white to brown. At this stage it is a good puffer.

Several related species have different sizes and arrangements of the surface decorations, which is one of many reasons to always carry a hand lens into the field. In our local beech woods an attentive forayer can have a close encounter with one of the less common and most appealing puffballs. Tucked down into the litter it looks very like a small, pale-brown, rolled-up hedgehog – a ball of spines, no less. This is the Spiny Puffball (*Lycoperdon echinatum*) and a little scraping around reveals the stem anchoring it to the woodland soil. I can think of no reason why resembling a hedgehog should confer any advantage upon this pretty fungus. The resemblance is only superficial as the spines are not particularly sharp.

Other kinds of puffballs are frequently found along path sides near *Lycoperdon*. The Common Puffball is often outnumbered by rounded, yellow or pale-brown fruit bodies that tend to form clusters, looking somewhat like potatoes emerging from a bank, or even from hard ground. A pair of them side by side can look distinctly testicular. In dry summers these fungi are often the only specimens that can be brought home, and they occasionally occur in such numbers that the ground appears to be blistered. These earthballs (*Scleroderma*) are pretenders. They are not true puffballs. The first thing you notice is that they have a different texture – they are hard when fresh, more like a genuine golf ball than a Field Mushroom. The flesh inside is marbled, resembling that of black truffles. They do not smell pleasant; the odour is sometimes described as rubbery – although I am not quite sure what that means. They are without a stem, but attached to pale mycelial cords in the ground, although some species do extend downwards into a gnarled 'pseudostipe'. Earthballs are designed to be tough customers. The commonest of them (*S. citrinum*) has a very thick yellow skin with a scurfy exterior – if you cut one through, the outer skin surrounds its innards in the same way the peel of a Seville orange encases the juicy fruit. Unlike the puffballs, the central spore 'factory' (*gleba*) is soon black, but remains very firm for a long time. Cavities develop within it that are lined with spore-producing basidia. It can take several months before the interior of the earthball is ready to become a puffer when the black spores are fully ripe, and the supporting tissues have degenerated. It then opens through a large, ragged vent in the top to make a crude cup. Every year I give a talk and lead a foray in October in the Harcourt Arboretum associated with Oxford University, at the edge of the attractive village of Nuneham Courtenay. On one occasion I was caught out in front of a small crowd by trying to make an earthball puff. The cup collects rainwater. My enthusiastic squeeze to demonstrate puffing projected a black, spore-filled soup into my face. It was the mycological equivalent of the custard pie. The small boys in the party were greatly amused.

There are many differences between these puffing pretenders and the true puffballs. They are not primarily saprotrophs, instead they are mycorrhizal partners with trees, which is why they accompany birches in such abundance in the part of Suffolk I know well. Their spores ripen in a different way and are about twice the size of those of puffballs. These terrestrial balls are also somewhat poisonous. They do not blow around like tumbleweed at any time in their life cycle. Their empty sacs endure for a long time in situ, sometimes breaking up into a crude star that becomes stained green with algae, at which point few would be able to guess their fungal persuasion. Earthballs have a separate evolutionary origin from other puffballs. DNA analysis has proved that they share a common ancestor with the fungus with which this book began – *porcini*. These inedible, tough, spherical survivalists are distant cousins of the boletes, the fleshy kings of the table that are all too soon decayed. The pore-bearing object of culinary desire has an undesirable alter ego, one that nobody wants to eat, not even snails. This may seem an astonishing transformation, but we have seen it before. It seems plausible that the processes of natural selection that made puffballs out of agarics made earthballs out of boletes. This would entail altering development so that spores matured while still enclosed, in the manner of the desert agarics. Certainly, earthballs cope well with dry conditions compared with their fleshy relatives – their outer skin ensures that they do not dehydrate, and they appear even in heat waves when the hopeful hunter searches in vain for *porcini* or one of its tasty relatives. They crouch down low in the ground, often partly buried. I sometimes think they are halfway to being truffles. Indeed, unscrupulous traders have used them to impersonate real truffles in patés and sauces. Their ingestion is known to cause stomach ache and nausea, but does not result in fatality, so death by earthball remains an improbable scenario.

★   ★   ★

On the north west side of the Chilterns the chalk scarp looks down on the fertile Aylesbury Plain below. For southern England the scarp is unusually steep, which has allowed it to escape the agricultural exploitation that has altered so much downland countryside. Sheep still graze on the slope and their tracks criss-cross the hillside. Towards the top of the hill, rock rose still blooms and has its own associated fungi in due course. Fragrant wild thyme and oregano decorate the tops of anthills, and the occasional orchid donates a splash of colour in June. On the flanks of Shirburn Hill above Watlington there is a strange, dark-green expanse of woodland hanging on to the steep side of the hill. On overcast days it can look almost black. It is a miniature forest of box trees (*Buxus sempervirens*).

A few years ago my wife Jackie and I were involved with a survey of such woodland, and found that most box trees were probably planted as game cover in large estates. These rare, dense, chalk-slope woods are something different. They are likely native. Box trees grow very slowly and spread by natural layering wherever branches touch the ground. In many places, as in Box Hill, Surrey, the hard boxwood has been used for centuries to make precision wooden tools – it is one of very few woods that can make a screw joint – as well as wind instruments and the boxwood rulers of the pre-plastic era. There is still a demand for the wood today, particularly from baroque revival orchestras. Such native box woodland is very densely packed. The outer branches lean down to the ground, making the whole mass of trees well nigh impenetrable. Nothing else grows there, except an occasional struggling mountain ash. Once the fortress has been breached by pushing aside branches and squeezing through, a strange world appears inside: the yellowish trunks of the trees make a series of supports as if the overarching canopy of leaves were a kind of enveloping tent. It is very dark. A hobbit would not seem out of place. Because so little light reaches the ground almost nothing grows there. It is not a little eerie.

When I ventured into this wood with a surveying party in the autumn of 2017, it did not seem the best place to prospect for fungi. People were stumbling around in the half-light getting poked by dead branches. The woodland floor appeared unpromisingly dry. Then the silence was broken by an excited cry: 'Earthstars!' Of all the puffers, the earthstars (*Geastrum*) are the most beautiful, and their discovery always causes a frisson of excitement. Here was a group of the largest and commonest species, the Collared Earthstar (*G. triplex*), each one a couple of inches or more across. A pale-brown, central spore-carrying sphere, with a distinctly projecting mouth (*ostiole*), was surrounded by six to nine outspread arms, like those of a starfish; on some specimens the arms had curved back and slightly elevated the fruit body. Several showed a collar around the spore sac. It was a delightful group. A tentative prod stimulated the expected spore puff. These earthstars had happily matured under this almost lightless, dense canopy. Further searching revealed some immature individuals, looking rather like onions with pointy 'noses', hunkering down on the forest floor. It was clear how the earthstar must have matured by the rays peeling back, almost like a flower opening from a bud, the outer layers of the 'skin' (*periderm*), making the star that allowed the inner one to achieve prominence as a special-ised sac helping the expulsion of the spores to the atmosphere. 'Earthflowers' would have been as good a name as earthstar.

Hardly five minutes had passed when another cry went up from a different part of the wood: 'Weather Earthstars!' Now this was really exciting because this earthstar (*Geastrum corollinum*) is very uncommon. We hoped it might be a 'first' for Oxfordshire here in this apparently most unpromising site: a group of three or so, about half the size of the Collared Earthstar but with a very prominent conical 'mouth' where the spores were expelled. This particular earthstar has a remarkable ability. When the weather is dry, the arms curl up around the spore body, but when it is wet they fold back to allow spore distribution to continue. Ours was out-stretched. In the enrolled state there is perhaps no more graphic example of water conservation in fungi. We carefully collected one sample to be sure of our identification, but we would bring it back to finish its work. Within a few minutes a third earthstar was discovered: the Striated Earthstar (*Geastrum striatum*), a smaller, elegant fungus with a pointy mouth scribed with parallel grooves, and the whole, rather small spore-bearing flask born aloft on a stalk. Not many of our party had seen it before. Nor did it stop there: eventually, we discovered that a total of five (possibly six) different earthstars enjoyed a living in this gloomy woodland – more than had ever been recorded together from a single locality. It was proving earthstar heaven.

Now was the best time for our group to discuss why this particular place so suited these peculiarly engaging, and almost certainly saprotrophic fungi. It was implausible that there was any particular association with box trees as mycorrhizal partners. The most noticeable feature of the site was the absence of almost everything else. The ground was bare except for box debris and soil. There were hardly any other mushrooms or toadstools to be found; the only common fungus was an orange patch that could be observed on many of the standing dead branches; I later identified it as *Peniophora proxima*, Box Crust. Hence it seemed likely that the absence of any kind of fungal competition had helped our earthstars to flourish (though it was always possible that there may have been other species only present as mycelium). The dry habitat may have eliminated potential competitors. Our Weather Earthstar was already adapted to conserve water by spreading or recurving its 'starfish' arms according to the meteorological conditions. All earthstars could bide their time until it was time to ripen their spores. There were also virtually no flowering plants in this dim underworld – except the remains of a foxglove or two, perhaps. Even that possible competition was removed. I like to think that the earthstars were able to colonise a habitat that discouraged virtually everything else, bringing their own curious beauty to a dark and secret place.

Shiplake Church is a pretty brick-and-flint building of medieval origin and largely Victorian restoration not far from the River Thames on the Oxfordshire side. It is close to an ancient manor (now a private school) and somewhat further removed from an affluent riverside village that is home to many commuters and their families. As in Blyford, churchyards and graveyards are profitable places to search for interesting fungi. They have generally escaped artificial fertilisers and the grass around gravestones has been mowed often enough to keep fertility low and encourage a mixed sward. In Shiplake churchyard a splendid cedar tree domi-nates the gate that leads to the church. The dense canopy of the cedar is such an effective umbrella that virtually nothing will grow underneath it. A dry patch of needle duff encircles the trunk of the tree. It might sound a little like Shirburn Hill under the box trees. In November 2008 I was thrilled to find more than twenty small earthstars in this dry area where nothing else grew.

These examples were different from all I had seen before because the spore bodies had been lifted from the ground on stilts! Though they were not much taller than an upside-down eggcup, there was something inescapably anthro-pomorphic about these fungi, as if they were tiny homunculi trying to break free of the ground. Each one had a strikingly lead-grey round 'head' the size of a small marble carrying a narrow pyramidal 'mouth' for the spores to exit. On closer examination it was clear that what had lifted up the 'head' were the rays that in most earthstars spread horizontally to give the typical starfish-like appearance. Here they had curved steeply downwards to achieve an elevation that would help spore release clear of the litter. When I dug one earth-star carefully out of the needle duff, I discovered that its structure was more complicated: each of the arms was attached to a point around the edge of a thin bag buried somewhat in the soft ground. Needles adhered to the outside of the bag. So the earthstar was lifted up twice. The number of arms was variable – four to seven in this collection – and the 'skin' enclosing the spore body must have been composed of several layers, the outermost of which formed the basal bag, the inner one the elevated arms. I could now envisage how this extraordinary earthstar must have arisen after emerging from an initial 'egg', raising itself up on its arms like a jack-in-the-box to break free of the needle cover. It was another wonder of the fungus world.

With the aid of *British Puffballs and Earthstars*, a 1995 publication of the Royal Botanic Gardens, I believed I should be able to identify this discovery in short order. There were several species illustrated that had some claim to be the same as mine – a small one, Rayed Earthstar (*Geastrum quadrifidum*), was about the right size and looked generally similar but four rays were usual in this species, the 'bag' was not well-developed and the 'mouth' was not surrounded by grooves. One species stood out as having a similar human-like appearance, complete with basal bag, and it was very rare: the Arched Earthstar (provocatively named scientifically *Geastrum fornicatum*). I already knew about this earthstar from an illustration in Roger Phillips' famous photographic guidebook to fungi, first published in 1981, and it must have been registered in my unconscious mind as an object of desire for many years. Could I have found it at last? It certainly looked similar in many ways. There were some reasons to be doubtful: not only were my specimens generally smaller, but the Arched Earthstar was typically four-rayed (most of mine had more), and the rays seemed to be more deeply split, and the covering on the spore sac was apparently not leaden grey as on the Shiplake specimens. I believed this was different. It was one of those occasions when the best thing to do is to dry a specimen and send it to Kew Gardens, where the reference collections for British fungi are conserved. I received a note back describing it as probably an unusual specimen of the Rayed Earthstar, *Geastrum quadrifidum*.

That might have been the end of the story, but there is another, and possibly final paragraph. In 2015 a scientific paper was published revisiting the European earthstars using modern scientific techniques, including DNA analysis.* A new species was erected for British specimens found in a churchyard in Cockley Cley, Norfolk – it was named *Geastrum britannicum*. I suppose it might be called the British Earthstar. It was without doubt the same earthstar that I had found in numbers in Shiplake, Oxfordshire, in 2008. It was also growing in needle litter. The *Metro* newspaper reported it in 2015 under the banner: 'These Newly Discovered Mushrooms Look Like Little Humans'. My misgivings had been correct – mine did not belong to *any* of the species named in the books I had to hand in 2008.

Although I may have been the first to wonder whether my collection was a distinct form, I was not the first person to discover it; the Norfolk collection had already been made by Jonathon Revett, a local naturalist, in 2000. I have been back to my site every year since my first discovery, and the

---

* J.C. Zamora et al. in *Persoonia*, Volume 34.

British Earthstar has reappeared in different numbers every year. Just a single fruit body survived the drought in 2022. Since 2015 there have been other discoveries in other church-yards, so this charming little 'hominoid fungus' had probably gone unrecognised for many years. If this is my 'I was right' story, I have a balancing 'I was wrong' story later in this book. When it comes to fungi, the one thing you cannot be is complacent.

The strangest and rarest member of the puffball tribe is the Pepper Pot (*Myriostoma coliforme*). When mature, it looks generally like an earthstar, but instead of having a single mouth through which the spores can exit, this weird creation of the fungus kingdom has a number of separate openings in the spore sac, which looks as if it had been pierced multiple times by a skewer. When the dusty spores emerge, it does, indeed, resemble a pepper pot. To make things odder still, the spore sac is supported by several pillars, like the bearers of a coffin. The figures in Roger Phillips' 1981 mushroom guide included the last specimen to be collected in Britain, from Norfolk in 1881, with the note: 'It is hoped that the publication of an illustration of this interesting fungus will lead to its rediscovery.'

After a hundred years that might have seemed a forlorn hope, but I always carried a secret wish that I might be the one to find it again in East Anglia, closest in Britain to where it was still known among sand dunes in the Netherlands. To the general astonishment of the mushrooming world it did reappear in our islands in sandy soil in 2006, at a site not so far from its 1881 home – I am not permitted to say exactly where. The rediscovery of the Pepper Pot can be credited to Neil Mahler, a diffident East Anglian mycophile of great persistence. He had already discovered the rare Arched Earthstar and spectacular Umbrella Polypore (*Polyporus umbellatus*) so he had a marvellous nose for alpha fungi. It remains a wonder that he spotted the Pepper Pot from a scooter.

Remarkable and strange though the 'puffers' and their lookalikes might be, few of them could be described as pretty, but that is the word that crops up when people first notice bird's nest fungi. The recent fashion for spreading bark on flowerbeds and under trees as a weed suppressant has suited these diminutive relatives of the earthstars very well, so they are now a common sight in public parks and new housing estates. They do not puff in any comparable way to the other fungi in this chapter. They do, however, begin as small spheres the size of a large lentil, at which stage they are easily overlooked, even though they may occur in swarms. When the spores are ripening, these vessels open up into little cups, and inside the cups are 'eggs' (*peridioles*) that contain the numerous spores, so at this stage they really do look like miniaturised bird's nests complete with a neatly stacked clutch. The spores have been packaged for a special kind of dispersal. The cups are no bigger across than your little fingernail (and some species are smaller) so to fully appreciate how pretty they are you have to get close. In the Striated Bird's Nest (*Cyathus striatus*) the little cups are slightly flared and subtly grooved along the inside. The eggs nestle in the bottom. The Field Bird's Nest (*C. olla*) is brown and hairy on the outside. The yellowish Common Bird's Nest (*Crucibulum laeve*) has many smaller eggs, and often grows in lines upon fallen sticks in damp places. There is even a species that grows on dung. The distinctive design of the nests is recruited to help dispersal of the eggs and spores. When a raindrop splashes into one of the little cups an egg is splashed out and may travel up to a metre away. After their outer covering decays, the spores released frequently germinate in an ideal place. In the Harcourt Arboretum at Nuneham Courtenay extensive patches of bark dressing under the conifers were completely covered in cups of the Striated Bird's Nest one year, so much so that it looked as if they had been deliberately planted to please the eye.

9.

Names names names

The writer of Ecclesiastes had a point when he complained: *Of making many books there is no end, and much study is a weariness of the flesh.* Students of fungi sometimes feel the same about the making of many species and the exhaustion engendered by trying to keep up with the new publications naming them. There are, it cannot be denied, an extraordinarily large number of different fungi, even if one only considers the larger ones that are the subject of this book. Geoffrey Kibby's recently completed splendid journey through northern Europe's larger fungi listed nearly 2,500 species, while the 2,800 described in Thomas Laessoe and Jens Petersen's 2021 two-volume European fungus book, even they admit is not comprehensive. I suspect that the reason fungi have not attracted the same popular following as birds or flowers is partly because of the sheer number of different species, coupled with the time it takes to learn how to recognise them. This leads to two obvious questions: do we really *need* all those names? If most people cannot recognise most mushroom species, do we really have to go into that sort of detail?

The language of nature is written in a multitude of species. The term 'biodiversity' has become bandied about by politicians who could not tell a sparrow from a chaffinch – but that does not diminish its importance. The unit of diversity *is* the species, and the business of identifying species is taxonomy. If you do not know how many species there are in a particular habitat, you have no handle upon its richness or otherwise. It is far from obvious that a piece of grassland in an old churchyard is more biodiverse than a bowling green, but a species inventory will quickly reveal the truth. This is not like collecting locomotive numbers, where satisfaction comes from ticking off a known list, and maybe collecting more than a rival. Taxonomy entails the very calibration of the natural world. It could not be more important than now when habitats are changing at best, and disappearing at worst. I spent much of my working life at the London Natural History Museum alongside some of the storm troopers in the battle to save the world's biodiversity, and their expertise was almost always the identification of species – including many that had up to then been unknown. They were paid less than they should have been, even as fellow experts around the globe celebrated their extraordinary work.

The name of an organism can prove complicated. At the very least, the scientific name is a label for the species, something to stick on a drawer of specimens – a unique identifier. For all species it is a binomial, a combination of the genus and species (or specific) name. *Homo sapiens* is the one we all know, particularly when used in slightly pompous pronouncements about ourselves ('Surely *Homo sapiens* ought to have more respect for the natural world' – that kind of thing). Every mushroom and toadstool known to science has its own binomial, and convention insists that the scientific name should be italicised, with the genus name given a capital letter and the species name lower case even if coined in honour of Winston Churchill – the species *churchilli* is correct. Two different species may not have the same name, and the one named first carries the day (it has *priority*, as we say).

Many of the older scientific names are based upon the classics and have Greek or Roman roots. A working knowledge of Latin was a sine qua non for early taxonomists; for example, the genus has a gender attached to it, and so the species name has to match it. To make up a hypothetical case, *Brutonius splendidus* would be correct and *Brutonius splendida* would not. If a species was named to honour somebody, the genitive case should be used; hence *Brutonius churchilli* (Churchill's Brutonius). If it happened to be named for Lady Churchill rather than Winston, it would be indicated by having a different (feminine) ending: *Brutonius churchillae*. Names are not meant to be offensive. I could not get away with calling a snail *Uglymuggia churchilli*, for example. Nowadays, the demand to obey nomenclatural rules has been somewhat relaxed, acknowledging how few living scientists are classically educated. A diagnosis of the new species in Latin is no longer required (thank goodness). As a former Latin student myself, I still like to understand how the old names were minted – if something is described in the original species name as *fragrans*, I know it has a pleasant smell, or as *coprophila* and I suspect it likes to grow on dung. This is still useful. However, before a new species can be accepted into the nation of organisms it has to be formally published, and that publication evaluated by a peer group, as being demonstrably something different from previously known species. As I know to my cost (Chapter 14), this is not foolproof.

The main puzzle and irritation to many people trying to hack their way through the nomenclatural jungle is that the signposts are continually moving. As one exasperated beginner put it to me: why do they keep on changing the names? What was wrong with the old ones? It is an understandable cry of pain. To comprehend the names we use today – and regard as the 'right' ones – it is necessary to go back to the beginnings of mycology as a science. Across nearly two centuries the scope and purpose of scientific names has changed. Nowadays the name is much more than a label to stick on a drawer.

One founding father of mycology is the Swede Elias Magnus Fries (1794–1878). His compatriot and close contemporary, the great Karl Linné (usually Latinised to Linnaeus), was busy describing and naming plants (and animals) in the early nineteenth century in what are still among the most important contributions to our understanding of the natural world. The Linnean binomial system accomplished a systematisation of nature that laid the foundations of much modern biology. However, Linnaeus described and named very few fungi, leaving that to others, most notably Fries. There were, of course, earlier attempts to depict fungal wonders, many of them beautifully executed. James Bolton's *An history of fungusses growing about Halifax* (1788–91) is a masterly account of more than two hundred species, the first of its kind in Britain, embellished with drawings of remarkable accuracy. When Bolton was making his collections, species of virtually *all* gilled mushrooms were assigned to one genus, *Agaricus* (the name derives from the ancient Greek for 'mushroom'), which was at least simple and memorable. For example, one of Linnaeus's few treatments of fungi refers to the familiar Fly Agaric as *Agaricus muscarius*; nowadays, it is universally known as *Amanita muscaria*. You could say that the subsequent history of mushroom taxonomy has been about hiving off progressively finer subdivisions from that original omnipresent *Agaricus* into many different genera.

Fries brought some of Linnaeus's system and rigour in grouping the mushrooms and toadstools into clusters of similar species that would become the foundation of subsequent classifications. The two men were at the pinnacle of European academia, both of them being professors at the ancient University of Uppsala in Sweden. When it came to stabilising nomenclature, the great works of Linnaeus and Fries would serve as the accepted base line for taxonomy, established by general agreement by the early twentieth century in order to 'sanction' the previously chaotic way different scientific names had been used by different authors – a rare example of successful 'science by committee'. From then on, the *Systema Naturae* of Linnaeus (1835) and the *Systema Mycologicum* (1821) and *Elenchus fungorum* (1828) of Fries became the works to refer back to if there was a dispute about what name to use. The Dutch Christian Henrik Persoon (1761–1836) had a matching claim to a seminal position in mushroom taxonomy, even though he was an impoverished recluse, without the clout of a major university. However, his work on puffballs and their allies published in 1801 also includes the 'sanctioned' names for this particular group of fungi. At about the same time, outstanding mushroom scholars were at work in France (Lucien Quélet), Italy (Carlo Vittadini and Giacomo Bresadola), Germany (Jacob Schaeffer) and England (Miles J. Berkeley), all of them generating names that are still in use today.

Elias Fries did not have a notion of biological evolution. He thought that species were created and defined by God, and had a belief in fourfold hierarchies that would seem decidedly odd today. However, he was unquestionably a very good observer. Most of the readily visible fungal features that are still considered important today were already recognised by Fries: the colour of spores, mode of attachment of the gills, presence or absence of ring and/or volva, sliminess (or not), scaliness (or not), smell, taste, flesh colour and bruising, and habitat. Most of the species he discriminated are still recognised today, which is a testament to his 'taxonomic eye', a strange gift I have come across in several exceptional scientists, including some of my colleagues in the Natural History Museum. They seem to latch on to the important features for defining a species and disregard the 'noise' of other characters. The problem with Fries is that he did not use microscopic features as he did not trust the instruments available at the time. Nor did he preserve fungi as part of his routine: specimens dried in the right manner retain both microscopic and DNA information that has become more and more crucial in recent decades. So if there is an argument about what Fries meant by a particular species, in many cases there is no possible arbitration based on his original material. This has caused many headaches and occasional spats among the cognoscenti, as disagreements arise over Fries' intentions.

Ever since evolution has been generally accepted as a fact, the scope of the genus has inevitably changed. It is no longer just a category to help file away a species, linked together by some characteristics that Elias Fries would have recognised; a combination of colour, smell and overall form, perhaps. The genus is now also regarded as an *evolutionary* entity: an assemblage of species that all descended from a common ancestor (technically, a clade). If the original concept of a genus had been founded on superficial similarities that arose more than once during the long course of evolution, then that genus should now be divided into groups that reflect the newer ideas about evolutionary pathways. The species names would remain the same, of course, as they are the pawns on the chessboard of life, but they would be reassigned new positions in other genera that truly reflect the trajectory of evolution. In a typical case, some species would remain in the original genus, while others would move to a new (or different) one, and there are many examples now where such a new genus finishes up in a completely different part of the fungus tree of life from its former home. This is how science advances. But the cost is the change of name, and particularly the generic name, that often leaves the amateur mycologist baffled and confused. This is the answer to that complaint *'Why do they keep changing the names?'* It can confuse those with the best intentions, even those like myself who love mushrooms but try to keep up with the science.

One example will make this clearer. An elegant mushroom is frequently found on forays under broadleaved trees in the late summer and autumn, and very often next to old tree stumps. Usually solitary, it has an obtuse, often wrinkled and viscid, pale-brownish cap the size of a small biscuit, pale and widely spaced gills reaching the stem, which, most importantly, is very long and thin and tough and has 'roots' reaching down deeply into the ground, with a spindle-shaped attachment connecting the fungus to its mycelium feeding on decayed wood. The common name Rooting Shank encapsulates this distinguishing feature very well. It is not surprising to find that it was one of the first mushrooms to be named at the end of the eighteenth century, as *Agaricus radicatus*, and the species name appropriately accounted for its most salient feature by incorporating the Latin word for 'rooting' in its designation. When the unwieldy 'genus' *Agaricus* was divided into several smaller genera, reflecting a better understanding of the great diversity in form of mushrooms and toadstools by the later nineteenth century, *Agaricus radicatus* was now included with a number of other white-spored 'tough shanks' into the genus *Collybia* – so at this point the scientific name became *Collybia radicata* (the ending of the species name changed with the feminine gender of *Collybia*).

This is where I enter the story as a schoolboy learning my mushrooms, because that was the name used in *The Observer's Book of Common Fungi*, by E.M. Wakefield, my first ever guidebook. I learned the Latin name with a sense of pride, and doubtless trotted it out to demonstrate my erudition to my bemused parents. *Collybia radicata* had a long life as the 'correct' name, and was used in the first more comprehensive field guide in English that appeared under the Collins imprint in 1961, based on J.E. Lange's beautiful watercolour illustrations from the 1930s published as *Flora Agaricina Danica*. But by the time that field guide was replaced by Roger Phillips' indispensable photographic atlas of British fungi in 1981, the label on the fungus had 'changed' to the rather inelegant *Oudemansiella radicata* – same mushroom, different name. Microscopic work had suggested that the Rooting Shank was related to the Beech Tuft (then called *Oudemansiella mucida*), so I had to unlearn the earlier name if I wanted to appear up to date, which of course I did.

Like many fungal names, *Oudemansiella* was named for a distinguished mycologist, in this case the Dutch professor Cornelius Anton Jan Abraham Oudemans, so one must be grateful that only the surname has to be used in nomenclature. As we went into the twenty-first century, by which time I had succeeded in thoroughly replacing *Collybia* by *Oudemansiella* in my mental filing system, I was surprised to find that the current name for the Rooting Shank was *Xerula radicata*. The familiar mushroom had now been placed in the same genus as some rarer species, one of which (*X. pudens*) I had been delighted to find in my home county of Oxfordshire. These two perhaps rather plausibly belonged together. By now, I was reconciled to any name changes whatsoever: they are correctly known as 'recombinations', and I would just have to learn to live with them. As more and more molecular evidence was being brought into play, it was only to be expected that 'Agaricus radicatus' would spring yet another surprise. So it proved. A scientific paper incorporating some of this new molecular science and published in 2010 concluded that a further name change was needed for our familiar mushroom: it has now become *Hymenopellis radicata*. To recapitulate our naming journey, it runs from *Agaricus* to *Collybia*, and thence to *Oudemansiella* and *Xerula*, and now to *Hymenopellis*: five different names for the same mushroom! It could be said that it is hard enough to remember one scientific name, let alone five, for one small fungus. This could be discouraging.

However, throughout this long and convoluted tale of names one of them remains the same – the common, or, if you prefer, English name Rooting Shank. In my earlier mush-rooming days I confess that I slightly turned up my nose at English names. I felt that using the Linnean terms demon-strated my command of the scientific sphere; it made me part of the club. It is still true that the 'Latin name' is the one that can be recognised in Yokohama, Toronto or Buenos Aires. It does fulfil the role of an international language of identity, and is the name that rightly appears in the scientific papers published in learned journals. Nonetheless, I have come to realise that the English name is often much more stable than the scientific one when a particular fungus is shuffled between genera in keeping with advances in science. Rooting Shank stays the same no matter how many times it has changed its name in the scientific literature. It does not strain the memory to hold that moniker in store; it is easier to explain to beginners; and it is appropriate to the fungus. If I had tried to rehearse the long tale of its changing scientific names while standing over the mushroom in the field, I can imagine that there would be much covert eye-rolling and stifled yawns among my would-be acolytes.

There is another problem; there are not enough traditional English names to go round. The suspicion with which mushrooms have often been regarded may have something to do with it, or maybe their capacity to disappear within days, or the sheer number of species. But some colleagues led by Elizabeth Holden have tried to fill the gap by adding to the meagre number of traditional English names by coining new ones. In 2003 a list of *Recommended English Names* was published, covering five hundred of the better known fungus species, which has achieved its aim of making fungus names less alien and more easily memorable, although not without grumbling from some mycologists who think that it would be as easy to learn the 'proper' scientific names as these new creations. Some are rather brilliant: the Flirt was coined for *Russula vesca*, a red-capped species often found with oak that rather demurely lifts its 'skirt' away from the edge of the cap.

A few names are not so much fun as they used to be: the beautiful *Porpolomopsis calyptriformis* (known for a long time as *Hygrocybe calyptriformis*) is to be called Pink Waxcap on the list, but I prefer the older name of the Ballerina, for the way the cap lifts and divides at maturity very like a traditional dress in classical dance. However, the intention to stabilise common names while the scientific ones are in a state of flux is thoroughly worthwhile; it reduces confusion among those who do not feel able to follow the latest research.

Amid many examples, the 'funnels' are descriptive of the old Fries genus *Clitocybe*, those white-spored agarics with gills running down the stem. Now, some of those species have been hived off into other genera with names like *Ampulloclitocybe* and *Infundibulicybe*. Surely Club Foot Funnel is easier to cope with than *Ampulloclitocybe clavipes*? This commonsense approach may go towards allaying that recurring complaint about changing the names.

A few names have come through the centuries unscathed. *Agaricus* is still with us, and that most familiar of all edible fungi, *Agaricus campestris*, remains its typical member – the Field Mushroom. This name is one of the few attributed to Linnaeus himself. As the original *Agaricus* was subdivided into many other groups, the old name pottered onwards, taking with it the Field Mushroom into the twenty-first century. Some names have tended to disappear. In the nineteenth century authors were fond of recognising 'varieties' (usually shortened to var.) – so a white form of a normally yellow toadstool like *Amanita citrina* would be called var. *alba*. Many of these varieties have since been shown to be genetically identical to their nominate species and have been forgotten. Occasionally, a 'variety' has proved genuinely different and become a species in its own right.

With the continual discovery of new kinds of fungi it is unlikely that the list of names will ever be complete. Fungi are different from all birds and most beasts in their endless richness. We are going to have to accommodate names and yet more names. The sheer magnitude of the task that needs to be completed to catalogue the fungi could be overwhelming, the parade of names an endless cascade. Even so, the naming of fungi is just the beginning. Will it ever be possible to know all their subtleties, their ingenious live-lihoods, or their elusive preferences? Imagine that invisible but pervasive mist of spores that fills the air, each spore only prospering if it reaches exactly the right place at exactly the right time to produce the mycelium that will eventually enable the propagation of its kind. An inconceivably large proportion fails to propagate. The abundance of species eventually found as fruit bodies fluctuates from year to year, according to rainfall and temperature, pollution levels and plain good fortune. Yet each spore does carry a name, which can only be made manifest if it is able to germinate and prosper. The spores are countless millions of specks of hope tossed upon the breeze, thrown into a changing world – a lottery of sorts, but one that is attuned to the fluctuations of our planet. The name of the species is the gate that has to be opened in order to explore the complexities of the world beyond.

10.

Stinkers

A few fungi can be smelled before they are seen. A walk through the woods in the late summer is often enlivened by a stench that proves a stinker is nearby. This can set the party to work to find the source of the aroma, which often takes a surprisingly long time. Lurking behind a tree or beneath the scrub, the culprit will be identified, resembling a white candle rising from the litter: a stinkhorn.

Stinkhorns are the most sexually explicit fruit body. The Latin name is *Phallus impudicus*,* which tells you all you want to know. The white stem of the stinkhorn arises from a pallid 'scrotal' bag to a foot in height or sometimes more, its penile qualities further emphasised by the glans-like cap atop the stem. When it is freshly arisen a greenish slime covers this cap. Those who discover it for the first time tend to express clearly their involuntary reaction to such a blatant object. A closer look allows fascination to take over. A search

---

* Latin: 'lewd'.

among the nearby leaf litter often discovers a white sphere – a little larger than a golf ball – tucked in at the top of the soil. This is the stinkhorn 'egg'. Prodded with the finger there is a certain rubberiness to its texture – there is no 'shell' to this egg, but rather a flexible white membrane surrounding it. Inside is a greenish jelly around a 'bud' that will expand into another malodorous phalloid. I have watched the process at work. Over the course of a day the bag of the egg is ruptured as the thrusting stem rises to its full glory. The white stem is quite unlike that of most mushrooms: a hollow centre is surrounded by a sponge-like, fragile network full of small holes – if anything, it reminds me of a brandy snap.

The slime on the 'cap' includes an extraordinarily rich brew of chemicals that might otherwise be found in excrement or rotting meat. This is not so much a cocktail as a witches' brew of pungent rot and shit; the word 'putrid' could have been coined to describe a mélange of more than two dozen volatile substances that otherwise belong with decaying carcasses and faeces. Since our deficient human sense of smell can detect the stinkhorn from some distance, it is not surprising that flies quickly discover this bonanza thanks to the exquisitely tuned organelles on their antennae. To them, stinkhorn must seem like the smell of the Christmas turkey rolled up with that of freshly baked bread. It summons them from who-knows-where. I have observed flies with their little sucker pads at work on the green slime, sucking at it with enthusiasm. However, they do not lay their eggs on the fungus as they would on a carcass of a dead mouse. Instead they seem to use the green gleba as food. They polish it off. When they have finished their work the stinkhorn remains behind as a white wand, and the 'cap' is revealed as conical, pale and coarsely netted without its glutinous covering. At this stage the pong is much reduced – indeed, it almost has a sweet component. The stinkhorn has done its work.

That work is the distribution of its spores. Stinkhorn spores are minute even by fungal standards, a few thousandths of a millimetre long and only one or two thousandths of a millimetre wide. To see them under the microscope, it is necessary to rack up the magnification to the point where the oil immersion lens must be brought into play. Now they look like tiny beans, yet each spore includes the capacity to generate a new *Phallus*. A fly may seem small, but compared with the size of a stinkhorn spore it is a monster. The fly's intestinal system is cavernous. As the insect flies onwards around the woodland it excretes the stinkhorn spores in tiny droppings. A very few of these may be lucky enough to land in exactly the right place for germination; and if a spore *does* germinate maybe it will be fortunate enough to encounter just the right kind of organic material for its life as a saprotroph. The stinkhorn's strategy may be seen as trading on luck, but its strange habits probably give it an edge over a hundred other fungus species that don't recruit a fly as an ally. Sooner or later a new stinkhorn will establish its mycelium. The mycelial 'roots' of *Phallus* can be found by gently scraping in the soil around an egg. It is more easily seen than that of other fungi, as it forms rather substantial white threads, resembling coarse cotton, which seek out new food among the leaf litter. If you pick up an egg the cords hang off the bottom, as if unwilling to let go of a stray leaf.

There is a second, scarcer *Phallus* species in Britain. It is only found in sand dunes in our islands, but is apparently more catholic in its tastes elsewhere in the world. Near Holkham in Norfolk, the Sand Stinkhorn (*Phallus hadriani*) regularly appears in the hollows between dunes that have become stabilised by coarse marram grass away from the seashore. The white mycelial cords seek out the decaying grass entrained beneath the surface sand. Even at an early stage the uncommon stinkhorn is distinguished readily enough from its common relative by having a pinkish-coloured egg. Whether the smell also differs is controversial. The pioneer British mycologist Reverend Miles Berkeley even described it as having a sweet smell of violets, or perhaps irises. It still seems to attract flies and small beetles, which appear as if by magic when the stinkhorn 'erupts'. Other accounts recognise an unpleasant odour not unlike that of its cousin.

When I eventually found this species in its natural habitat, much of its slime had already been consumed by insects, and in the Norfolk wind the odour was not particularly unpleasant – but then the regular stinkhorn is much less noisome after the flies have been at work. I had assumed that the species name might have related to Emperor Hadrian, builder of the eponymous wall, although his connection to stinkhorns was unclear to me. The real reason is more curious. The fungus was first named and described by a Dutchman with the Latinised name Hadrianus Junius, as early as 1564, from sand dunes in Holland. It thus is not only one of the first fungi to be described (and the origin of the name *Phallus*), but was actually named *before* the much commoner stinkhorn of woods and copses. Hadrian's Phallus led the way.

It may seem unlikely that stinkhorns have any use as food. I have seen dried *Phallus* species on sale in China, in a shop decorated with all manner of exotic plants and anonymous things in jars, where it was doubtless part of their vast traditional pharmacopeia. At the egg stage, however, the 'nut' inside is reported as edible because the smelly component only develops when the fruit body has expanded. My foraying friend Stuart demonstrated this to appropriate effect, after showing a small party of naturalists the adult *in flagrante* to induce a proper measure of awe. After demonstrating the egg phase, he neatly cut it open to show the 'nut' in place, pushed it out and popped it into his mouth to an accompaniment of horrified gasps. It had, he declared, a nice crunchy texture and a nutty taste. I doubt he made many converts.

A commoner, smaller species is the Dog Stinkhorn (*Mutinus caninus*), which does indeed resemble the genital equipment of a male canine, with a red tapering tip that shows through once the brownish gleba has been consumed. It would have to be a rather small dog. Like its larger cousin, it arises from eggs – smaller, and more elongate than those of the stinkhorn. These are occasionally found in 'clutches', concealed among damp leaf litter in most kinds of woodland. It is rather a feeble phalloid, with the pinkish spongy stem usually not much thicker than a pencil, and often flopping over. The smell is fetid, although it hardly matches that of *Phallus impudicus*, but is enough to ensure the attention of flies.

A decade ago I was approached by a neighbour in my small hometown in Oxfordshire who thought some kind of alien had landed in his garden. Several extraordinary structures had appeared at the back of his flowerbeds. They were bright red in colour, so they could not fail to attract attention. He thought they looked as if they had fallen from the sky rather than erupted from the ground. About the size of a small grapefruit, the structures were a sort of cage constructed of corrugated coloured struts that joined together to make a small number of polygons. They were quite fragile, so a strut could be severed with the poke of a stick. The fungus suggestion occurred to him simply because nothing else seemed to fit the weirdness of this bizarre organic production – if it is strange enough it must belong to that eldritch kingdom! It could have been something from an H.P. Lovecraft story (who also loved the word 'eldritch'). 'When I saw how weird it was,' he said, somewhat unflatteringly, 'I thought of you.' I was relieved he did not mention the obtrusive smell.

However, I did establish that the 'structures' had emerged from a slightly irregular white sac – the remains of the egg. It was indeed another phalloid, and one that is apparently becoming commoner in the United Kingdom. I had recently seen it in the gardens of a *palazzo* by Lake Como in Italy, and I had heard reports of it from Hampshire. The database for British fungi has scattered records, and it is frequent in the Isle of Wight in some years. Now here it was in Oxfordshire. It may be one of those species that is becoming more frequent with the warming of our climate, although John Ramsbottom noted British records of this distinctive fungus as early as the mid nineteenth century, and it may well be native to our islands. By any measure it is an extraordinary production, appropriately called the Red Cage Fungus (*Clathrus ruber*). It, too, has malodorous spore-carrying slime on its surface to attract flies. I convinced my neighbour that he was extremely fortunate to have such a visitor next to his compost heap, but it did not turn up again the following year. Fungi are never biddable.

Clathrus species provide an interesting test case for thinking about what is native and what is introduced. An even more extraordinary species than the Red Cage Fungus is *Clathrus archeri* (formerly known as *Anthurus archeri*) that rejoices in two alternative common names: Devil's Fingers or Octopus Stinkhorn. Both names have something to be said for them. The first impression made by this fungus is of a lurid red, stranded sea creature with spread-eagled arms. An octopus is appropriate (although fewer than eight arms are usually present), but it could equally well be a starfish. In either case it looks *most* inappropriate arising from a mossy bank in the middle of Oxfordshire, which is where I found it in 2022. It is a startling thing to discover. When something so anomalous appears apparently from nowhere, it is perhaps not so surprising that the devil himself is invoked – so here are his fingers. By now, we will know what to expect of a phalloid, and once again we find that originally all-enclosing bag and the fetid slime spread on the 'fingers' of the fruit body that insects find so irresistible. It is not so difficult to see how this relates to *Clathrus ruber* either, since the 'fingers' of this fungus are at first conjoined into the beginnings of a cage. It is such a distinctive species that it must have attracted attention wherever it turned up. It is known to be a native of New Zealand and Australia, from where the Reverend Berkeley originally described it in 1859. It seems to have arrived in England close to the beginning of the First World War; perhaps the spores were carried on the boots of an Anzac soldier recruited from the wilds of Tasmania. Unlike some invaders, and in spite of its name, the Devil's Fingers seems to have done no damage upon its arrival, but is here to surprise and delight us with its alien form.

The phalloid fungi are probably the most fantastical of all the fungi that produce spores on basidia (Basidiomycetes). Many of them are tropical, or originated from the southern hemisphere. A review of these fungi published in 2021 recognised twenty-two different genera of which only three are regularly found in Britain. They span a spectrum of size and colours, some with pallid 'arms' raised like gothic arches, others looking like coarsely crumpled paper, a few almost agaric-like in proportions; all arising from 'eggs' and attracting flies. In Australia I saw stinkhorns that were orange in colour covering whole flowerbeds in a park in Adelaide; they were more spectacular than any of the flowers nearby. Some stinkhorns (*Phallus indusiatus*) have what can only be described as a perfectly lacy dress hanging down below the cap – a 'garment' whose shape resembles the skirts of Turkish whirling dervishes. It is a structure without parallel in the natural world. I saw these wonderful fungi while I was working in Thailand; they were lurking in the shadows of a bamboo forest. They seemed to be a kind of hallucination, too extravagant to be true. This must have been the same species as the dried packets on sale in the Chinese herb shop, since they are the only phalloids to have culinary and medical applications. The American diplomat Henry Kissinger was served them on a mission to China in the early 1980s but he was, perhaps, rather an unlikely candidate to be vulnerable to their alleged hallucinatory properties.

Another extraordinary antipodean species has rarely been recorded as an 'escape' in Britain, the Starfish Fungus (*Aseroe rubra*), which looks remarkably like a scarlet sea anemone on a contrasting white stalk, arising from compost heaps or rich soil. It has a spectacular radial array of 'tentacles' spread out symmetrically, often splitting into two towards their tips, and the brownish, smelly gleba lies at the centre. In cooler climates this spectacular phalloid has been found in greenhouses, but the practice of mulching flowerbeds with woodchips and organic matter may encourage it outdoors. Wherever it grows it is likely to attract attention and amazement at the inventiveness of the fungal kingdom.

The phalloids demonstrate a successful variation on the saprotrophic lifestyle, and have evolved concomitantly special designs, although it is hardly possible to guess why some species should find making a cage or a 'starfish' an advantage in the circus of life. You might imagine that a fly is unlikely to be concerned with the architecture of the fruit body, only with the tastiness of the lunch provided. Can it be that recruiting insect partners somehow teases out the inventiveness of natural selection? Among the flowering plants those species that have adopted flies as pollination agents are also often spectacular: the parasitic Corpse Lily *Rafflesia* from Sumatra not only has the largest flower in the world, but has also 'created' the stench of rotting flesh to

attract its pollinators. The small succulent *Stapelia* has dispro-
portionately large flowers with a similarly unpleasant odour,
and at least one species produces blossoms very like starfish,
inviting a comparison with *Clathrus archeri*. There is even a
preference for reddish colours in these flowers – suggesting
meat perhaps?

Plants and fungi have been on separate evolutionary pathways for more than a billion years, but can still contrive
similar complex tricks to hoodwink invertebrate animals that
have been on yet a *third* trajectory through unimaginable
stretches of geological time. History weaves patterns, and
these patterns can be recruited across the great kingdoms
of life. It could be argued that the fungi have been most
successful of all in subverting the senses of insects for their
own ends. Stinkhorns and their allies are probably more
widely distributed around the world than any of the flowering plants that have devised comparable tricks. Creeping
unseen through the forest floor, these fungi are masters of
deception, weirdly dressed as starfish or dervishes.

11.

Parasites

Not far from the boundaries of our own morsel of Chiltern woodland a footpath runs alongside a large open field underneath a line of mature oak trees. Between the path and the field an untidy border with big patches of nettles has occasionally yielded Giant Puffballs – one of the few species that enjoys nitrogen-rich soil. Towards the end of October 2012, Jackie and I were enjoying a stroll along the path to see 'what was about', which is mycological shorthand for grubbing around under bushes and turning over logs. Extending from the trees towards the field and into the nettle patch a huge fairy ring of Clouded Funnel (*Clitocybe nebularis*) comprised dozens of large, pale-grey toadstools.

This is one of the commonest of autumnal saprotrophic species, easily recognised by its pallid, solid and stout fruit bodies with the margin of the cap at first rolled downwards, and having yellowish-tinted, rather crowded gills sloping on to a relatively short, sturdy stipe. It is distinguished from typical funnels in having a thick-fleshed cap that is hardly depressed in the centre, and has a distinctive fruity odour that may have encouraged over-confidence in its edibility in the past (it is best avoided). Typically, the middle of the cap carries a whitish 'cloud' of mycelium, looking as if a cobweb-thin sliver of tissue paper had been applied there. A forayer may pass by a circle of Clouded Funnels with little more than a nod of recognition, happy enough to see them but no further investigation required. Jackie's years of rubbing along with a mycologist has honed her instinct for discovery, and something prompted her to wade into the nettle patch, following the fairy ring. There she discovered a fungus I had been trying to find for more than fifty years.

When I first began my long love affair with fungi in my childhood the only identification book that was widely available was *The Observer's Book of Common Fungi* by Elsie M. Wakefield. This is where I first learned to recognise the Clouded Funnel (or Clouded Agaric, as it was then known). A few years later, in John Ramsbottom's New Naturalist *Mushrooms and Toadstools*, a novel mushroom was introduced – in a footnote – appended to his mention of the Clouded Funnel; it was, he said, 'the host of the rare *Volvaria Loveiana* [*sic*] which grows in clusters on the cap'. What a wonderful fact to learn! There could be mushrooms that grew on mushrooms – and, what is more, this was a special species that grew only on one particular host. It seemed to me to be the ultimate tribute to the wiles of evolution. When I was a schoolboy, mushrooms were already exotic enough, but here was curiousness piled upon exoticism.

Somehow, the current common name Piggyback Rosegill for what is now called *Volvariella surrecta* is hardly adequate to encapsulate the extraordinary idea of the fruit body of one species growing on top of another. The additional remark about its rarity only added to its allure, and ever since I first learned of its existence I had wanted to find it in the wild. The *Collins Guide* published in 1963 upped the stakes by describing it as 'extremely rare', with a good illustration showing a few pretty, white mushrooms arising from neat white cups (*volvas*) atop a decaying funnel, as if they had been modelled in porcelain. Thus began decades of hopefully scanning fairy rings of Clouded Funnels; and no year passed without many sightings of this common fungus dotted over the woodland floor. I never found an example of the 'piggybacking' toadstool, until I believe my inspection of funnels became a perfunctory ritual rather than a gesture of hope. I was probably becoming resigned to the idea of never seeing the perching parasite, but here it was, at last, hidden away among the nettles. Jackie had finally discovered it. If I got stung I didn't notice. Remarkably, there was not just one of the funnels carrying the alien toadstools aloft. It seemed as if every other fruit body in the fairy ring had been instructed to burst forth its rare passenger at the same time. They hatched from white 'eggs' made from the volva, but most had already pushed out to open their caps and spread their spores. When this happened the gills became a pleasing shade of pink. The small boy interred somewhere deep inside my old body clapped his hands with delight. A clumsy attempt was made to immortalise the moment with a photograph on my mobile. I still automatically rake my glance over any group of Clouded Funnels, but it is now just an old habit that is hard to break, a mycological tic.

I later discovered that I *had* already seen the elusive Piggyback Rosegill, only I did not know it. The nebula-like 'cloud' in the specific name of the Funnel (*Clitocybe nebularis*) refers to the faint white patch that decorates the centre of the cap. Sometimes it looks slightly fluffy. This is actually the mycelium of the piggybacking parasite. I must have noticed it a hundred times without making the connection. Whatever its potential, most mycelium tends to look like other mycelium, so perhaps this unspectacular dusting does not really count as a sighting. Only once in a rare while does the superficial passenger 'decide' to produce a mushroom, and eventually I was privileged to see that moment at the edge of a wood in Oxfordshire. That does invite some intriguing questions. The obvious mystery is what triggers that rare fruiting, and why it does not happen more frequently.

It is particularly curious that the trigger for fruit body production – whatever the cause – simultaneously affects the whole fairy ring of Clouded Funnels. There is apparently no connection between the *Volvariella* on one funnel mushroom and that of its neighbours, yet it is as if a clarion call was sounded to produce their spores at the same time, to awaken their hidden mushroom. It might be plausible to invoke some concatenation of external events – a combination of rainfall, nutrition and season perhaps. However, another ring of Clouded Funnels not far away was apparently not obliged to allow its mycelial passengers to announce themselves, and if it were just down to meteorological conditions there should surely have been more piggybackers nearby. Maybe some strains of *V. surrecta* differ from others in a propensity to produce fruit bodies, or possibly the necessary 'mating types' to make a fruit body rarely come into contact. How typical of the fungi to leave behind two questions for every one answer.

Although the Piggyback Rosegill is the most glamorous hitchhiker, it is not unique. Some other agarics have developed a similar trick, and they are commoner. The most frequent member of the mycorrhizal genus *Russula* in our woodland is the Blackening Brittlegill (*Russula nigricans*), a chunky toadstool, typified by very widely spaced gills, that begins almost white and finishes up completely black, in which state old fruit bodies can hang around on the forest floor for many weeks. By then, most of the fungi that came up alongside this durable species will have decayed away. If October is wet – and it often is – some small powdery lumps may appear on the old wrecks of the Blackening Brittlegill. In a few days these will have assumed a mushroom shape, usually in a cluster, with caps no larger than a small coin, looking as if they are covered with pale yellow-brown dust. Then they are quite conspicuous (if you know what to look for) emerging from the dead corpse of their host.

Discovering them on a foray is always exciting. This Powdery Piggyback* (*Asterophora lycoperdoides*) – a long name for a small toadstool – is as curious in its way as the Piggyback Rosegill. The superficial powder that covers its cap is a mass of spores, but not the usual kind that are born on the gills. Instead these are tiny bits of fungal hyphae derived from

---

* Although I have never found it on any agaric other than the Blackening Brittlegill, I should add that there are reports of it growing on other species of *Russula* and on some species of milkcaps (*Lactarius*).

the parent fruit body. Blown by the least puff of wind these can be carried to another blackened wreck rapidly to produce a clone of the parent. I have noticed that if you find one Powdery Piggyback you will often find others nearby, and this easy form of propagation may be the reason. The gills of this toadstool are rather poorly developed, and may not be as important in reproduction as in most agarics, thanks to its special fairy dust. A related, white-coloured species (Silky Piggyback, *A. parasitica*) found on the same host has more normally developed gills and lacks the exterior dusting. In my experience it is less frequently encountered than its powdered cousin.

All these piggybacking agarics are using the host mushroom to provide them with a source of food, in order to further their own reproductive ends. None of them affect the host's ability to grow to maturity and shed its own spores. Nor is the parasitic habit confined to agarics. A few boletes have developed a similar trick. I had a close encounter with one of these specialists near the village of Walberswick in Suffolk, which lies about as far to the east as it is possible to go in the British Isles. The ground nearby is sandy and relatively infertile – good for encouraging heathland, with a scattering of oaks, sweet chestnuts and birches. From late summer, often the only fungus that is seen in profusion along the path sides is the Common Earthball, the yellow, scaly spheres of which emerge from even the most compacted ground, looking as if some careless customer had allowed potatoes to drop at random from their shopping bag.

It is one of those fungi that the walker tends to ignore after a while, because it is so abundant. In 2015, during one of my familiar strolls to the sea, one cluster of earthballs on a bank looked a little unusual – too crowded together perhaps. A large specimen appeared to be surrounded by a group of three other smaller fruit bodies. To my surprise and delight these proved to be diminutive boletes, almost the same colour as the earthball, but with an obvious stem and cap and the yellow pores typical of their kind. The texture was clearly softer than that of their host, and it would have been easy to walk on by without noticing the Parasitic Boletes (*Pseudoboletus parasiticus*), but once alerted to their presence it was clear that several other earthballs had similar smaller companions. The attentions of these freeloaders did not obviously stunt their hosts, so these may not have been particularly demanding as parasites go. Further along the same path, one of the curious boletes was itself looking sickly. It had been almost completely colonised by a white or yellow velvety covering that served to obscure the pores. The covering made the *Pseudoboletus* cap more conspicuous by the wayside. It was obviously a mycelium blanket. So here was a fungal parasite on a fungal parasite! The Bolete Eater (the asco *Hypomyces chrysospermus*) changes from white to golden yellow as it matures. It commonly 'mummifies' boletes from head to foot, to the disappointment of humans who like to eat the same fruit bodies before a fungus beats them to it.

The pinnacle of this parasite narrative has to be another, very rare bolete that was found in the same sandy ground a few years earlier. With a domed, warm yellow-brown cap that is usually markedly rolled under along its perimeter, and bright-yellow pores that bruise blue when touched, *Buchwaldoboletus lignicola* is an exciting find for any mycologist.

My friend Stuart and I discovered two examples emerging from dry sandy ground near the base of an old pine tree along the Blyth estuary. The fungus is sometimes called the Wood Bolete, which is probably a literal translation from its Latin species name. This is mistaken, because the rare bolete does not grow on wood; it is another parasite – this time upon a common bracket fungus called Dyer's Mazegill (*Phaeolus schweinitzii*). The latter is a large, often broadly fan-like fungus with a thick, meaty texture; it appears at the base of ageing pine trees. It is typically yellow when young, but becomes umber brown as it matures, and is perhaps best identified by its dark, finely porous, maze-like spore-bearing lower surface. We were gratified to be able to find an example of these unusually durable brackets near our discovery of *Buchwaldoboletus*. The apogee in this cascade of parasitism is that *Phaeolus* is itself a parasite of pine trees. So in the Wood Bolete, we have a parasite living off a parasite. It is not too fanciful to surmise that the very common Bolete Eater might in turn infect the Wood Bolete (perhaps sadly, ours wasn't). Were that the case we would have a parasite depending upon a parasite parasitic on a parasite. To recall a famous rhyme by Augustus de Morgan: *Great fleas have little fleas upon their backs to bite 'em, And little fleas have lesser fleas, and so* ad infinitum.

There are much more malevolent parasitic fungi known to science than the relatively benign agarics and boletes,*

---

* I should note that there are many ascos parasitic on other ascos. They can be spotted through a hand lens sitting on top of their host species, but there are too many and they are too small to deal with here.

which do at least allow their hosts to shed their spores, and in the case of *Asterophora* the host is already defunct. As an evolutionary strategy this would seem to make sense because the parasites depend on the continuation of their host for their own survival. There are other scenarios. An invading parasite could completely take over another fungus, hijacking it for its own reproduction. This is the technique of the stranglers.

I first learned of these fungi in the pages of a very dry book of keys to fungi by Professor Meinhard Moser, but the name of the genus *Squamanita* leaped off the page as something exotic, carrying with it a hint of the lethal glamour of the Death Cap *Amanita*, but mixed with the esoteric attraction of something rare and remarkable. All the species of *Squamanita* were very seldom encountered, said Professor Moser, so here was a challenge just as there was with the Piggyback Rosegill. The stranglers have specific hosts – they are choosy about their victims. They are body snatchers. They do not wait for their intended target to make a mushroom, but they take over – hijacking their unfortunate quarries to produce their own fruit bodies – and obliterating their fungus hosts in the process. The typical species of *Squamanita* is parasitic on *Amanita* (I suppose that is how it got its generic name) and makes the most extraordinary fruit body – with a massive base like a turnip from which arises a handsome agaric (sometimes more than one) with white gills and a fibrous-looking cap which is unlike that of any *Amanita*, though like that genus it does have a ring on the stipe and white gills. In the end, there is not much left of the host fungus.

The thickened base has been termed a gall (a recent scientific paper recognises its unique character with a different name – *mycocecidium*) and is where the parasite takes hold; DNA analysis suggests that both *Amanita* and *Squamanita* are present within it at this stage. Thereafter, the lethal intruder takes advantage of the fungal network of its host to reproduce its own kind. The *Amanita* is simply obliterated. It is hard to escape a grisly comparison with the horror film *Alien*. This particular fungus (*Squamanita schreieri*) has not yet been collected in Britain, despite some claims to the contrary. It is listed as endangered in Europe, and I think it is now improbable that I will ever see it in the flesh. It is sobering to know that some fungi are so uncommon that a lifetime is not long enough for site and season to intersect with exceptional good fortune.

I felt I must meet one of the British stranglers before I could write this book. The most well-known species (can I use 'well-known' for something so rare?) parasitises a common yellow grassland mushroom, the Earthy Powdercap (*Cystoderma amianthinum*), a familiar species favouring short turf, distinguished by a powdery covering of loose cells that often form tiny teeth around the edge of the cap, and similar bands of cells on the slender stipe below a small ring. After a lifetime of reducing the fertility of my garden lawn, I was rewarded with powdercaps – but not accompanied by their exotic parasites. I was obliged to look elsewhere. Recent work on the DNA of the stranglers has shown that British species, including the Powdercap Strangler, should now be placed in a different genus, *Dissoderma*, so with a tear in my eye I bade farewell to the exotic *Squamanita*, which I will now never meet face to face. Science has to move on. Professor Gareth Griffiths of Aberystwyth University, who has minutely studied the stranglers, kindly put me in touch with Torben Fogh, who lives deep in the Lake District. Torben knew where the stranglers hide.

It may seem a trifle eccentric to drive five hundred miles to see a mushroom the size of a ten pence piece, but in October 2023 a message from Torben propelled us northwards: *Dissoderma paradoxum*, the Powdercap Strangler, had arrived! The southern part of the Lake District is not as rugged, bare and bleak as the country beloved of fell walkers. Relatively gentle hillsides are clothed in broadleaved trees – birch, oaks and beech – and sheep farming predominates. We admired the stone walls that kept the Herdwick sheep confined; they were carefully constructed from grey grit and coarse slates in alternating layers, and capped by vertical slabs, serious walls, meant to last. Some of the fields on lower ground looked too lushly green to be rich in fungi – fertilisers had done their worst. The pastures we were looking for would have been grazed short, but not artificially fertilised. The open fells themselves occupying the high ground tended to be covered with bracken, which is generally bad news for fungi.

In the early morning, the mist hung low over Lake Coniston. Torben proved to be a tall, bearded, lifelong Lakesman and naturalist, with a gentle manner. He told us he had been determined to find stranglers once he had learned of their existence. On a perfect sunny autumn day he led us uphill across several fields, past quite a few of those admirable walls, to a farm he said had been run in the traditional way for generations. Sloping fields were wonderfully free of the nettles and brambles that soon disfigure 'improved' pasture. It was not long before we found brilliant yellow caps of the Golden Waxcap (*Hygrocybe chlorophana*) and the slimy green ones of the Parrot Waxcap (*Gliophorus psittacinus*). We knew that waxcap grassland is the preferred habitat for powdercaps. It was a perfect site. A small beck marked by scrubby hazels and alders tumbled across the fields, providing a tinkling accompaniment to our close scrutiny of the sward. While not exactly on hands and knees, this process involved slowly quartering the field peering at the ground. After a few minutes the first fairy ring of powdercaps was spotted, even though rain had stripped the caps of much of their typical dusting. Carefully plucking one from the grass, we could see the somewhat shaggy lower part of the stem. We soon discovered several such fairy rings, but none of them obviously 'strangled'.

Torben had been here earlier, and I am not sure we would have found the strangler at all had he not done a reconnaissance – he had left a small cairn to mark the spot. And there they were, near the top of the field; in a ring of powdercaps, three had been taken over by the parasite. Close inspection showed that the lower part of the stem was still that of the Earthy Powdercap – but the upper part had been converted to that of a very different toadstool with a purplish cap. One species captured by another! You could even see the point on the stem where the crime had taken place. There were probably better specimens, and they would have grown further given another day or two, but I had at last seen this perplexing toadstool for myself. Torben then told me he had discovered a second, shaggier and even rarer strangler (*Dissoderma pearsonii*) on the same host, but growing in a different meadow. We had better come back to see that one.

The stranglers lead to so many questions. It is difficult to understand why the powdercap is particularly vulnerable – so much so that *two* parasites had evolved to take advantage of the same species. After all, the Lakeland field was full of other toadstools – not least waxcaps – that could have played host. Perhaps it is because stranglers are more closely related to the powdercaps than to the other fungi. They are like the ne'er-do-well cousins that sponge off His Lordship in the big house: only blood relatives could get away with it. Then we need to know why they are so excessively rare; if the parasitic lifestyle could succeed in one spot in a field, why not all over? Why not in my garden? If this parasitic lifestyle is viable on powdercaps, there seems to be no reason why it should not have arisen multiple times with other kinds of mushrooms – but that is not the case. There are no Milkcap Stranglers or Parasol Stranglers. And if stranglers need powdercaps to complete their life cycles, one has to wonder where they lurk for the rest of the time. The wonderful thing about mushrooms is that for every question answered there are a dozen posed.

12.

Morels and allies

In April the bluebells are at their best in the Chiltern Hills, carpeting the same areas under the trees that in autumn are scattered with mushrooms. The fresh, pale-green leaves of the beech unfurl at different rates: some are already clad in a cloudy garment of foliage; others have barely started to wake up. Sunlight streams on to the ground. It is quite different in late summer when the main mushroom season gets under way. Then the canopy cuts out most of the light and the brightest things on the forest floor are shining brittlegill fungi; in spring, everything is illuminated. Many of the ash trees may fail to unwrap their leaves altogether if they are succumbing to the onslaught of ash dieback. For a short while, the forest floor belongs to bluebells and lesser celandine. This is the time when an annual ritual takes place: the search for the most delicious of all fungi – the Yellow Morel (*Morchella esculenta*). It is a specialist for spring fruiting, on or around St George's Day. It is also the object of a search when hopes run high, but disappointment is just as likely as success. The great morel hunt sharpens when rumour stokes expectation: a whisper from a colleague, perhaps, or maybe an online post. They are out there – somewhere.

Morels are saprotrophs, so they can be found in many different sites. I have had encounters with them along path sides, on mossy banks, or on the ground inside an old apple tree. They often turn up where you don't expect them, and fail to turn up where you *do* expect them. They are only around for a few weeks, so delay is out of the question. There are traditions that suggest morels like old fire sites, prompting many a search, but I have never found them there. John Ramsbottom noted that morels appeared in abundance in France after the First World War in burned-out buildings. In April 2023 my nephew told me they were present on the north side of the South Downs in Sussex on the chalky slopes. A basket was immediately put in the car in the expectation of a good haul after an hour's drive. The steep hills looked just right: a good covering of dog's mercury, promising-looking patches of open chalky ground, scratchy scrub where we thought nobody else would have searched. Up and down we went, basket in hand. We poked under bushes, braved bramble patches and were mocked by magpies. Not a single morel was discovered – maybe my informant had scooped the lot. A few years earlier I had found a dozen of them near my home in an apparently identical site. They are as frustrating as they are desirable.

The morel is also a very distinctive fungus. It is sometimes described rather loosely as 'a brain on a stalk', but it is probably better compared with a rather coarse, spherical, yellow-brownish bath sponge carried on a white pillar. The cap is really an irregular array of small pits separated by prominent ridges, a folded surface designed to allow a generous area for spore release. Both cap and stem are hollow inside, and the flesh is rather brittle. The Yellow Morel is perhaps the most sought-after and elusive. There are other species, the commonest of which is the Black Morel, usually called M. *elata*, in which the cap is both darker, reflected in the common name, and elevated into a tall cone as the Latin tag might suggest. It is still undecided exactly how many different morels there are: a recent French review lists fourteen of the black ones alone. No matter, they are all equally edible. The Black Morel could almost be described as cultivatable. Yet again, the fashion for dressing flowerbeds with tree bark and woodchips as a weed suppressant has resulted in this species appearing more regularly as a pioneer coloniser of treated areas. We had our best-ever haul of Black Morels from our local supermarket! After the usual perfunctory building had been erected, the car park was laid out with a number of beds containing young trees to divide one rank of cars from another. Dark-coloured bark mulch was thrown down in some quantity. The following spring Black Morels were dotted around the car park. They looked like little black protruding pixie hats. I filled my largest collecting basket with them. I could not suppress a smug feeling from harvesting a valuable crop for nothing outside such a temple to consumption, full of plastic-wrapped food that had travelled halfway around the planet. I have seen Black Morels on mulched flowerbeds in new housing estates, though never in such quantity, and I have never felt comfortable with stealing from someone else's garden. They only seem to have one year of glory. A different succession of fungi follows the next year; the morels must have moved on to the next new supermarket.

Morels are among the largest of the ascos. In the early days of mycology there was a concept of greater 'perfection' in fungi measured by the complexity of the fruit bodies.* On this measure *Morchella* lies at the top of the asco league, with such a well-developed stipe lifting the spore-bearing part above the ground, and with a complex cap atop, folded cleverly into small pockets. When the spore-bearing asci were discovered, they formed a palisade lining the depressions on the cap, and, when they were ready, spores would 'puff' into the breeze to aid their distribution. The White Saddle (*Helvella crispa*) had a comparable stipe, but the spore-bearing apparatus had but a few folds; it was one notch down from the morel. Such a hierarchical view of fungal complexity is thoroughly misleading in an evolutionary context, but it does resonate with the stature and complex shape of morels compared with their 'simple' cup-like disco relatives.

Where the morel can genuinely claim a top position is in flavour. This is a delicious blend of succulence and smokiness, completely different from the taste of the regular mushroom – perhaps that is not so surprising since agarics are such remote relatives of the ascos. Morels have been part of the gourmet's wish list for centuries, which indicates

---

* A similar idea placed *Amanita* at the apex of agarics, because these large toadstools had both a ring and a volva – another measure of complexity. This notion lingered for some time, even if unacknowledged. For example, *Amanita* was placed first in J.E. Lange's magnificent *Flora Agaricina Danica* (1935).

that picking them has not greatly diminished the supply. By the time they have grown to full size they have already ejected many millions of spores, so picking them at this stage may not greatly affect their fecundity. They do like wet spring weather, and climate change could yet impact their abundance. They are certainly commoner in some regions than others. A friend of mine in New England sent me a picture every year showing his brimming baskets of morels gleaned from the apple orchards near his home. I have only seen such morel mountains in my dreams.

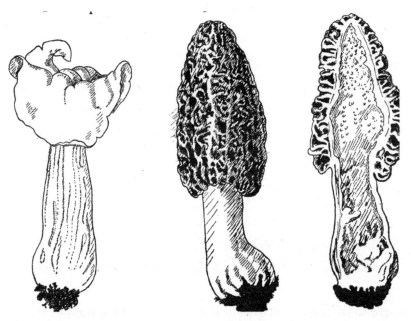

Morels and relatives: the White Saddle (*Helvella crispa*) (left) and one of the morels (*Morchella*) (right).

Caution demands that I mention a morel 'lookalike', the False Morel, *Gyromitra esculenta*. In general construction it is similar to *Morchella*, but the cap is more genuinely brain-like and convoluted, a tangle of thin lobes, and is a rich chest-nut-brown colour. It seems to be particularly fond of growing under pine trees and in sandy soils. It is rather uncommon in Britain, but I was once brought a basket of them from Surrey by somebody who thought they had hit a morel bonanza. The reputation of False Morels for edibility is most confusing. In continental Europe they have been traditional and sought-after edible fungi, yet they have been associated with fatalities. The original describer, the great Dutch mycologist Christian Hendrik Persoon, gave it the specific name *esculenta* ('edible') in 1800, presumably because it was a familiar comestible in Europe. Cooking methods have varied: some recommend drying first, and all agree that the fungi should be blanched. The flesh of the False Morel does indeed include a notable poison called (unsurprisingly) gyromitrin, but its concentration seems to vary among different wild populations, and cooking helps destroy it.

Some people seem to be less vulnerable to its effects than others. In Poland, the country where the love of consuming fungi is unbridled, False Morels were responsible for a fifth of fungus fatalities in 1971. Several European countries have banned its sale, but not Finland, where it is a common species and a favourite food, and where many tonnes are consumed every year. However, it is a legal requirement that cooking instructions have to be displayed wherever the fungus is sold. The precautionary principle undoubtedly applies in this case: the False Morel is best avoided. Recent molecular evidence has proved that *Gyromitra* is not as closely related to the true morel as was once believed, so this is another example of 'parallel evolution' in fungi. Both probably evolved from fungi with simpler, ground-dwelling, cup-like fruit bodies having the asci lining the insides of the cups. Both fungi are solving a common problem: how to raise a fruit body cup off the ground to launch as many spores as possible into the air stream. Required: a stipe, and a way of folding the spore-bearing cup surface to get the maximum number of propagules into the smallest possible space. Result: a morel (or, alternatively, a False Morel).

Morels are only the most spectacular and complex of a very large group of ascos that have cup-like or discus-like fruit bodies. At the microscopic level the asci of many species release their spores by way of defined, terminal lids that open when they are mature. Many of them are very small, a few millimetres across or less, but their interest is greater than their size. They may be seen as white or yellow swarms on old nettle stems or fallen twigs, but their endless variety renders too many close encounters impractical here. I have saved a few for my account of the dung fungi I reared during the COVID lockdown (p. 257). The old term 'discomycetes' for these fungi no longer applies, as it is now known (thanks to DNA sequencing) that ascos with cup-like fruit bodies are derived from possibly as many as five different ancestral lines – but I still like the informal term 'discos' for species whose spore-producing surface is open to the air. It is simple and descriptive. Once you get to know them, a walk in the woods is transformed, because discos are everywhere in due season: on the petioles of leaves, inside acorn cupules or old hazelnuts, on the damp bases of ferns, on logs – and on lichens. The collaboration between discos and algae (and other photosynthesising organisms) that make lichens among the toughest living things on Earth is a great story, but it is not mine here, as I have always left the lichens to the lichenologists. At the Natural History Museum I worked alongside Peter James, the charming and self-effacing Prince of Lichens in the late twentieth century, and to try to learn lichens then would have been like picking up a violin next to Paganini.

The commonest large discos are saprotrophic cup fungi, usually found on the ground, that compete with mushrooms and toadstools for attention in the autumn, although many can be found all year round. Exceptionally, they can be as large as the palm of your hand. The simple cups of *Peziza* species can be any shade of yellow or brown, or even an alluring violet colour. One species is found very commonly on piles of rotting straw. The Blistered Cup (*P. vesiculosa*) is named from the appearance of the exterior, infertile part of the cup, which has an off-white, scurfy appearance, like unhealthy skin. It is one of the few fungi that can tolerate nitrogen-rich habitats, so the piles that farmers leave at the edge of the field are fruitful places to search, although staring closely at a gently steaming heap can attract odd looks from passing walkers.

My sister once found fawn-coloured disco cups dangling from her ceiling. They were growing happily in a corner from some damp wood that was decaying out of sight. *Peziza domiciliana* seems to favour our human dwellings (to judge from the scientific name), but presumably has somewhere it likes to grow in the wild. Unlike dry rot (p. 263), it is not invasive. Most other *Peziza*s are found on the ground, where they often last longer than agarics, but can be well disguised among fallen leaves of a similar colour. Ear fungi

(*Otidea*) are rather more prominent forest floor discos, often clustered, in which one side of the cup is cleft, so they resemble what P.G. Wodehouse called the 'shell-like' ears of his young heroines. Small bouquets of the Hare's Ear (*Otidea onotica*) seem to favour path sides in our woodlands, where their pinkish apricot colour could hardly fail to attract attention. This species is the best candidate to illustrate the release of ascospores. Kneeling down close to the cups, I exhale a careful puff of breath towards the open 'ears' – not as if blowing out a candle but more as if I were delivering a gentle breath to polish up a wine glass. If it is done correctly, and the fungus is sufficiently mature, a pale, wisp-like white smoke is ejected from the cup to vanish into the air. This is a cloud of many thousands of spores, and they disappear when they are dispersed into the slightest breeze. It is a good moment to invite my fellow forayers to imagine how the air we breathe is charged with countless emissaries dedicated to the survival of the species, invisible but omnipresent.

One of the most conspicuous and common discos is the Orange Peel Fungus (*Aleuria aurantia*), whose name exactly describes its appearance. It is usually found on rather bare ground, and its scattered fruit bodies look as if somebody peeling an orange had strewn small pieces of discarded peel over the soil. Decorating the path on a country stroll the bright patches immediately attract attention. Sometimes the fruit bodies are rather flat and distorted, or they can be relatively round and neat. It is one of many discos that have acquired red, orange or yellow pigments; these are invariably carotinoids, which help prevent cellular damage caused by sunlight. There are numerous tinier and less conspicuous discos,* but masses of the brilliant yellow Lemon Disco (*Bisporella citrina*) are readily visible in winter as bright splashes of colour decorating rotten wood, with little discs a few millimetres across swarming in their hundreds to make an obvious patch: beta-carotene provides the yellow paint of this common saprotroph.

Both Orange Peel Fungus and Lemon Disco have to vie for attention among a plethora of excitements from across the entire fungal kingdom on a typical autumn foray. At other times of year there is less competition, but more dedication is needed to bring home the mycological bacon. It requires a good pair of gloves and several layers of woollen clothing to poke among dead and damp willow branches lying in a swamp in February. I know several suitable localities in the Thames Valley. On one ornithological walk to identify winter visitors on the lakes near Twyford, I discovered piles of cut willow branches that had been left to decay. Willows grow promiscuously and every year the paths need tidying to keep them open for walkers. Cleared branches roughly piled in a damp corner offer exactly what is needed to encourage a winter specialist. The Scarlet Elf Cup (*Sarcoscypha austriaca*) looks almost like a tropical flower, absurdly out of place on a misty and chilly winter's day. It is a large cup fungus that has its interior painted richly red; on this occasion half a

---

* There are thousands of species of small discos that require microscope work for their identification. A rather wonderful website called Ascofrance reveals a network of dedicated people, mostly amateurs, who are committed to their study and freely share information. It is a model of how natural history can be furthered internationally with the help of computer technology.

dozen specimens were aligned along a decaying branch, almost as if they had been planted there deliberately. The strange thing is that only one branch was so favoured, and similar branches lying nearby carried no such bonus. The Scarlet Elf Cup is unquestionably one of the most beautiful of all the ascos, and its unexpectedness only adds to its glamour. A close colour match for the Scarlet Elf Cup appears later in the year on damp, decaying wood, however the Eyelash Cup (*Scutellinia scutellata*) is only a fraction of its size, although it occasionally occurs in sufficient numbers to become conspicuous. It does, however, bear a fringe of dark, graceful, spiky hairs around its rather flat disc, which, so far as it is possible for a fungus, makes it look somehow flirtatious.

13.

Things on sticks

If there is an autumn season favoured by agarics, and a vernal season favoured by discos, then there is a period in between when the Scarlet Elf Cup appears to be one of few fungal pleasures remaining. Soft fungal tissue – being largely water – generally cannot endure sub-zero temperatures. The first hard frost reduces most agarics to a sad pulp, a floppy relic of their former elegance. Even tough brackets stop shedding spores. There are a few survivors. The Winter Agaric (*Flammulina velutipes*) seems to be supplied with anti-freeze, having caps the size of large coins clustering on dead trees, their bright orange contrasting with darker, velvety stems. I have seen this fungus happily shedding spores while dusted with snow. Among other winter specialists, jelly fungi are curious basidios with fruit bodies that are frequently foliar or wrinkled, or make brain-like hemispheres, or maybe just pale blobs. When it rains or when the atmosphere is humid, they have a jelly-like texture that some people find repulsive. In this state they shed their big, sausage-shaped spores. When the sun comes out they dry away to practically nothing – no more than a papery wisp – but they can rehydrate perfectly in the next shower and shed their spores once again. Frost does not deter them either – they can freeze and thaw without ill-effect. Yellow Brain (*Tremella mesenterica*) is the most distinctive species because of its bright colour and folded form, somewhat like a banana-coloured slice of the cerebral cortex. After a gorse fire in the summer of 2017 in Southwold, Suffolk, the blackened stems were decorated all winter long with yellow jellies, hanging like frilly garters. The colourless members of these gelatinous fungi can be quite inconspicuous when clustered on twigs – my son suggested they looked like 'bogies', which was hardly flattering but was not a bad description. It has been proved that all these jellies are parasitic upon other fungi – which are often rather inconspicuous crusts. They are not closely related to another batch of winter jellies that are saprotrophs, including dark Witches' Butter (*Exidia glandulosa*) that forms stumpy, black growths on fallen oak twigs. This is one example where the common names are ambiguous. You might think that butter (not brain) is more appropriate for *Tremella mesenterica* – after all, it is the right colour. Another sinister-looking black jelly is 'Warlock's Butter' (*Exidia nigricans*), which forms contorted masses on dead beech branches in winter. A different naming question attends what is the most familiar of the jelly-textured saprotrophs – the Jelly Ear, *Auricularia auricula-judae*. This fungus really *does* look like a pinkish-brown ear, and usually grows communally on elder wood. When moist it is gelatinous and somewhat flabby, and when dry a crisp, in which state it can be stored indefinitely: to revive, just add water. Once rehydrated, it is perfectly edible, although some people don't enjoy its gelatinous texture. The Chinese Cloud Ear Fungus is a close relative. In China in the 1980s I met it at the bottom of a bowl of clear chicken soup and was informed that it was 'very good for old age', and since I am now old I presume that it worked. The problem with the Jelly Ear is its species name in Latin, which obviously means 'Jew's Ear' – an unacceptable name for reasons I do not have to explain. But there is a rule in scientific nomenclature that valid names cannot be changed, so there it will remain as a reflection of past attitudes; the name was already in use before the end of the eighteenth century.

Attempts to prolong the fungus 'season' into the winter months led me inexorably to study 'pyrenos'. If you know where to look, fungi can be found along country lanes and by tracks through woodland even as early as February. Many of them show up at first glance as no more than black patches lurking on dead or dying tree trunks, or painting twigs or the stems of herbs. They could easily be passed by unnoticed, but once their fungal nature has been recognised they seem to be everywhere. They may cover the whole length of a fallen beech trunk – an entire tree wrapped up in a fungal sheet! The surface is rough to the touch and pimply, like the skin of a lychee. A casual glance might have suggested that the trunk had somehow been set alight, blackening the surface with a patina of carbon, but this is a *living* covering, a pioneer wood-rotting fungus that has covered itself in a funereal cloak, black as tar. Under a hand lens, the rough surface is revealed to be the result of thousands of tiny pyramidal warts, each one fluted delicately to a pointed tip. This Spiral Tarcrust (*Eutypa spinosa*) must be the largest, but least-noticed organism in the forest.

If the surface of the crust is cut with a sharp knife its secret is revealed. Below the warty exterior are a series of diminutive chambers, each one filled with a gooey substance. These little flasks (*perithecia*) contain a lining of many asci, every ascus including eight smooth, sausage-shaped spores. The gooey tissue is their nursery. The asci ripen in sequence, when they elongate into a channel in a corresponding wart above them, where their spores are ejected into the atmosphere. The spores are only about seven thousandths of a millimetre long. When the fungus has done its job of spreading its spores, the flasks remain behind, all hollow and empty, and they will endure in this state for months. This reproductive activity mostly happens during the wintertime, when you might imagine the whole forest is asleep. It is actually invisibly seething.

The vast number of spores produced from a single log defies computation, though doubtless the numbers of stars in galaxies would be a measure. The blackness of the fruit body explains why these fungi were called pyrenomycetes, from the Greek for 'fire' (as in pyromaniac), and the obvious difference from discos is that the asci ripen inside closed vessels rather than open to the air; but, like the discos, it is now well established that these flask-bearers include several groups that are only remotely related to one another.* It remains appropriate informally to continue to call them all

---

* For example, one large group of pyrenos has a double, rather than single, wall to the ascus, a feature requiring microscope work to identify.

pyrenos. They *are* united by black walls – a wrapping of black melanin, the complex polymer that protects from ultra-violet damage and resists just about everything, be it natural (or unnatural) acids or laboratory solvents. It stops living tissues drying out. Maggots cannot get to the soft bits. If you were of a sensitive mycelial disposition, you could not have a better covering.

Once I had started looking at pyrenos I found them everywhere, and not just in winter. In our wood I noticed that dead beech branches carried small, round, densely scattered dark-grey blisters dotted with spore-releasing apertures; they broke through the bark, peeling it delicately back around their perimeters – this was Beech Barkspot (*Diatrype disciformis*). Trunks of the same tree were decorated with swarms of what might have been undersized rusty-coloured strawberries, Beech Woodwart (*Hypoxylon fragiforme*). My hazel branches carried less knobbly spheres of a similar size and colour (*H. fusca*). I saw fallen, small branches belonging to broadleaved trees wholly blackened by a covering of Common Tarcrust (*Diatrype stigma*). Each dry nettle stem had lines at its base of tiny black flasks carrying prominent necks, which somebody with a sense of humour had named Nettle Rash (*Leptosphaeria acuta*). It became a routine on country walks during the winter months to carry a linen bag to pop in what my family referred to – sometimes with a hint of exasperation – as 'things on sticks'. And indeed there proved to be a great many different things on sticks.

I was fortunate to have learned the British flora when I was still a schoolboy naturalist. I didn't know the Latin names, but I did know the old English names like Garlic

Mustard, Hogweed and Cow Parsley. There was no practical purpose to acquiring this catalogue of identities – it was just what young naturalists did at that time. Like many skills learned young, the old names stayed with me. They finally proved very useful to help with identifying things on sticks, as many of these fungi were confined to single hosts. A fat book by East Anglian naturalists Martin and Pam Ellis was organised by host plants (rather than fungal names) so if I identified the host I was well on my way to making an identification of some small black fruit body on a stick. I soon learned that some of these pyrenos fruited *inside* the stick – using the thin layer of bark as a protection – and only the small mouths (*ostioles*) of the spore-bearing flasks protruded through the bark to release the spores.

These fungi were more easily detected by touch than sight, and I found myself lightly stroking dead twigs, as might a blind man, to detect the tell-tale roughness produced by fungi that were ready to release their spores through small protruding mouths. I occasionally had to explain what I was doing to some perplexed dog walker. When I found a productive twig it went into the bag for further investigation. Things on sticks proved to be inexhaustibly varied.

At this point one of the great books should take a bow. Many biologists know the work of Ernst Haeckel, whose images of organisms – particularly invertebrates – combine astounding accuracy with artistic delight. They have been reproduced countless times, and adorn the offices of many scientists who have never picked up a pencil in their lives.

Very few biologists know the work of the Tulasne brothers, let alone have handled a copy of *Selecta Fungorum Carpologia* (1861–3). Yet their work on fungi combined advances in knowledge with astounding and beautiful drawings, one of which is reproduced here. They surely deserve to be more widely appreciated. Charles and Louis Tulasne died in Hyères in France within a few months of one another in 1884 and

One of the Tulasne brothers' incomparable drawings for *Selecta Fungorum Carpologia* (1861–5), a mycological landmark that linked anamorphs bearing conidia with sexual fruit bodies bearing asci. This shows *Trichoderma delicatula* with finely branched structures carrying conidia on the left, and ascus stage the spheres to the right.

1885 respectively. As appropriate for mycologists, they had a symbiotic relationship. Charles illustrated what Louis described, turning what could have been exercises in microscopy into art. So solid are Charles's images that the viewer feels as if she could wander into these strange groves of monstrous flasks and waving threads, bombarded with spores of all shapes and sizes. A lesser artist would have illustrated the bare minimum to characterise a particular species, but Charles created vistas. His pyreno flasks bubbled over with asci. He drew at every scale from twig to spore. The word 'surreal' is rather overused to apply to anything a tad weird, but I do believe that some of the strange landscapes painted by such surrealist artists as Yves Tanguy are no more effectively realised than the fungal illustrations of Charles Tulasne.

As for the science, the Tulasne brothers broke new ground that changed everything that was known before. They proved that fungi could exist in two forms, with apparently little that was obvious to connect them. As the subtitle to the 1931 English translation of their work put it rather pompously and not wholly accurately, they showed 'those facts and illustrations which go to prove that various kinds of fruits and seeds are produced, either simultaneously or in succession, by the same fungus'. Many of the pyrenos they investigated were split personalities. The mature fungus embodied in its black phial full of asci was not the whole story. At another stage in its life cycle that same species could look completely different, and its spores were not necessarily enclosed in a receptacle. It might well be a white fuzz of hyphae decorated with spores like a Christmas tree with baubles, or maybe a minute pad dedicated to producing spores like a production line in a factory – or perhaps a black flask containing odd-looking spores that were not produced in asci. Some of these fungi might once have been called 'moulds', but now they were recognised as stages in the life of an asco. The spores produced by the alter ego growth stage were often different in shape and size from those of the ascus stage. Many of the details of this double life magnificently laid out by the Tulasne brothers have been proved time and again by the researchers who followed in their footsteps, and are now routinely tested by molecular evidence. Their newly characterised phase in the life of the fungus was later termed the 'anamorph' – which taken literally means 'without shape', but it would be better to say that they had a bewildering variety of *different* shapes. The spores produced by the anamorph are called *'conidia'* to distinguish them from those produced inside asci.

The ascus-bearing fruit body is the sexual stage in the life cycle of the fungus (the teleomorph). The conidial stage is asexual. It provides a way of producing prodigious numbers of spores very rapidly when the going is good. Conidia, carried by the slightest breeze to a favourable site, may be able to germinate successfully almost immediately and start a new mycelium. They are mycological storm troopers. If the fungus in question is a pest, fields of crops might be devastated within days, courtesy of hordes of microscopic invaders. The ascus stage has been described in the past as the 'perfect' stage, which naturally makes the anamorphic stage 'imperfect', even though it is perfectly adapted for its function. Though many conidia-carrying fungi have now been linked with an ascus-bearing stage, there remain others that have not. Many of the details of the anamorph require microscopic examination, which takes them out of my purview here, but they have proved of great importance in identifying genera and species – and are often more reliable than the features of the 'perfect' stage alone. Many ascos pass most of their life as mycelium in the growing state.

This complex lifestyle may be a little hard to comprehend for a novice. The mycelium of the anamorph carries one set of chromosomes in their nuclei – in the usual terminology, it is haploid, as are the conidia that are produced in such profusion. The spores produced inside the asci during the sexual, diploid stage of the fungus are the product of complex 'mating' of two compatible haploid partners. Only once conjoined can the asci develop the spores that carry the future of the species into subsequent generations. Most asco species need to find and 'marry' a compatible mycelial mating type before they can complete their life cycle. There is no equivalent to male and female here (they are conventionally just represented by + and -). To parody a well-worn phrase from *Star Trek*: 'It's sex, Captain, but not as we know it.' This is also the place to emphasise that a comparable mating ritual also applies to basidiomycetes before they can develop their diagnostic basidium on which the four spores are held like jewels on a coronet. Haploid mycelium must find a compatible partner before the fruit body can develop. The situation is more complicated in basidios because there are often more, and sometimes many more than two mating types – and not every pair is compatible.* The intricate particulars of these

---

* A number of basidios also have anamorphic alter egos, differing profoundly from the larger fleshy fungi. I do not deal with the more complicated sex lives of smuts and rusts in this book.

mating rituals have been studied in more than microscopic detail by the intellectual successors of the Tulasne brothers, but they have never been illustrated with such panache as in the original.

The different personae of ascos may seem a tad theoretical and hidden out of sight but they play out on the ground in dramatic fashion. When Jackie and I acquired our small piece of Chiltern woodland in 2011, we noticed a plethora of young ash trees. There were so many that we wondered whether we should thin them out before they overwhelmed the small beech trees that were competing for the same patch of light at the edge of the canopy. Ash is always the last woodland tree to unfurl its leaves in the spring, but then it makes up for lost time with prolific growth. When I wrote the story of our wood in *The Wood for the Trees*, passing reference was made to the appearance of ash dieback in the Chilterns. I had encountered the disease two years earlier when making a television programme about fungi. At that time dieback was found in Norfolk, but its potential for causing a major crisis for ash woodland had already been acknowledged. It was believed that it had been introduced from the Netherlands on infected saplings. The film crew and I had to splash through a footbath of disinfectant at the edge of the affected woodland to make sure we did not carry spores to a new site. It was already too late.

By 2021 we were accustomed to the sight of dead ash groves in the midst of our hills; straight trunks topped with twigs that all turn upwards towards their tips made them all too recognisable from afar. The National Trust was soon felling trees next to public footpaths, because those that have suffered dieback rot on the inside and suddenly drop. In our own woodland all the young trees were dead or dying – displaying typical outlines with the highest twigs and small branches carrying no more than a few blackened, dead leaves. They were becoming both leafless and lifeless. A few viable shoots struggled on nearer the ground. We need not have worried about them crowding out our young beech trees. We were now more worried about losing all our ashes. Larger ash trees are apparently more resistant, but will succumb in the end. Some of them are centuries old.

The pathogen that causes dieback was given the scientific name *Chalara fraxinea* as recently as 2006. For several years the agent responsible for ruining many a woodland was referred to as chalara in the press, usually accompanied by a picture showing the diamond-shaped lesions below small branches that were typical when the microfungus blocked the vital 'plumbing' of the young tree. Chalara was the anamorph of a lethal fungus; it was the asexual, rampant invader, and an invisible killer. When ash dieback is mentioned now in the media the reader (or listener) might be confused to see it named rather as *Hymenoscyphus fraxineus*. It is, of course, the same fungus as chalara! But the current name is its sexual stage – and this name carries the day. *Hymenoscyphus* is a genus of small, white discos with short stipes, and this is where the sexual, 'perfect' stage of ash dieback belongs. It is usually just a few millimetres across. I have found it on the petioles of the fallen leaves of ash trees, looking as if tiny, white tacks had been inserted in a line.* The 'split personality' of this invading asco was central to its rapid spread and subsequent survival: the chalara stage as aggressor, the disco stage to ensure survival of the species. Mighty trees have been brought down by something that is as small as a pinhead.

There is hope for the ash tree, in spite of its fungal foe. Dieback probably arrived on an imported exotic species of ash, and the European species offered no resistance to infection. It is now widespread across continental Europe and in the United Kingdom. When we were driving through France in 2023, the spindly skeletons of dead ash trees were a frequent sight along the autoroutes. But as we passed progressively upwards along the Isère valley towards the French Alps, it was noticeable that healthy looking ash trees were everywhere. They abounded on the steep slopes of the valley sides, where they were among the commonest of the deciduous trees. Maybe the long and cold winters of that region are not tolerated by *Hymenoscyphus fraxineus* and alpine habitats may offer a redoubt for these beautiful trees. A more domestic recovery might also prove possible. Ash trees are prolific seeders and among the many seedlings are a few that resist dieback. Natural selection will favour such trees; although it may take many years for this obduracy to feed back into the landscape, the ash will not be lost, and

---

* The nomenclatural details are somewhat complex. A very similar, native species found on ash is called *Hymenoscyphus albidus*, which apparently causes no harm to our native trees; ash dieback was briefly known as a newly differentiated species termed *Hymenoscyphus pseudoalbidus*. However, the older species name was *fraxinea*, and that is the name that finally took precedence. Hence *Hymenoscyphus fraxineus*.

as I write human selection of resistant strains is speeding the process.

Sadly, the same cannot be said of Dutch elm disease. The fungus that administers the *coup de grâce* to the majestic elm is a tiny, flask-like pyreno called *Ophiostoma*. The lethal fungus spreads from tree to tree carried by a bark beetle – a weevil of the genus *Scolytus* – which carves out feeding galleries beneath the bark that make handsome traceries on bare trunks, until their lethal effect confounds admiration for their symmetry and execution. Once the disease is established, the conducting tissues of the tree become blocked, and the poor plant essentially starves to death, deprived of its photosynthetic nourishment. Its foliage yellows and then turns brown, as if scorched by an invisible flame. Dead trees can be seen in every other hedgerow in East Anglia where once fine, almost feathery crowns allowed John Constable a chance to display his mastery of portraying grand trees. Alas, poor Norwich! The trees do not die completely, because they regenerate clonally from suckers, but when these get to about twenty feet high the disease returns, so that affected hedgerows develop an unattractive mixture of dead standing wood and living shoots. The English elm very rarely sets seed, and its clonal reproduction means that it does not have the same potential as ash to produce immune strains.

Today, the only stands in England that Constable would recognise are around Brighton, seaward of the South Downs, which act as a barrier for the dispersal of the beetles. Vigilant local naturalists look for telltale signs in the foliage of these survivors that indicates when the barrier has been breached, and infected trees are immediately destroyed. There is historical evidence that 'waves' of Dutch elm destruction have happened in the past, and eventually trees do regenerate, but this is scant comfort for those who would love to see the stately trees rising above the ditches in eastern England. It is some consolation that the related wych elm does set abundant seed, allowing for more genetic variation, and resistant strains of this attractive tree are evolving to feed the many insects, especially moths, that rely on elms as part of their life cycle.

14.

Mea culpa

As we have seen, fungi do not disappear at the first frost, although the more flamboyant mushrooms vanish as cold weather takes a grip. Even in the middle of winter the unpredictable British climate can throw up a week or so of comparatively warm, wet weather, and then the serious fungus aficionado can have fun turning over rotting logs or examining moss-covered branches. Some tiny bonnets even seem to prefer such warm episodes, or maybe we just notice them because there are fewer glamorous distractions. The Bark Bonnet (*Phloeomana speirea*) grows in small troops exactly where its common name says it should; no more than a few millimetres across, it has a bell-shaped cap and flesh so thin that you can see the gills through it like the struts of an umbrella. The Dewdrop Bonnet (*Hemimycena tortuosa*) is as small, but pure white, and seems to have a penchant for ash (*Fraxinus*) logs in winter. Its stipe, no thicker than a pin, carries tiny water droplets that have condensed around minute spiral hairs. Once you get up close, these diminutive toadstools are beautiful and charming in a way that contrasts with their more burly autumnal predecessors.

On such a warm interlude on 10 December 2006, I ventured from my home town to the nearby National Trust property of Greys Court, an Oxfordshire manor house in which medieval towers are blended with a Tudor building and Regency trimmings, an architectural pot pourri that somehow all hangs together rather well. The grounds are famous for an ancient wheelhouse where a donkey once worked relentlessly to lift good, clean water from a great depth for the benefit of the manor. Not far downhill from the wheelhouse, the verges of a somewhat overgrown and very narrow country lane were covered with dead plants and sticks to tempt the unseasonable fungus forayer. Warm, wet weather had encouraged lots of small fungi to display their particular charms. From the base of a nettle – no more than a stick but still somehow able to inflict a sting – a little cluster of small, shining white goblets erupted in a line along its length. They looked like little discos, but I had met them before. They were actually minuscule mushrooms doing their best to mimic the cups of a typical ascomycete – even to the extent of having the *inside* of the cup lined with spore-producing basidia (where flask-like asci might be expected). Of course, a microscope was later necessary to confirm the identification, but a little flush of satisfaction was allowed for not being fooled by this pretty pretender.

Further along the roadside, stout stems of burdock over-topped the nettles. Burdock (*Arctium*) is one of those plants that prompt a measure of caution, because the rounded seed heads are composed of hooked seeds that have a special adaptation for catching on to your winter pullover. In nature they must be distributed on the backs of animals. They can embed themselves in your hair very effectively, and it is a painful business pulling them out. I was hoping to find a modestly sized and inconspicuous black disco (*Pyrenopeziza arctii*) that erupts through the surface of the stout burdock stems and it was not long before I had succeeded in my quest, even at the cost of some burs hanging on to my back. As I pulled the stem from the ground I noticed that its base carried more fungi, one a simple white patch (a 'crust fungus'), the other something orange that extended for some centimetres along the damp burdock. I put the latter into a sealed box and continued my hunt.

When I got back to my little home laboratory, I examined the orange patch more closely. It proved to be a poroid – that is, much of the fruit body was a closely packed array of approximately hexagonal pores, on the sides of which the spores were produced. This fertile area was surrounded by a fringe of sterile hyphae, forming a skirt around the patch, closely pressed to the burdock's surface. Another puzzling feature was the very soft texture. I was accustomed to finding poroids like this one, but their texture was usually quite firm, even corky. They tended to resist squishing under a microscope slide, whereas a sample from this one offered no resistance at all. Under the high-powered microscope, the hyphae were orange-coloured and slender, and the spores proved to be colourless, narrow cylinders only about four thousandths of a millimetre long.

I looked for something like it by thumbing through my many reference books – hundreds of pages of frustration.

If I found the right colour, the spores were wrong; if I found the right spores, the colour was wrong; nothing seemed to have the correct soft texture. It was a complete puzzle. Under these circumstances I might have been forgiven for leaving the specimen unclassified and moving on to something more tractable, but this little patch seemed so interesting that I carefully dried it. Gentle heat from an old-fashioned light bulb in my somewhat Heath Robinson homemade contraption is sufficient to drive off the water that makes up the bulk of the fungus but preserves the microscopic features. Once dry, the specimen is ready to become a voucher, and, carefully stored, can last indefinitely. The microscopic features survive this treatment unscathed; but it still looked like an orange patch in the dried state.

One deeply knowledgeable mycologist in the Jodrell Laboratory in the Royal Botanic Gardens, Kew, had a special interest in this kind of fungus. Nick Legon was, like me, an amateur, but after an unsatisfying life in advertising now devoted his time to fungi to great effect. At Kew he also had access to more of the literature than I did, so he was able to look for a match in North America or – who knows? – the Far East, or indeed anywhere. I sent him the dried voucher specimen, retaining a part of it for myself. After a couple of weeks I heard back: he had drawn a blank. He, too, could not find a match for the mystery poroid, despite having looked through many more books than I had to hand. There was a final step to solve the mystery. The world authority on these kinds of fungi is Professor Leif Ryvarden of Oslo University. Maybe the voucher should take a trip to Norway to see if such an experienced eye could make anything of it.

Some weeks passed before I heard back. The professor had not seen its like before, and it was a new species! Although during my long career as a palaeontologist I had named many new species of trilobites and graptolites, this was the first time I had found a fungus that was, in the correct jargon, 'new to science'. It did seem rather wonderful that such a discovery could be made virtually on my doorstep rather than in some rarely visited jungle in Papua New Guinea.

A new species does not officially exist until it is published in a scientific journal. It must be described and illustrated there and given a scientific name. Just about eighteen months after my December discovery, *Ceriporiopsis herbicola* (Fortey & Ryvarden 2007) appeared in *Fungiflora*, a journal published in Norway. It now had an identification tag; it was one tiny addition to the catalogue of biodiversity. The biological world was richer by one species! I knew some other species of *Ceriporiopsis* from my years of fungus hunting, and these were commonly encountered as white or yellowish patches on the underside of more or less rotten wood. The new species name *herbicola* indicated the preference of ours for a herbal substrate – even if burdock is rather on the substantial side for a herb. So far as we knew the Greys Court collection was the only one. It was clearly very rare.

My 'new' fungus had a life of only nine years. First, I heard of another record of the species from Denmark, this time on a dead stem of the most invasive and ineradicable plant known in Europe – Japanese knotweed. People have moved house when they discovered this plant in the garden, because even Agent Orange would have trouble eliminating its grip. It is another unusually solid herb like burdock – so far so good. Then I learned of a study based on DNA analysis of a series of fungi that took *herbicola* far away from where it was classified in *Ceriporiopsis*. This paper, published by O. Meitennen and colleagues in a journal called *Mycotaxon* in 2016, included material from my original (type) dried collection, and the DNA sequence that they studied showed that it was, in fact, a species called *Hapalopilus eupatorii* – belonging to an entirely separate group of fungi from *Ceriporiopsis*. *Mea culpa!* My small contribution to living global biodiversity was no more! Had I but applied some alkali to my specimen it would have turned deep purple – a reaction I knew from another, rather common species of *Hapalopilus* that grows on woody debris – this being a bracket that superficially does not look at all like my discovery. *H. eupatorii* had originally been found on hemp agrimony (*Eupatoria*), a common plant of wet places, but also a stout herb as herbs go – so one thing that had not changed was the preference of my inconspicuous species for robust plants. It had first been recognised as a species different from all others and named scientifically by the renowned Finnish mycologist Petter Adolf Karsten in 1884 (from French material), but it must be a very rare fungus, because it was missed out in subsequent published summaries of pore-bearing fungi. I had thumbed relentlessly through what I believed was the definitive volume on fungi of this kind: the 'standard work', one of a multi-volume series called *Fungae Europeae*, that appeared just before my discovery. It isn't in the index. Professor Ryvarden had not seen it before. It was lurking in obscurity. Maybe I should not beat myself up about not knowing what it was. It was already a fungal mystery.

Even if my 'new' species proved to be nothing of the kind, the record of *Hapalopilus eupatorii* was still the first for the United Kingdom, so if it was not a brick in the edifice of knowledge it was at least a splash of cement to hold another brick in place. The details are interesting, not for reasons of pedantic scholarship, but because they illustrate how the sheer numbers of species of fungi can defeat even expert eyes. It is impossible to imagine a bird species slipping through the batteries of binoculars to emerge as a new discovery. So many fungi are rare, but for some of the less conspicuous varieties it is genuinely hard to know whether the rarity is a fact, or an artefact. Can it be that some things are rare just because nobody goes to look for them? Since I knew about *H. eupatorii*, I have studied patches of hemp agrimony along the valley of the River Thames without finding my orange-coloured former friend. It is not likely that it is common on Japanese knotweed in Japan, not least because its discovery by the learned Professor Karsten pre-dated the arrival of that aggressive interloper in Europe. It must maintain a sufficient population to allow its spores to find a suitable host, presumably robust herbs of several kinds (maybe *herbicola* was not so far off, after all). What I do know is that my mycological antennae will be tuned to finding it again, but I will put up a modest wager that this will not happen. What is much more likely is that the search will turn up something else that has not been seen for a long time, which will stimulate poring over many books once again.

15.

Eaters

One of the rewards of knowing about fungi is eating the delicious ones, confident in the accuracy of your identification. Some mycologists maintain that this is damaging to the natural occurrence of edible species. Whether this is true or not is still vigorously debated, not least by those who enjoy their Ceps and their Lawyer's Wigs. In the other camp I have known hypersensitive mycologists who will not pick toadstools at all, even examining their gills from above by wielding a tilted mirror stuck to a pole.

Nearly all the food we eat is farmed, but only a few kinds of mushrooms are cultivated, and at least in the United Kingdom by far the commonest cultivar is just one of them, found as everything from tiny 'buttons' to meaty giants on supermarket shelves – its scientific name is *Agaricus bisporus*. For many, this white agaric is simply synonymous with 'mushroom', and the only kind that finds its way on to the dinner plate alongside the steak and garden peas. It is very popular. In 2020 nearly a hundred thousand tonnes of the supermarket mushroom were produced in Britain. I find it impossible to visualise what this quantity of fruit bodies would look like if piled on top of one another, but it would surely make a shining mycological mountain. I visited one of the largest mushroom farms in Scotland, housed in a series of huge, low sheds, imitating the caves in which mushrooms were traditionally cultivated. The carefully controlled dim light eerily illuminated the simultaneous fruiting of thousands upon thousands of mushrooms on raised beds, looking like a snowfall over pebbles. All stages in cultivation were rigorously protected from infection by other fungi that would have liked to dine on the same rich compost as *Agaricus bisporus*, so, by a strange twist, sterile conditions were most important in this cathedral of decay. Mycelium is known in the trade as 'spawn' and actively growing spawn is inoculated into new sterilised beds, which are then brought up to the ideal growing temperature. When the mycelium has completed its work, conditions are changed again to induce fruiting. The mushrooms duly oblige. Picking and sorting follows in order to separate buttons from more mature mushrooms intended for individual packs. A torch shone into the air at this stage picks out a swirling mist of billions of spores. As we have seen, the astronomical numbers of mushroom spores are routinely compared with the number of the stars in a galaxy, and this feels as if you were staring into your own murky Milky Way.

The protocols supplying the demand for common mushrooms can only be described as industrial. Even the special varieties with brown caps known as Portobello Mushrooms are just one variant of the same, ubiquitous cultivar. Oyster

Mushrooms (*Pleurotus ostreatus*) are now becoming more familiar on supermarket shelves and often (I suspect disingenuously) appear on menus in restaurants as 'wild mushrooms'. They do, indeed, commonly grow in the wild, with a preference for recently felled wood, but they can very easily be cultivated on dead tree trunks, or indeed on just about any source of cellulose, including old books. *Pleurotus* come in all kinds of pleasing colours, including yellow, white or pink, so these mushrooms appeal to those who like to explore rainbow cuisine. Packets of this good edible species are nudging their way on to the shelves of the more discriminating food shops, where they join Shiitake (*Lentinula edodes*), another fungus that readily colonises woody substrates, and has been cultivated for centuries in the Far East. Shop mushrooms, Oysters and Shiitake can all be bought as do-it-yourself packs to bring on at home in the cellar or in the garage. It could be said that these saprotrophs are all tamed. They do not affect the wild species. You can grow as many as you need.

The same cannot be said of the unpredictable Field Mushroom that appears in great numbers in some years, but is hard to find in other seasons if conditions are unfavourable. When these mushrooms are abundant even people who never normally pick wild fungi go into the fields with baskets to collect everything they can. Enthusiastic pickers can leave a favoured pasture almost completely denuded of its bounty. Wild mushrooms do prefer fields that have not been drenched in artificial fertiliser, but they will pop up next to horse manure or sheep droppings; they appear preferentially among short grass, although it could be that longer grass just makes them harder to spot. In spite of centuries of exploitation, the Field Mushroom is not a rare delicacy. If there is a diminution in their abundance it is probably because pastures that have been left alone without a boost of fertiliser are not as common as they once were. Button mushrooms are particularly sought after: these are golf ball–sized specimens whose gills are still pink and immature so that they have not yet started to shed spores. If anything, this might be expected to have a deleterious effect on the survival of the species. Yet the millions upon millions of spores shed by Field Mushrooms that *have* managed to mature on the ground until the gills are black seem to be sufficient to keep *A. campestris* on the menu. Its abundance is controlled by the availability of the right grassland and plenty of rain at the right moment rather than by the eagerness of pickers to seek out the last one.

Parasol Mushrooms (*Lepiota procera*) can be seen from afar, even from a speeding car. Their stately bearing above the rough grassland they favour makes them recognisable at a glance, and on occasion has distracted me sufficiently to stimulate excoriating remarks from fellow drivers who fail to appreciate that their aesthetic qualities demand a slower pace. When you see one mushroom, you are likely to find half a dozen nearby, as they quite often form fairy rings in old grassland. They are reliable, often appearing early in the year compared with Field Mushrooms, and their mycelium obviously lives for many years in the right habitat. The 'roughs' of golf courses are a predictable source for these mushrooms, and I regard such locations as fine Parasol habitat interrupted by uninteresting green bits. Apart from their overall size and shape, and the innate scales roughly zoned on the cap, their ruff-like ring on the stem and its brown 'snakeskin' markings below make them one of the most distinctive of fungi. Among mycophagists it is favoured food and has been for many years, yet I have not detected any diminution in its abundance over the last half-century. By the time it is visible from the Volkswagen it has already done much of its reproductive work; even picking leaves the network of fungal threads intact, and the real challenge to their survival comes from their habitat becoming overgrown with brambles or being turned into a housing estate. For these grassland mushrooms I conclude that the current and past rates of gathering for food does not impact their survival and abundance, but loss of the right habitat might yet do so.

Mycorrhizal fungi could well be different. This book began with the Cep (*Porcini*, Penny Bun, etc.), which in central Europe is regarded as the definitive edible mushroom. It cannot grow far away from the tree to which its underground network is connected. In the United Kingdom, this is frequently beech, though allied, equally delicious species (Dark Bolete, *Boletus aereus*) are associated with oak. Factory production along the lines of the standard supermarket varieties is impossible – there is no equivalent to a Portobello Mushroom. This increases the pressure on wild populations. A living is to be made from scouring the woods for fresh Ceps to bring to upmarket chefs who will weave them into some wonderful concoction. Worse, the gastronome favours baby Ceps when the tubes are still white, the maggots have not yet got going and the texture is almost like that of hazelnuts. This is before the fruit body has started to shed spores. Any Cep eaten at this size is a drain on the network for no return. For a Cep to release as many spores as possible it should grow to full size (and that can be over a foot across); the tubes go yellow, and eventually the texture becomes quite spongy, as hundreds of maggots mature into fungus gnats.

Because I am able to recognise such soggy remnants, I can vouch for the fact that even in well-known fungus woods a few Ceps escape the eyes of collectors; hence we can safely assume that many millions of spores must have been released despite the searchers' best efforts. The burden the Penny Bun bears from collectors must be a heavy one, but still they keep on fruiting despite the depredations of the hunters, as I described in Borgo Val di Taro at the start of this book. A preference for the 'king of mushrooms' is not a recent choice. The Roman naturalist and philosopher Pliny the Elder, who perished in the eruption of Mount Vesuvius in AD 79, appreciated the virtues of what he called *fungi suilli*. For several thousand years this mushroom formed a special part of the human diet; not merely being *edulis* (edible) but recherché, desirable, delicious and coveted. If collecting alone had spelled its destiny it would now be so rare that nature reserves would have been established to protect the last few specimens. Fortunately, this is not so. All over Europe those who know about edible fungi set out with a deter- mined look on their faces to beat the Duponts, Schmidts, Berggrens or Spolinis to the best fruit bodies, but still the Cep (Steinpilz, Karl Johan Svamp, *Porcini*, etc., etc.) survives. This must be a tribute to the enduring properties of its fungal network, safe in the ground where *B. edulis* surfs the time between good and bad years. However, the demand is always growing, and now there is hardly a country in Eastern Europe that does not export some Ceps to wealthier nations.

A contrarian mycologist I know even suggested that the more you pick Ceps, the more will come – rather like the principle of pruning roses, when the harder you prune back, the more you will be rewarded with blooms. Although this is most implausible, it is undoubtedly true that numbers of this mushroom fluctuate greatly from year to year. Prolific rain in late summer certainly helps, particularly if this is followed by a warm spell. It is not uncommon to hear of a good year in Scotland while a hunt for woodland treasure in the south of England is completely fruit(body)less. I find no reason to believe that picking by amateur collectors is solely in charge of the numbers of fungi, particularly if their harvest includes older examples that have already shed spores.

Wholesale removal of 'button' mushrooms over many years might prove a different matter. In the New Forest there is something profoundly depressing about coming across an area under the beech trees that is known to have yielded many fine Boleti in the past, in which all that can be seen are the neatly cut signatures of the professional pickers going over the ground with the efficiency of a combine harvester. Now nobody will be able to appreciate the beauty of the full-grown mushroom, its elegantly swollen stipe and tan-brown cap, with the slightest hint of white around its margin, slightly glistening in the morning dew. If this harvesting were carried on relentlessly year after year, it could well outlast the enduring underground partnership and that would certainly damage the survival of the species in its favourite habitat. Making mushroom-picking illegal within the National Forest area is a necessary precaution. Despite much coverage in the press, it has proved difficult to enforce. Pickers can slip in unnoticed and leave promptly. Although hefty fines (and even imprisonment) are available as deterrents, court actions are expensive and the enforcing authorities seem to be relatively toothless. Natural England has been underfunded for years, although they are empowered to protect Sites of Special Scientific Interest (SSSI) such as the New Forest. The Forestry Commission can impose a fine of £200, which is hardly draconian. Cases have even wriggled through a legal loophole exploiting the original wording of the statutory protection offered to 'plants'. Fungi are *not* plants – as we now recognise – and therefore not protected. The law sometimes really is an ass.

If the Cep is the most desirable autumn prize, there are several other delicious fungi that also form subterranean collaborations with trees. It is a delicate matter whether these should offer a free-for-all, or whether the precautions relating to *Boletus edulis* should be more widely applicable. Apricot yellow chanterelles abound in some parts of Scotland. In Newfoundland, they are so abundant that the mushroom fancier could fill a bucket with them if she pleased. Piles of them are on sale in provincial French markets, so numerous that their sweet scent may be picked up *en passant*. At first glance they do not seem vulnerable to over-picking. Unlike Ceps, by the time they get to collectable size chanterelles are already releasing spores; they are also rather long-lived

for a mushroom. So it could be assumed that their reproductive business has been largely conducted by the time they
fall into the basket.

Even so, there is evidence of over-exploitation. In 1950s
Saarbrücken, on the border between Germany and France,
six tonnes of chanterelles (there called *pfifferlinge*) were sold
annually, but by the seventies this had reduced to a small
percentage of that. Again, it may be that persistent over-
picking for financial gain was responsible, if that onslaught
outlasted the life of the mycorrhizal association. The poor
pfifferlings had no chance to recover. There is another caveat.
Several other species of *Cantharellus* are much more
uncommon than the familiar chanterelle, and might be
picked by accident. One that blackens on handling (*C. melanoxeros*) is seldom seen, and I suspect that one amateur
mycologist of my acquaintance ate most of the British population after he made a collection from a beech woodland
on the Isle of Wight.

Some relatives of chanterelles are also long-lived, lasting
for days, even weeks, among leaf litter, and continuing to
increase in size if the weather is warm and damp. The
Hedgehog Mushroom (*Hydnum repandum*) is one of my
favourite edible mushrooms. Although it looks like many
other rather uniformly buff-coloured fungi that can be found
in woodlands in autumn, it differs from all other common
species in having ranks of spines where in an everyday agaric
the gills might be expected. The spines can be rubbed off
easily with a fingernail. It belongs with a group of 'tooth
fungi' that are readily recognisable by their very distinctive,
spiny spore-bearing surfaces.

Some of these fungi grow directly from dead wood, where the spines hang down like mycelial icicles. The Hedgehog has a good, firm texture, which may be why the French call it *pied de mouton*. It likes to grow in clumps in mossy hollows in woodland, and has a very particular, slightly lumpy appearance, as if it were moulded from dough, that makes it easy to recognise once its search image is implanted in the brain. The Horn of Plenty (*Craterellus cornucopioides*) is shaped like a thin-fleshed chanterelle, and is wholly black – the outer, somewhat wrinkled spore-bearing surface as if grey-dusted. It can form troops in autumn on beech forest floors if conditions are in its favour, when it looks as if pieces of black paper had been strewn among the brown fallen leaves. It is much sought after for its distinctive, slightly smoky flavour, and is an excellent comestible despite its French name *Trompette de la Mort*, which refers to its funereal colours rather than any effect on the body. It dries very readily and can be revived to give a mycological lift to winter dishes.

I had always gratefully picked both Wood Hedgehogs and Horn of Plenty whenever I found them, and made the assumption that by the time I had harvested them they had already shed enough spores to perpetuate their kind. I figured that if it was the slugs or me finishing them off it might just as well be me. In the last decade – maybe longer – I have noticed a decline in their abundance. They tend to be loyal to site, but those sites are more frequently disappointing. I may have to revise my opinion about the effects of gathering for the table. On the other hand, we also know that the effects of climate change in southern England are now undeniable – it is indeed getting warmer. Droughts are becoming more regular, and most fungi do not like dry weather. New species are arriving and others are moving northwards to maintain the conditions they prefer. It may be that my favourite three members of the Cantharellales are part of a pattern of southern decline that has nothing to do with my culinary predilections. Changes to grassland fungi (p. 224) may be part of the same pattern.

What I now know is that I cannot be as complacent about picking edible fungi as I once was. The rise in the fashion for foraging wild food sometimes seems to ignore the sustainable survival of the organism being foraged in favour of a kind of generalised 'back to nature' ambience, as if nature was there simply to nurture human beings and contribute to their mental well-being. Fungi are indifferent to human ends, and exist solely to propagate their own kind. They are not there to make us feel good about ourselves. If we can derive food and pleasure from fungi without harming their primary function then that is how it should be. I am left wondering whether I have been too lenient on my picking regime in order to enjoy my mycological treats. The thought that I might inadvertently contribute to making an empty woodland fills me with horror.

16.

Fielders

A small village church near my home in Oxfordshire is surrounded by a graveyard, where generations of local farming families have been laid to rest. The grander folk are remembered inside the church, with memorial brasses to the de Greys, who founded the nearby stately home, and extravagant monuments to the Knollys who followed them and were intimates of Queen Elizabeth I. While those inside have escaped most of the depredations of time, the gravestones outside have been sculpted by the elements over the centuries. Many of the inscriptions on them have weathered away, and the simple headstones have become home to spreading lichens, dappling the faces of the graves even as they obscure the names of those who were buried centuries before. For many years the grass between the graves has been mowed to keep the space tidy. Once, there may have been sheep to do the job, but a petrol mower took over in due course. The grass cuttings were removed to keep everything spick and span. There was no worrying about biodiversity or optimal conservation strategy – this was just about being respectful. Herbs like Mouse Ear Hawkweed, Lady's Bedstraw and Self Heal vied with mosses and grasses to make a sward. A green carpet thrived between the gravestones. This proved to be the ideal habitat for a cohort of mushrooms and toadstools, a special band of grassland fungi that needed just the conditions offered by this out of the way country churchyard.

In the autumn of 1999, fungi were everywhere. Even the most casual visitor to the church could not have failed to notice brilliant red, gently convex caps dotted among the short grass. Ivory-white mushrooms an inch or so across offered a contrasting attraction; and, nearby, toadstools of an almost luminous green hue dripped with slime. From behind another grey, lichen-covered stone sharply conical caps poked up as if Walt Disney cartoon pixies were crouching down among the autumn flowers – some of these caps were bright red, others banana yellow. These show-offs offered a distraction from other, grey or brown toadstools with more modest claims to attention, but the more closely one looked, the more variety was revealed; best to get down on hands and knees and crawl about. Strange, slender white spindles that emerged from the moss hardly looked like fungi at all at first glance. Another common species was branched like a miniature bundle of twigs and tucked well into the sward – and this oddity was bright orange in colour, which somehow established its fungal credentials. An occasional white Field Mushroom was a familiar friend, its cap still glistening with dewdrops and beginning to open as the sun warmed the soil. Large pinkgills (*Entoloma*) would have to wait a while for attention. The whole churchyard was suddenly alive with fruiting fungi that must have been waiting for this perfect combination of rain, turf and warm sunshine to burst forth in decorative profusion. Their mycelium had surely been feeding in the same short sward until the ideal conditions were reached and then the whole habitat revealed its diversity in short order.

Fungi that grow in grassland are a different cast of characters from those that live in woodlands, and they are very choosy. Very few species other than dung lovers are found in fertilised meadows – the diet is too rich in nitrogen. The old grasslands that fungi prefer have been largely left alone, but that is not the same as neglected. Cutting or grazing is an important part of the process, as is a good mix of plant species – and not just grass. Creeping plants like clovers and Yarrow and Heath Woodrush are ingredients in the recipe. Coarse grasses like Cocksfoot and False Oat Grass are negative indicators; fine-leaved grasses are best, such as bents, with their delicate sprays of flowers like pink mist. Moss killer also seems to impact the fungi. Artificial fertiliser is a veritable poison in this habitat, though sheep and rabbit pellets may be permitted. Close cropping by herbivores serves to keep the coarser plants in check. Unthinking 'rewilding' may just encourage the coarser grasses and aggressive herbs like nettles that spell doom for the fungus-rich grassland. My churchyard in 1999 had had just the right treatment for many years. Nobody set out to do the right thing to honour a diploma in biodiversity management; it was just housekeeping.

The brightly coloured fungi whose caps dotted this

makeshift lawn were dominated by waxcaps. When a waxcap is picked the soft, even greasy texture of the flesh is immediately apparent – the gills often feel silky to the touch and offer little resistance to a probing finger. Waxcaps come in all colours except blue: white, pink, red, yellow, green, grey and brown. It may not be *de trop* to describe them as the orchids of the fungus world. Their spores are invariably white, regardless of the colour of the gills, which often follow the tint of the cap. None of them have a ring on the stem. In Britain, species of waxcaps are found in meadows by the seaside all the way to high pastures flanking mountain peaks. All these mushroom jewels were once placed in the genus *Hygrocybe*. The Scarlet Waxcap (*H. coccinea*) first attracted my attention in the churchyard for its vivid coloration; the pixie hats belonged to the Blackening Waxcap (*H. conica*) and the Golden Waxcap (*H. chlorophana*) or one of its allies.

These are among the commonest of some forty species that can be found in the British Isles, a few of which are exceedingly rare. The green and glutinous species was the Parrot Waxcap, and the white one the common Ivory Waxcap *Cuphophyllus virgineus*. One species had a curious odour. *Cuphophyllus russocoriaceus* looks very like the Ivory Waxcap, but differs in having an intense smell. The species name means 'Russian leather' and presumably that would have been a familiar fragrance in 1848, when it was named. The only reason I know what Russian leather smells like in the twenty-first century is because I can recognise the fungus! I have considered going to an antique shop to see if any item of Russian leather might allow me to test the accuracy of my identification. Fortunately, the common name of this little white mushroom has solved the problem: it is Sandalwood Waxcap (and everyone knows what sandalwood smells like). You don't have to know much Latin to appreciate that *Hygrocybe aurantiosplendens* was both deeply golden-orange and splendid. Other waxcap species were smaller and more discreet. I sat for an hour checking with a monograph by David Boertmann on my lap, ticking them off. Species by species, an inventory of waxcaps was compiled from this bounteous churchyard until the list totted up eighteen different species. This was a nationally important site.

The little branched orange fungus tucked away in the grass bore no resemblance to a mushroom, but this Meadow Coral (*Clavulinopsis corniculata*) was equally a basidio – but one in which the spores were produced directly on the twig-like branches, rather than on specialised gills. Such clavarioid fungi include even simpler fruit bodies – the white, un-branched and elegant rods that I had noticed emerging from the moss were White Spindles (*Clavaria fragilis*) that were little more than tapering batons clothed in spore-manufacturing machines. Much larger Smoky Spindles (*Clavaria fumosa*) looked like some strange, grey spaghetti had been extruded from the ground. Unlike the waxcaps, these corals and spindles have close relatives that grow in woods, but the species themselves are diagnostic of species-rich grasslands. The same is true of a variety of pinkgills (*Entoloma*) that flourish in meadows. In my churchyard the Lilac Pinkgill (*E. porphyrophaeum*) was a comparatively large and stately toadstool, with a pink-brown cap extended like a parasol and an elegant, slender stipe of similar colour that looked slightly twisted. The deep pink gills of the mature specimens set it apart from all the other agarics. If the herb-rich sward is just right, an observant naturalist will be rewarded with a festival of colour and form that is the match of any woodland at the height of the fungus season.

Such a grassland habitat is precious, not just for the biodiversity (though that is vital) but also for the aesthetic richness that can be enjoyed even within a small area. Near the village of Stoke Row in Oxfordshire a protected monument known as the Maharajah's Well is an extraordinary and very Indian structure in the middle of a typical English country village. It was completed in 1864, paid for by the Maharajah of Benares to provide good water to the villagers, in recognition of the work that the local squire had done in bringing water to many inhabitants of the Subcontinent. Nowadays, it is reached by way of a small path; the grass to either side is kept short and is full of herbs. It is not a big area, no bigger than a small suburban garden. Here I met a waxcap I had always wanted to see – the Ballerina (aka Pink Waxcap, *Porpolomopsis calyptriformis*) – a larger waxcap with a beautiful flared, pale pink cap that as it ages lifts at the edges like a dancer's skirt in motion. I had never found it in my church-yard, but here it was with several other waxcaps just a few miles away. It was one of those occasions when even an ageing gentleman is entitled to do a little jig.

Waxcap grassland has been recognised as an important habitat, and it is becoming very rare in England. The special fungi associated with it have been lumbered with an inele-gant acronym to highlight CHEGD ('chegged') species. These comprise the first letters of the most typical grassland fungi. We have met Clavarioids (corals and friends) *Hygrocybe* (waxcaps) and *Entoloma* (pinkgills). G is *Geoglossum*, the Earth Tongues, which are strange-looking ascos producing black, spatula-shaped fruit bodies about the same size as those of *Clavaria* that often appear late in the season after everything else. D is *Dermoloma*, a genus of grey agarics with contrasting white gills, which might seem dowdy compared with most waxcaps, but have their own charm among their 'cheggy' neighbours. All these fungi live in dynamic equilibrium within the sward. Waxcap grassland is often described as 'nutrient-poor', with low levels of nitrogen a particularly important factor in promoting diversity of fungi. It is not altogether surprising that these special fungi are now known to have complex interactions with plant roots that are comparable, if not so fully studied, as the mycorrhizal intimacy between many woodland fungi and tree roots. DNA sampling from beneath nutrient-poor grassland reveals the presence of mycelium of numerous CHEGD species, even in the absence of fruit bodies. A lawn-wide web? It is likely that there is trade between plant and mycelium of sugars in return for fungally scavenged vital elements, but I doubt there is fungally mediated conversation between daisy and dandelion. It is quite marvellous enough to lie on the grass and see the interplay between flowering plants and insects, and enjoy the brilliance of the waxcaps, reflecting on the intertwined lives that go to make up this special habitat.

It is also unsurprising that waxcap grasslands are only found in sites that have escaped intensive farming, and since so much of our countryside has been drenched in fertiliser and insecticides, the special habitat needed by these choosy fungi are little nooks that have been overlooked. Waste ground is not enough: this can soon become the kingdom of nettles and coarse herbs. Old orchards are often good places to start looking, particularly if the grass has been kept short between the trees. Lawns in front of neglected stately homes host some delicious waxcap sites, as old Jenks the gardener has continued to mow and remove the clippings during his lifetime. Fortunately, the National Trust is now aware of the importance of these special patches along the avenue or between the topiary yews. I have been leaving my own lawn unfertilised for more than thirty years, and only now are a handful of CHEGD species appearing, so it could take a century to get to optimal diversity. Naturally nutrient-poor meadows with short turf can be found near the sea. One of the best I have ever seen was on a golf course on the small Scottish island of Colonsay, where an unobservant golfer might easily swipe a crouching fungus imagining it to be a ball. The west of the British Isles, with clean weather systems arriving from the Atlantic Ocean, has more than its share of important waxcap sites, and particularly in the Lake District, which is both west and wettest.

On a global scale, our country is an important redoubt for waxcaps. Some of the most distinguished students of these fungi come from the Netherlands, where there is little protection from pollution compared with that bestowed on us by friendly westerly breezes off the Atlantic Ocean. I recall the unfeigned delight of one Dutch professor when he found a rare *Hygrocybe* species during a foray in the west of England; it had disappeared from his native country many years previously and he had never seen it before outside a book. Nonetheless, there is little public awareness in Britain of the importance of low-nutrient grasslands with their CHEGD fungi when compared with similar sites that retain populations of rare orchids (although they sometimes coincide). Flowers seem to trump mushrooms. There is a fashionable trend to allow churchyards to be left alone 'for the benefit of biodiversity', which usually means allowing coarser grasses to grow and mostly benefits the ranker flowering herbs. It does *not* benefit the waxcaps and their associates, nor the creeping plants that are a defining part of short sward. The 'no mow' policy saves hard-pressed vicars the cost and trouble of frequent grass-cutting; thus, linking inaction with biodiversity allows perceived virtue to be allied with thrift. It is understandable why the practice of benign neglect has caught on – but in my view it would be far better to close-cut two-thirds of the churchyard, removing the cuttings, and leave one-third to nettles and cow parsley.

I have returned many times to the churchyard where this chapter began. In the last twenty years I have watched the number of waxcaps and their associates dwindle. It has been a slow decline. The rarities went first, like some of the more unusual coral fungi, but maybe (I reasoned) they would reappear when the conditions were exactly right. The manifestation of fruit bodies is hardly predictable at the best of times, so perhaps after a few years' 'rest' I would be delighted once more by the profusion of shapes and colours of the waxcaps and their allies. It was not to be. One year the graveyard was decorated with large Pestle Puffballs (*Handkea excipuliformis*) rising from the ground as if angry fists were on display among the memorials. It might have been a warning. That golden and most splendid waxcap never reappeared. My record lists got shorter. In recent years only the Scarlet Waxcap, Ivory Waxcap, Parrot Waxcap and Blackening Waxcap have been regular treasures emerging from the grass. If I had not known its history this churchyard would be just another average piece of waxcap grassland, nothing special at all – though *every* waxcap is a pleasure to see. Nor is this particular graveyard unique. The grounds that surround another, nearby church in the middle of Henley-on-Thames have similarly declined in fungal variety and are no longer fully 'chegged'. A common cause must surely be sought.

Since neither of these churchyards has been fertilised, it is likely that direct application of nitrogen-rich chemical compounds can be ruled out. Nonetheless, nitrate enrichment seems to be an established cause of disappearance of sensitive species. Some of the sprays that are applied to agricultural land are as fine as mist, so it might be possible for chemicals to spread beyond their legitimate target simply by breezes blowing from the wrong direction. This is unlikely in my test cases, because one of the churches is backed by a 'natural burial ground' that acts as a buffer from agricultural activity further afield, and the other church is in the middle of a small town, well away from plough and pasture. The remaining option must surely be that something untoward has come down from the heavens. Rain has been the carrier of disappointment, the subtle eraser that has wiped away a diverse ecology. I may be imagining that the grass has become lusher and darker green than it was before, and that the sward is not as rich in flowers and moss. There is no quantifiable record of before and after in my notebooks, but I would swear that this perverse 'greenwash' has happened little by little in the years that I have visited the same place. It is like the face of a loved one, with which you are so familiar that you hardly register that youth has passed and the wrinkles of seniority have taken command. Old age still comes as a surprise. As to the cause, atmospheric nitrification seems to be the plausible option. Particulate pollution has increased in the twenty-first century, with the release into the atmosphere of molecules of oxides of nitrogen that have damaging effects on the fungi of nutrient-poor grasslands. These are the subtle killers brought down to earth in the rain. They simultaneously fertilise grass species in the same habitats, to the detriment of a varied sward. Brambles and nettles are encouraged at the expense of delicate herbs.

Diesel engines are a proven source of particulates. Until transport becomes largely electric-powered, we will not know whether removing diesel fumes can halt the decline in our special grasslands. Intuitively, the retreat of sensitive fungi seems to link up with a well-documented decline in numbers of insects in Britain that has indisputably happened since the later decades of the twentieth century. Small creatures seem to be sensitive to minute quantities of certain pollutants or agricultural chemicals in a similar way to fungi. It could be that the mushrooms and toadstools of *Hygrocybe* grasslands could provide a useful bellwether for the health of the environment as a whole. It is comparatively simple to make an inventory of different fungi growing in grass, even if precise scientific names require more taxonomic knowledge. Climate change may also be part of the story, as it is in many of the changes in bird distribution that are happening right now. The predominant direction of movement is from south to north as the climate warms. New species of fungi appear on the British lists every year, and the southerly Isle of Wight might be expected to offer the first comfortable billet for a new arrival. I have seen diverse CHEGD species growing on the sparsely vegetated downland that makes up the high ground of 'The Island' – as the locals call it – which argues against climate warming as the prime cause of decline; my graveyard lies well to the north in chilly Oxfordshire. If warmer climates favoured fewer waxcaps we might expect to see that first on the Isle of Wight. It is important not to over-simplify; some of the rarest waxcaps only seem to occur along the Atlantic seaboard, and it may be the extra rainfall in those regions that is a limiting factor. There is still so much we do not know.

17.

Survivors

B lenheim Park hides more ancient oak trees than almost anywhere else. That part of the estate known as High Park is home to most of them, largely because it is a survivor from medieval times, when open woodland with pasture was much more common than it is now. Such continuity of usage is rare, and perhaps unsurprisingly associated with the traditional demesnes of the aristocracy, where oak trees escaped from being a crop harvested for beams or boat building. Since royalty is always the top tier in any former hierarchy, Windsor Great Park remains Blenheim's rival for these arboreal Methuselahs, left to grow old in peace. Such trees do not grow crowded together, but are scattered, with grassy glades between, allowing a full development of the crown in their youth and middle age. High Park is still full of light. Cattle continue to be grazed there, but inevitably the park is used for pheasant shoots, when anyone looking for fungi would be most unwelcome, so access is strictly limited by the modern estate office, whose smart vehicles regularly patrol the public right of way running through High Park. Some of the oaks are readily visible from the path, which is open to the public at all times. They present a parade of extraordinary, wizened personalities. No one ancient tree closely resembles any of its confreres. The trunks often have a huge circumference, but there is much variation in this feature around the seven metres that is often cited as typical of ancient trees. Some trunks are grey and fissured and covered in knobbles, a few of these sporting aborted bristly shoots below. These are Chaucer's 'knotty, gnarly, oakes olde'. Most are hollow, and some of the hollows are big enough to crawl inside. Others are only apparent if an admirer stands on her toes and peeps in through a hole where a branch once was. Dark and cool and moist, and protected from predators, it is easy to imagine how bats might find the interior of such trees a comfortable home. The great majority of the ancient oaks carry 'stag's horns' – dead branches held aloft and taking years to decay. Each oak differs in their extent and arrangement. Some trees have more stag horns than living branches, but they are still distinctly alive, as leaves erupt each year from a few brave limbs, defying mortality as decades roll by, shedding acorns to outlast their rivals. These are oaks to satisfy the Rackhams (no relations): Oliver Rackham the great tree historian, and Arthur Rackham the great arboreal fantasist – whose trees all twisty and furrowed housed goblins and sprites, and were not altogether benign. Methuselah is also curiously appropriate, as the Bible tells us that he died when he was 969, and oaks are claimed to last a thousand years. He lived as long as an oak.

These ancient oaks are actually smaller than the veterans that preceded them. At full maturity an oak allowed to grow freely spreads its main branches high and wide, almost into a hemisphere around the trunk. As old age approaches branches may be lost, or die back to make a stag's horn. Eventually, in many ancient oaks the tops of the trees begin to contract, and then look out of proportion to the great trunks that support them. Like some valiant old timers they carry on, more stooped perhaps, even their roots retracting, playing the long game. Ancient oaks can be found that carry uninvited passengers, those other trees that germinate and take root in some rotting crevice in an oak's trunk. Hollies are commonly seen where a bird excreted a seed, or maybe an elderberry arrived in similar fashion; but still the oak persists, dignified in its decline, if ever more twisted and decorated with strange growths.

Dr Aljos Farjon is the doyen of ancient oaks. After many years at Kew Gardens as their conifer expert, in retirement he became obsessed with ancient oaks. Aljos was born in the Netherlands, and has the kind of characterful face surrounded with a fringe of beard that Rembrandt would have painted for pleasure; that face becomes animated when ancient oaks are mentioned. He has visited almost every oak of sufficient antiquity in the British Isles and in 2017 published a wonderful book summarising what was known about them. Our islands are fortunate in retaining many more ancient oaks than anywhere else in Europe. A majority are, as in Blenheim High Park, situated in the grounds of stately homes or ancient estates, some of which were established just after the Norman Conquest. Deer parks were then an important status symbol among the incoming aristocracy, and the trees that were planted at the time have carried on growing peacefully, undisturbed by wholesale revolution. No baying crowds surged through Windsor Great Park, demanding the felling of the king's trees. Oaks elsewhere are often boundary markers, perhaps at the junction of two parishes, where their longevity has provided an indisputable point of reference in more temporal disputes. Aljos has examined some of the accepted notions about the age of oaks. There are enough historical documents that take specific oaks back some six hundred years. The traditional method of ageing a tree is to count the number of annual growth rings when it is felled, or to bore out a small section across a living tree, from which a ring count can be taken. The problem is that ancient oaks almost invariably become hollow, so their early history is lost to the bats. Aljos told me that exceptionally sound trees can indicate an age of eight hundred years. Some huge survivors may well be older but it is difficult to prove. What is not in dispute is that ancient oak parkland is a special habitat, and that invites further questions about whether the fungi associated with these survivors are as distinctive.

Aljos spearheaded a five-year synthesis of the biodiversity of High Park, finishing in 2022, bringing together specialists in everything from lichens to beetles. A party from the Fungus Survey of Oxfordshire – a group of amateur mycologists with which I have been associated for many years – was augmented by the erudite professional mycologist Dr Martyn Ainsworth, from Kew. With the approval of the estate, the group was permitted to wander freely through all the ancient oaks, many of them far from the public right of way. Aljos had already recorded every tree in detail. He greeted some of the oaks like old friends, although tree hugging is not allowed in scientific circles. Visits were arranged at different times of year, in the hope that we could be comprehensive, but on some occasions we were excluded whenever shooting parties moved through, which sadly sometimes happened just when the fungi were at their acme. It was soon obvious that many other kinds of trees were also established in the park, including birches everywhere, willows in damp hollows and the occasional beech. Because root systems spread widely, it would sometimes be impossible to associate fungi definitely with oak if there were other kinds of trees in the vicinity. Quite a few ancient oaks had fallen, and their grey carcasses lay among the herbage waiting for a century to pass before they could decay away. For some reason they reminded me of a dead, beached whale I had once come across on the shores of the island of Newfoundland.

One July visit, not far from the main track and quite high up on a bare, dead oak branch protruded a yellow, lobe-like bracket fungus. It seemed to emerge almost perversely from the exposed grey wood as if making life as hard as possible for itself. If such a difficult-to-reach specimen could be considered a close encounter, this was my second meeting with the rare and special Oak Polypore (*Buglossoporus quercinus*). Many fungus fanciers pass their whole foraying life without seeing an Oak Polypore. When I got a closer look it did resemble the extremely common and paler Birch Polypore (aka Razor Strop Fungus *Fomitopsis betulina*) and indeed they were once classified together. It had firm texture, not at all crusty like that of so many brackets, and minute pores giving an almost velvety feel to the spore-bearing under-surface. There was ample chance to make the comparison between the two species as almost every dead birch in Blenheim carried the commoner bracket. Martyn Ainsworth has a special interest in the Oak Polypore, which is rare enough to merit a Biodiversity Action Plan, one of few so privileged. Even globally, it is a threatened species, and classified as Vulnerable. Curiously, it had a Blenheim record in 1949 (then the first from the county of Oxfordshire), but that proved to be an identification error, and one made by a party of professional mycologists to boot. This specimen – fortunately, it had been curated at Kew – was shown in 2001 to be the common Blackfoot Polypore (*Cerioporus varius*), and it was growing on beech. The *real* Oak Polypore was the subject of an intense search effort and was eventually found on twenty-one different ancient trees, living and dead, in High Park. If Windsor Great Park is the champion with a hundred records, Epping Forest comes next with twenty-eight trees and Blenheim follows closely behind. Although most of the reports in the literature are of fruit bodies on standing trees, one of those recumbent 'whales' yielded a good example, as did a hollow tree and a root-plate. For once, Britain is the world centre for the conservation of a species. It is interesting to reflect that the survival of that very species depended on the medieval love of hunting and the subsequent survival and conservative habits of the upper classes.

My earlier close encounter with the Oak Polypore happened

nearly twenty years before Blenheim, and it is one of the rare occasions when, in a mushroom context, the injunction 'seek and ye shall find' actually worked. I already knew that ancient oaks in the grounds of country houses in summer were the best places to find this rare bracket. In eastern Suffolk close to our cottage I had noticed Sotterley Hall marked on the map, and the way the country roads took a generous circular detour around the house was a sure indication of the boundary of an old estate. A public footpath also crossed this estate to allow public access to the church next to the hall, which is a legal right of way rather than a privilege. My mycologising friend Stuart and I went to take a look, and it was indeed a rather wonderful estate, even though it was then slightly ragged at the edges. We quickly took in the presence of some old, but probably not ancient oaks, and started towards the church. From a distance we noticed that several of the trees had suffered some storm damage. The church turned out to be one of a hundred in Suffolk constructed in flint, absolutely unpretentious, without unique treasures, but somehow utterly charming in its setting and sense of continuity, with the big house still in view. We read a few plaques dedicated to the dead, brave and pious, and set about returning. When we reached the oaks, we briefly trespassed to have a closer look. One of the damaged trees held dead wood, and on the dead wood well off the ground was a yellowish bracket fungus that neither of us recognised immediately, although we knew what it ought to be. A small sample was taken – enough to look at the spores. It proved, indeed, to be a new record for the Oak Polypore, growing in the right time and place on the right tree, and found by the right people (and with the right spores). We had sought and we had found. The usual story with fungi is going somewhere in the middle of a wood on the assurance that some wonderful and exotic species is sure to be there, and coming home empty handed after spending an hour in a cloudburst, being swiped by nettles and brambles, and being laughed at by dry locals.

The total number of species of fungi recorded as fruiting bodies during the five-year Blenheim survey totalled 428, and the survey hardly touched the microfungi. Martyn Ainsworth said that another ten years would have added many more to the list, and while that is undoubtedly true, the number 428 is already more than a little intimidating. If each of those species had a biography as brief as that I have just given for the Oak Polypore, this book would have been as long as *War and Peace*. Fortunately, they do fall into natural categories, as far as their ways of earning a living are concerned. About a quarter of all the fungi discovered are mycorrhizal with plants – more specifically ectomycorrhizal, associated with tree roots. They are contributing to the health of the whole habitat by this mutually beneficial collaboration with trees. Only 2 per cent of the fungi we collected are pathogens, affecting oaks (and others), although some of these species are a necessary part of the whole life cycle of the signature trees. Nearly all of the balance are saprotrophs, breaking down the organic matter that plants had made through their photosynthetic activity, and ultimately responsible for organic recycling. The saprotrophs that break down wood account for 43 per cent of the total list, while those that predominantly feed on leaf litter or acorn cupules on the ground are 21 per cent. To generalise, one could say that almost two-thirds of all the fungi recycle while nearly a quarter collaborate. Imagine what the habitat would be like if the fungi were removed! Sickening trees would soon be surrounded by impenetrable brash and debris as the whole environment interred itself in its own waste. There would be no future.

In summer, a walker following the path that runs through High Park will almost certainly have a close encounter with a red knob the size of a tennis ball protruding from close to the base of an ancient oak. To the touch it is cold and firm, and it is rather mysterious. The same observant walker strolling along the path a few weeks later will see how the knob has grown into a deeply red-coloured bracket, perhaps glistening and slick in the morning dew. The underside of the bracket is now somewhat paler, but the whole does look very much like a piece of raw beef. Even the soft but firm texture is like that of a cut of good fillet steak. This is the Beefsteak Fungus (*Fistulina hepatica*). The gnarled bark from which it emerges belongs to a living tree, so it might seem rather obvious that this bracket must be a parasite, its mycelium feeding on the body of the oak out of sight and dooming the tree to ultimate perdition. This assumption is wrong. The Beefsteak Fungus is playing an important part in the life story of the oak. It *is* feeding on the oak, but not damaging the cylinder of tissues that comprises its living skin. Rather, it is consuming the middle of the tree as one of the 'brown rotters' (p. 267) – its mycelium is equipped with enzymes that break down and use the cellulose component of woody tissue. The degraded, brown 'wood' that remains behind shrinks and cracks into a mass of character-istic small cubes. This is a stage in the hollowing out of veteran oak trees into the almost cavernous old characters that dot the Blenheim landscape. The special habitat on the interior of ancient trees would not exist without this fungoid filleting. Some researchers claim that the tubular trunk created this way makes the tree less brittle than it would be if it were still solid: it can better face out a battering wind that might snap a younger and apparently more solid version. Certainly there is not much evidence of snapped Methuselahs – more of these trees seem to be tipped over because their root plates are not so well developed as once they were. Perhaps the oak owes its last century or so of existence to the activities of the Beefsteak Fungus.

The Beefsteak fruits on the outside of the tree where its spores stand the best chance of distribution, connected to its interior world of working hyphae. It is no problem for the hyphae of the fungus to pass through the tree, much as ghosts were supposed to pass through walls. The bracket's flesh is soft enough to be readily cut with a knife and the meaty appearance continues within its substance. It tends to ooze a little juice, adding to the carnal illusion. The spores are born in tiny tubes on the lower surface, but under a lens they are different from the usual poroid surfaces of common brackets like Turkey Tail (*Trametes versicolor*) – for the Beefsteak's tubes are separate from one another rather than forming a closely packed array. I know of no other fungus like it. The Internet shows happy gastronomists enjoying it as food, and a friend who will eat anything from locusts to Japanese knotweed recommended it to me thinly sliced, raw with lemon juice. I believe the Beefsteak Fungus is much better left to get on with the useful job of adding years to the life of characterful oaks.

Now for the case of the missing bracket. The Oak Mazegill (*Daedalea quercina*) is another oak specialist, like many more fungi with *Quercus* hidden in the name. This one is as tough as the Beefsteak is soft. I had my first close encounter with it on a massive, fallen old oak trunk lying in state near the National Trust property of Greys Court, near Henley-on-Thames. Several wedge-sectioned brackets with rock-hard, greyish, concentrically zoned caps as much as a foot across stuck out conspicuously from the side of the log. Their undersides carried very coarse ridges, which branched and split into a range of wonderful mazes from the walls of which the spores were dispersed. That explained the generic name, of course, for Daedalus was the maze maker who designed the Labyrinth for King Minos of Crete. In these tough brackets, each maze was different from that of its neighbour, an exuberant inventiveness that must have arisen by chance during development, but which gave every appearance of being working models for some perfect maze yet to be designed.

I kept one of these brackets for years. The books describe the Oak Mazegill as common, or even very common, and certainly it is a regular sight on dead old trees: but not in High Park. Since High Park is one of the densest areas of old oaks in Britain and many fallen trunks lie there waiting to decay, it seems almost inconceivable that we could not find one example of *Daedalea* in our five years of research. Fungi are supposed to be gifted with the means to find their appropriate place to develop. That is what their uncountable millions of spores are for. This significant absence reminds me of the famous Sherlock Holmes story ('Silver Blaze') wherein 'the dog that didn't bark in the night' led to the identification of the perpetrator. This is the fungus that didn't turn up, and I am sure it is telling us something. Could it be (for example) that there is a negative correlation between Oak Polypore and Oak Mazegill? Or could it be that Oak Mazegill prefers oaks that are not quite as ancient as those in Blenheim Park? Unlike Sherlock Holmes, we have no answer to these questions, and they may not even be the right questions to ask.

As work continued it was clear that the Oak Mazegill was not unique. Other common fungi failed to present themselves during five years of searching. The False Death Cap was one of the most perplexing because it is one of the most regularly recorded species on British lists, and should have been a routine addition to the High Park list. In some woods it is the commonest autumn find, its pale yellow caps almost illuminating the dark leaf litter. Even the Fly Agaric failed to turn up, the scarlet show-off that is the very emblem of all toadstools, and usually common under birch trees, which abound in High Park. Both these toadstools are typical tree associates because they are strictly mycorrhizal and form long-lived partnerships with their hosts. Could it be that High Park was too ancient a habitat to be suitable for these familiar *Amanita* species? Maybe ageing oaks 'let go' some of the partners that they would have nourished in their youth and middle age. Even the Death Cap itself had only a couple of records in High Park.

However, we did find the Snakeskin Grisette (*A. ceciliae*) several times, which is normally a rather rare species. It is a distinctive and stately fungus with a pale-brown cap carrying a few whitish scales, a long stem lacking a ring and displaying irregular bands of colour below towards the volva, and flesh that gradually turns black. I remembered it from the frontispiece of the original *Collins Guide to British Fungi*, but failed to see it in the flesh until a visit to the New Forest many years later. It does seem possible that this elegant species is favoured as a partner with ancient oaks when the familiar species have taken their leave. The other common oak partners are brittlegills and milkcaps, and although they were represented by a fair selection of species in Blenheim, some that might have been expected had left without making their excuses. I was amazed that the Blackening Brittlegill failed to make any appearance, as in my own piece of woodland, and almost everywhere else in Oxfordshire in similar sites, it is probably the commonest of its tribe and sometimes almost carpets the autumnal leaf litter. Unlike most toadstools it does not decay away quickly, and its dark carcasses hang around for months, so it is inconceivable that we missed it in our backwards and forwards under the trees. Was this another 'dog that didn't bark'?

There is a scientific adage attributed to the astronomer Carl Sagan that 'absence of evidence is not evidence of absence'. Such a caution is appropriate for any hypothesis cooked up on the basis of something *not* being there, and in fungi there is always the possibility that a species is in hiding rather than absent. Maybe the mycelia of our 'invisible fungi' are present on tree roots or concealed within dead wood and a mere five years is not yet enough for the culprits to reveal themselves. If there were only one or two 'no shows' that might be plausible, but it becomes less so as the list grows. Now that species can be identified from mycelium alone, thanks to DNA techniques, if our absentees were present in soil or wood it should still be possible to identify them, which would potentially harden up that 'evidence of absence'. At the moment, we are left wondering what it is about High Park that apparently discourages the Blackening Brittlegill and False Death Cap and many others.

One peculiar and rather scarce fungus that undoubtedly likes being in the vicinity of senior citizens of *Quercus* is the Zoned Rosette (*Podoscypha multizonata*), which sprouts close to the ground under the old trees and looks like no other fungus. Rosette is an appropriate name for its concentric batteries of brown, plate-like spore-bearing folds, which resemble something that might have been sported around the cuffs by an eighteenth-century dandy. It is a root rotter, so it is not difficult to imagine why it favours oak trees in the latter stages of their life cycle. Before Blenheim I had only seen it once under a mature oak in Sussex, when I wondered at first whether I had stumbled across a weird relative of the Cauliflower Fungus (*Sparassis crispa*). Like the Oak Polypore, southern England is one of its strongholds in Europe, and it is similarly a conservation priority. Only two oaks in High Park produced fruit bodies during our survey, but it is very likely that other *Podoscypha* individuals lurk underground, attached to roots waiting for exactly the right conditions to spring a mycological surprise.

Many of the other fungi found in High Park on oak

stumps, fallen branches or twigs are familiar from almost any other oak woodland, and account for a sizeable chunk of the 428 mentioned earlier. It is curious how their recognition becomes almost instant after many years of slow walking and spotting under trees in the autumn season. Sometimes the name of the fungus bubbles up spontaneously, almost without a thought. The eye has summarised the salient features – size, colour, the way it clusters (or not), or the outline of the cap and colour of the gills – and short-circuited the deductive process that would have laboriously worked through an inventory of features to arrive at the identity. It is as if the mind can move faster than the words it needs to scan a taxonomic key. In High Park the bonnets are a case in point: nearly all share pointed and delicate caps, and are often clustered or found in small troops. I recall having trouble identifying the Angel's Bonnet (*Mycena arcangeliana*) when I was learning my way around these fungi, having to look at microscopic details along the gill edge before I was confident to give out a name. Now I believe I can identify it at a glance, but I am pushed to say why: something to do with a hint of yellow in the cap and bluish tinges in the stipe and the way it emerges in groups on dead wood. It is a lovely thing by any account.

The similarly clustered Burgundy Bonnet (*Mycena haematopus*) has a strange way of looking pinkish and half transparent, but its identity is soon confirmed by breaking a stipe, when the dark reddish-'burgundy' juice oozes from the wound. The Bark Bonnet is tiny with arched gills, and the cap is pale brown with a darker dot in its centre – not much, but enough for identification. I once went out in the field with a skilled ornithologist who could identify small brownish birds as they flitted past into deep cover. He seemed to see things in a moment that I simply could not register. Many years of observation had fed into his appreciation of the mere flick of a tail or flash of a feather. Mushrooms stay put, which allows for the slow and systematic approach if it is needed, but a quick identification still feels better.

Among the leaf litter some of the saprotrophic toadstools – especially the funnels – made rather neat fairy rings outlined by more than a dozen fruit bodies. I could imagine the mycelium scavenging for nutrients as it spread outwards in a circle in the damp debris under the trees, until the signal to clot together to make toadstools passed through the whole system, mysteriously coordinated to make a simultaneous show of tan to greyish caps. White puffballs were more randomly dotted about, but Stump Puffballs decorated rotting roots in profusion. In a moist October the toadstools were so numerous that it was hard to avoid treading on them, as dapperlings (*Lepiota*) vied for fruiting space with toughshanks (*Gymnopus*) and knights (*Tricholoma*). Clustered Brittlestems (*Britzelmayria multipedata*) burst forth together from the ground in a mass like some mycological bouquet. Rooting Shanks with slimy, wrinkled beige-coloured caps had tough stipes that continued downwards into the ground to unseen buried wood. Small brown mushrooms of several dozen kinds would test the patience of those who took them home to identify. Smaller fungi required getting down on hands and knees. Even the oak leaves in damp hollows had their own minute specialist toadstool, the Pink Oakleaf Bonnet (*Mycena smithiana*), with a cap just a couple of millimetres across, and delicately pink, and a stipe no wider than a hair. There were ascos, too, hidden among the litter: a group of small, brown cups on stems (Oak Goblet *Ciboria batschiana*) arises from a half-buried acorn. Everywhere in the woodland a sense of profusion reigned, providing an almost bewildering array, and everyone on the survey was too busy to notice that some familiar species had not made an appearance.

There were further 'invisible' fungi in High Park, but their identities could still be determined. These were the species associated with oak roots that had yet to produce fruit bodies. They can persist for years under the ground before the conditions are just right for them to produce their characteristic toadstool, but their molecular identity is still all there in the mycelium. If oak litter is brushed aside and the surface of the soil beneath teased with a fork, it isn't long before tree rootlets are discovered, with the slightly puffy, almost coralline appearance that is typical of mycorrhizal associations. Root collections made from beneath trees can be analysed for critical parts of their DNA sequences, and these are then computer-matched with those already on the database. The match identifies the species. This technology has improved hugely over the last twenty years, and the results have opened up a new understanding of what goes on in our forests.

Our 'below-ground survey' from seven trees in High Park found thirty-two species that were known to form ectomycorrhizal partnerships with tree roots, but it was surprising that only a paltry three of these had been matched with actual fruit bodies we had collected from the park (an earthball, a brittlegill and a knight). Twenty-nine additional fungal species were present on the roots that had yet to be found under oak trees above ground, although they mostly did belong to genera similar to those we had already collected. Such a mismatch between what is found on forays and what lurks within the soil has been found in other surveys, and is probably always the case; the mushrooms and toadstools gracing the autumnal forest floor augmented by their shy companions hiding beneath our feet.

The total ecosystem in High Park shimmers with fungal activity: no standing wood is really dead, for it harbours recyclers, as does the smallest twig or fallen leaf; the litter is alive with questing mycelium; tree roots are like an unconscious mind beneath the visible woodland, sending fungal messengers to the surface when the time is ripe, or concealing another world that may never see the light of day. On a warm, dry summer afternoon nothing of this world is visible; it is then held in abeyance. Just add water, and wait.

Blenheim Park is well known in mycological circles for one other fungus: it has been the home of the Devil's Bolete (*Rubroboletus satanas*) for many years. This is a striking, large and uncommon bolete, with a domed white cap that contrasts dramatically with a bloated bright red, even vermilion stem and pore surface. It is the most poisonous of the boletes – hence its satanic label. It does not grow in High Park, but nearer the lake that sets off the stately home to such advantage; it is an obligate associate with beech on calcareous ground, and is a rare companion of oak. The distinguished naturalist Peter Marren has told its Blenheim story. The British Mycological Society held an official foray there in 1949, among their number John Ramsbottom, whose New Naturalist *Mushrooms and Toadstools* sparked my interest in fungi well before the Beatles had their first hit. (Ramsbottom spent forty years in the Natural History Museum, nearly as long as I did.)

Discovery of the remarkable fungus caused much excitement, but also a difference of opinion as to its identity and edibility between Ramsbottom and another well-known mycologist, A.A. Pearson. To resolve the dispute, Ramsbottom ate a chunk of the toadstool. He had cause to regret his misidentification for at the end of the day he had to be guided back to the waiting bus having been 'quickly and abundantly sick'. Curiously, Ramsbottom never mentioned this event in his book; indeed, he wrote that its 'evil reputation had diminished with the years, and it is commonly eaten in Czechoslovakia'. There are now known to be a number of species that are somewhat similar to Satan's Bolete, and perhaps these *are* eaten in Czechia, but the toxicology of Satan's Bolete has been investigated and justifies its original reputation. Perhaps this part of the 'long awaited book' (according to his frustrated editor) was completed before Ramsbottom's unpleasant experience. It is certainly a wise precaution to avoid all boletes with scarlet colours. As for the devil himself, he continues to appear where he always did under the same beech tree in Blenheim Park.

18.

Dung stories

While the world was shut into lockdown as COVID-19 was spreading out of control, I spent much time contemplating dung of various kinds. There were probably not many people who took up this pastime to help with their mental health and wellbeing during a period of pestilence, but droppings, pellets and manure quite quickly developed into a minor obsession for me – from a fungal perspective, of course. My home laboratory is a small room at the top of the house, well away from the usual living quarters, so that my experiments did not impinge greatly on Jackie, or anyone of a nervous disposition. During that difficult time we were permitted to take exercise in local areas, and since we live very near open countryside it was pleasant to take a stroll in the open air. I always took a lidded box or two with me in case I encountered anything of interest along the way. I should say that my collections were confined to the excreta of herbivores – even for a mycologist, there are limits.

Rabbits oblige by neatly depositing their droppings on anthills. Our chalk meadows are favoured habitats for both ants and rabbits. Although it is possible to find rabbit pellets that are not on anthills, it is unusual to find a living anthill *without* its covering of neat, round pellets the size of garden peas. Many of the same anthills also have a close covering of fragrant wild thyme, but it is doubtless fanciful to imagine that the anthill is the bunny equivalent of the perfumed bathroom. However, when an anthill dies – as many of them seem to do when their tireless hosts move elsewhere – it is very quickly recolonised by grasses, and then it is not nearly so popular as a latrine. Old pellets become almost white, and it is better to discover darker, moister and more recent deposits for what happens next.

My wife and I also walked through many of our fine local beech woods. Deer have greatly increased in abundance over the last thirty years. This has not been to the benefit of the trees, as the seedlings are browsed relentlessly, preventing regeneration. Roe and fallow deer herds are shy: they are most often observed bounding off to get somewhere else fast. By contrast, tiny muntjac deer are solitary, creeping discreetly through cover; they specialise in nipping off orchids in the bud, which is probably why the early purple orchid has become rare in the Chiltern Hills. All deer leave their droppings in dark clusters among the leaf litter, and they are obviously larger than rabbit donations; they, too, are candidates for the little box. I believe I can distinguish small and pointed muntjac excreta from the larger deposits of other deer, but I am not confident to recognise fallow or roe deer droppings to species. Both deer and rabbits are

Parasitic Bolete (*Pseudoboletus parasiticus*) parasitising Common Earthball (*Scleroderma citrina*). Photo by Jackie Fortey

Piggy Back Pinkgill (*Volvariella surrecta*) growing out of the cap of Clouded Agaric. Photo by Rob Francis

The ultimate fungus on a fungus: the Strangler (*Dissoderma paradoxa*) takes over the fruit body of the Powdercap (*Cystoderma amianthinum*), whose typical stipe is still visible at the base of the fruit body. Photo by Torben Fogh

A bonanza of highly sought-after Morels (*Morchella esculenta*), growing in April.

The most beautiful of fungi, Silky Pinkgill (*Volvariella bombycina*). Photo by Linda Seward

Scarlet Elf Cups (*Sarcoscypha austriaca*), a winter asco growing on damp willow wood. Photo by Linda Seward

Common Chanterelles (*Cantharellus cibarius*) on a mossy bank. Courtesy of Jackie Fortey

Parasol mushrooms (*Lepiota procera*), common in grassland. Photo by Stuart Skeates

Blackening Waxcaps (*Hygrocybe conica*) growing on my low-nutrient lawn.

Courtesy of Caroline Lawrence

Ancient oaks in Blenheim High Park.

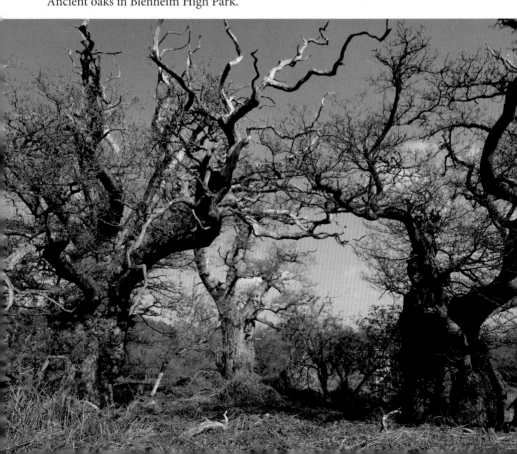

A lovely yellow Coral Fungus (*Ramaria*) in beech woodland.
Photo by Jackie Fortey

Associate of ancient oaks, Zoned Rosette (*Podoscypha multizonata*).
Photo by Aljos Farjon

Oak Polypore (*Buglossoporus quercina*), a rare specialist on ancient oaks. Photo by Aljos Farjon

Beauty arising from dung: Snowy Ink Cap (*Coprinopsis nivea*). Photo by Derek Schafer

A close-up of a deer pellet with the minute hairy discs of asco (*Cheilymenia fimicola*).

Photo by Derek Schafer

The remarkable asco Nail Fungus (*Poronia punctata*) on New Forest pony dung.

Photo by Stuart Skeates

Spalted wood, with black lines demarcating the realm of each rotting fungus.

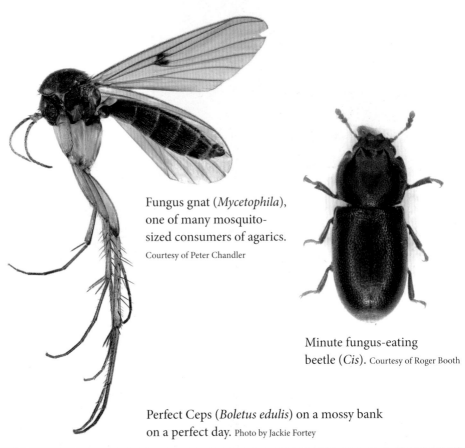

Fungus gnat (*Mycetophila*), one of many mosquito-sized consumers of agarics.

Courtesy of Peter Chandler

Minute fungus-eating beetle (*Cis*). Courtesy of Roger Booth

Perfect Ceps (*Boletus edulis*) on a mossy bank on a perfect day. Photo by Jackie Fortey

properly wild, which means that they feed on natural vegetation and do not ingest the kind of chemicals that are often
fed to domesticated animals – including antibiotics and
supplementary nutrients. Such drug-free animals have the
potential to yield a natural fungal biota from what they
excrete.

The fungi are brought on by incubation. I do not mean
that they are heated to speed things up. Rather, the pellets
are placed in plastic vessels with slightly loosely fitting lids;
I usually put the specimens a few together on damp pieces
of blotting paper, as they should be moist but not sodden.
It is important that the relative humidity remains very high
– hence the lid. In nature you tend to find fungi appearing
on dung only under very damp conditions, and often the
fruiting bodies do not have time to develop fully if the sun
returns too soon. The laboratory allows optimum conditions
to be maintained for as long as it takes for several successive
species to appear. Rabbit pellets are particularly easy subjects
as they are the right size to be grasped in a pair of forceps.
Mike Richardson, one of the high priests of coprophilous
(dung-loving) fungi, refers to rabbit pellets as 'pearls', and
indeed they are the size of larger examples of that precious
gem, even if in this case beauty is in the eye of the beholder.
When the fungi start to appear, the 'pearl' can be readily
lifted out of the pot and placed on a small tray to examine
under the low-power binocular microscope. If some tiny
species requires higher magnification a specimen can be
detached from the side of the pellet with a scalpel, placed
on a microscope slide and protected with a glass cover slip.
A drop of water placed next to the cover slip gets sucked

under it by capillary action, and then if it is tapped with the blunt end of a pencil this usually splays out the tiny specimen in such a way that it can be examined under the higher-powered light microscope. It is a simple enough technique, but it takes a while to master.

As we have seen, most fungi avoid nitrogen-rich habitats, and indeed, many kinds of toadstools are killed by nitrogenous compounds – these fungi could be described as 'coprophobes'. It is not surprising that coprophilous fungi are specialists, and are hardly ever found elsewhere. They relish their special role. For them, the compass of a single rabbit pellet can be their own entire small world. It is surprising how many individuals of several species are supported by such a tiny ball of nutrients. Fungal mycelium must move fast once a spore has germinated, feeding on the rich broth that other fungi eschew. The next generation will be released as spores from some kind of fruit body, which must, of course, release them into the atmosphere to be carried to the next 'pearl' on the adjacent anthill. A fully occupied pellet might be covered in tiny mouths ejecting spores into that special microhabitat close to the ground where ants and beetles ply their various trades. Sometimes during my experiments I have been surprised to see a fly in the same sample box with a dropping or two; it wasn't there before. Its maggot must have fed on the dung alongside the diminutive fungi – maybe even nourished by the mycelium that secretes enzymes to make excreta more digestible. It pupated within the pellet, but when it emerges it may yet repay its fungal host by carrying spores to another site, where they can germinate in fresh offerings. To understand this world one has to think *small*.

Ecological succession is a theory that recognises that in many habitats particular species (sometimes several species) follow one another more or less in order during colonisation. In our local nature reserve, for example, grassland left untended soon gets birch seedlings all over, joined quickly by hawthorn and willow, followed in due course by longer-lived trees like beech and oak, when the woodland gradually attains its mature structure. It is not an invariable law, and has been criticised as a concept lacking in rigour, but in general it appeals to commonsense and experience. A version of this notion is an important part of 'rewilding', although it is not often acknowledged. A sequence of trees takes years to follow through; but a rabbit pellet can show ecological succession in fast frame. A parade of fungus species takes just a few weeks to complete the cycle in a specimen box. Mike Richardson showed me that it is an exemplary demonstration of the principles involved: it costs nothing, and can be set up in even the most modest laboratory. The order of species is not invariable, but some of the actors merit investigation as they make their entrance one by one.

On the cultivated 'pearl' the earliest activity is enigmatic. Tiny, glassy bodies appear on the surface: under a lens they look like rocket launchers drenched in dewdrops. Over the course of a day the tops of these minute transparent threads thicken and puff up. Many of them lean in the same direction as if propelled by some inner urge. Their translucent stems grow; they now resemble minuscule, un-pigmented tulips. By now they can be readily seen with the naked eye. Within a day or two each stalk is topped with a black dot. This fungus is *Pilobolus* – the Spore Shooter – one of the advance guard on excreta of many kinds. Sometimes it is so abundant that the original poo cannot be seen for a festoon of threads not much longer than a fingernail, all seeking the light. The black dot is a package of spores, the basis of the next generation of *Pilobolus*.

Although it is so delicate, the Spore Shooter is able to propel the little package for considerable distances – anything from a centimetre or two to three metres. In a laboratory dish the whole of the lid is rapidly covered on the inside with a spattering of tiny black dots – rather like the dots at the end of every sentence in this book. A shoot-out. The analogy of a human athlete lobbing a tennis ball over the Eiffel Tower seems appropriately dramatic. Compared to the size of the fungus, it is a prodigious throw. In nature, the spore capsules are catapulted far enough to attach to a neighbouring herb or blade of grass. They even carry a dab of adhesive to help the process. When a herbivore eats the grass the capsule is carried happily into its digestive tract. When the nourishment has been extracted from the grass within the animal, the capsule is carried inevitably towards the anus of its host, but the spores will not germinate until they arrive on the ground embedded in pellet or cowpat, and then the mycelium gets to work apace to produce the next generation. It is an extraordinary and finely tuned mode of life.

The mechanism of the 'gun' that shoots the spore package has been investigated in detail. The force necessary to fire the 'gun' is developed in the inflated part of the stem – it builds to a pressure of 7 atmospheres, or even more. When the spore package is released, it accelerates in a mere two microseconds to 20 kilometres an hour, which, of course, slows rapidly in air, but is sufficient to help the parcel to be delivered to the right place. The inflated sac below the spore package also acts as a lens, and contains chemicals sensitive to light which prompt the orientation of the tiny threads, and guarantees that the spores will be propelled into the clearest space to help them on their way. Even the capsule itself has a dusting of chemicals that react with the smallest dewdrop to turn the spore package towards the blade of grass so that the sticky side adheres. This tiny species is as marvellous in its way as the most glamorous mushroom – and far commoner, as any field or footpath will harbour its secrets.

The Spore Shooter is a pin mould (Mucorales), a member of one of the most primitive and ancient fungal groups, for all its sophisticated adaptations. Next to emerge from the rabbit dropping is a regular toadstool, if a very diminutive one. Several tiny, shining white finger-like projections emerge from the side of the pellet and within a day they can be recognised as having a cap and a stem, though at this stage the cap is folded down like an unfurled umbrella, so the whole fruit body looks something like a tiny chicken drumstick. It is covered with a glistening powdery cover as white as snow. Under the microscope the cover is revealed to be a mass of minute spheres, mixed with threads, loosely piled together to form a veil. The toadstool is rather beautiful at this stage. Within a matter of hours the stem extends, growing upwards to lift the toadstool well above the pellet that gave it succour. At the same time the cap opens out, exactly like a miniature Chinese parasol, with radial ribs supporting a thin membrane between them. The remains of the snowy veil dust the surface. Now you can see the gills, the same number as the 'struts' on the surface of the parasol. Almost as soon as the cap has unfolded and expanded, the spores dust the surface of the gills and the spores are obviously dark in colour – a striking contrast to what went before. It is easy to imagine the spores being released into the breeze to travel to the next rabbit dropping. Before long, the tiny cap has blackened completely, the gills melting away to nothing. Soon, just the stem remains. This dissolution reveals the tiny white toadstool as an inkcap, one of several small species specifically adapted to dung.

The life of a single toadstool is brief, but if conditions are right, new examples will emerge and go through the same short cycle. When I came to look at deer pellets, this Dung Inkcap, *Coprinopsis stercorea*, turned up regularly, but it was soon joined by other inkcaps like the delicate *C. radiata* and smooth brown *Parasola misera*. Deer dung supported a greater range of species than rabbit. Some of the tiny inkcaps I discovered carried a thicket of tiny, spine-like projections on cap and stem, and were identified as *Tulosesus pellucidus* and *Coprinellus pusillulus*. Clearly, this ecological niche was ideal for the transient inkcaps, some so delicate that they could be destroyed inadvertently just by breathing a little too hard. It intrigues me that these fragile, evanescent productions of nature were recognised by early mycologists, even though they grew on what most people instinctively avoid. Elias Magnus Fries had discriminated '*Coprinus*' stercoreus by 1838, taking the species name from a still earlier publication. The curiosity of the dedicated naturalist evidently has always trumped squeamishness.

Some bowl or disc-shaped 'spore shooters' appear early in the parade of species on dung. Most walkers will know at least one of them. In damp fields with herds of cows the cowpats are often coloured orange, and this is noticeable even from some distance. If you get down on your hands and knees and gingerly approach the object in question, you will see that they are covered in small, bright orange discs just a couple of millimetres across. This is often one of the first fungi to appear on a fresh deposit as soon as a crust has formed, and has, somewhat optimistically, been dubbed the Cowpat Gem (*Cheilymenia granulata*). It often appears as early as *Pilobolus*. The spores are carried on the waxy-looking outward-facing orange surfaces; they are located inside little sacs (asci) in lines of eight. When mature they are expelled from the asci and get carried on the air currents to nearby cowpats, or on to grasses where they will wait until a cow decides to munch that particular bunch, when they will enter the cow's digestive system.

A great variety of other 'discos' colonise all types of dung. Most really belong to the microscopic realm, since they all require careful examination at high magnification to identify, but I cannot resist visiting one or two of them. Their identification kept me engaged while the COVID pandemic was at its peak. Such fungi usually appeared as tiny gelatinous discs, drums or lumps on the surface of my rabbit pellets, and can be almost any colour except green and blue. Their spores are very small, so they are usually completely invisible to the naked eye unless seen en masse. However, those on *Ascobolus* are visible even under a magnifying glass. That is because the tiny top-shaped disc of this fungus is often semi-transparent, and a hand lens reveals scattered minuscule black dots on the surface. These are the asci that contain relatively large spores, which are darkly pigmented and often show up purple-brown under a microscope. They carry an interesting surface sculpture of darker ridges, which are important in identifying species. Now they are displayed inside transparent asci on the pallid, spore-bearing surface, like minute chocolate cakes laid out on a platter.

One of the species I identified was *Ascobolus hawaiiensis*, which, as the name implies, was originally recognised in Hawaii. This is surely a case where the fungus was transported to Hawaii with the cows when the islands were colonised, rather than spreading from the remote archipelago back to Europe. Farm animals can carry their biota much as a traveller might carry his or her hand luggage. *Saccobolus* appears early on as dark humps on the surface of the 'pearl' – quite well disguised until you realise what they are. They include arrays of asci, within which the eight dark spores huddle together as a package rather than separating into individual spores. Maybe this is a similar strategy to that of *Pilobolus* to increase the chances of being picked up by a grazing animal. Some of the other early species that appear on rabbit and deer dung even break the rule in ascomycetes of eight spores in each spore-bearing ascus, which holds true for thousands of species. The inconspicuous bag-like asci of *Thelobolus* can contain hundreds of spores; prolonged cell division during their development continues to double and redouble their number. Counting them is almost impossible. It seems reasonable to suppose that this is a simple way of increasing the chances of any one spore reaching a suitable place for germination: safety in numbers.

After the early fungal species have had their way the rabbit pellet can look quite different. A mass of small dark flasks takes over. Most conspicuous are a few species that sit on the surface, but elsewhere the apertures – you want to say mouths – of the flasks protrude from the surface. It can occasionally look almost prickly. In these fungi the asci are concealed inside the flasks rather than exposed as in the 'discos'. Their spores are lemon-shaped and very black in colour, but many have colourless gelatinous appendages at each end. When the spores are ripe the ascus holding them extends and pushes up into the 'mouth' (ostiole) of the flask and ejects them into the air. One of the first species I investigated broke the 'eight spore rule' but the other way round – *Schizothecium tetrasporum* only has *four* spores per ascus. There are examples in other dung-lovers of 'spore killing' where half the spores in an ascus that lack a particular gene are eliminated by the other four that have that gene. Many of the common flask fungi belong to the genus *Podospora* and have interesting arrangements of hairs on the surface or around the 'mouth'; they, too, employ the numbers game with their spores . . . 8, 16, 32 . . . all the way to 256 in one ascus. It is intriguing why dung-loving fungi should play tricks with spore numbers; although more spores give a reproductive advantage, it cannot be all about that since some species have gone the other way – to fewer spores.

Perhaps durability has something to do with it. *Sporormiella* is another immersed fungus, with a brown cellular 'bag' occurring commonly within in all kinds of dung that house asci with eight very peculiar-looking spores – each one rather like a string of short sausages, four in a row. These distinctive spores (which can break into four pieces) are very durable and survive in many sediments, so they have an excellent fossil record. Because they are so common in herbivore dung, their relative frequency as fossils should be a sound proxy for the abundance of large herbivores: the more animals, the more excrement, and the more *Sporormiella* spores. In western North America it was discovered that the numbers of these spores had a precipitous decline in abundance 12,900 years ago, coinciding closely with the extinction of giant herbivores like mammoths, mastodons and sloths, and even horses and llamas. Since this also coincided rather closely with the arrival of modern humans into that continent across the Bering Strait, the inference was drawn that it was the hunting activities of our own species that so depleted the number of *Sporormiella* spores, not to mention removing some of the most impressive herbivores that have ever existed. I cannot think of a better example where the study of something that is apparently tiny and obscure to most people intersects with an issue of mammoth concern – and where the word 'mammoth' can be used literally rather than metaphorically.

My rabbit and deer (and a few sheep) excreta became exhausted after only a few weeks. I had also tried horse dung in the laboratory, but domestic issues involving flies (and threats) meant that it was politic to cut that study short. I did not even attempt to bring home a whole cowpat. It is perhaps not surprising to find that horse and cow droppings yield scaled-up versions of the tiny mushrooms and other fungi that made their home in my rabbit 'pearls'. Near my home I know a piece of parkland where artificial fertilisers have been withheld, and the grazing animals are not so numerous as to add too much nitrogen to the habitat. When it has been damp and humid for some time – usually in spring and autumn – fungi are soon evident among the grass, either growing directly upon or next to the waste products of the grazing animals. The common Dung Roundhead (*Protostropharia semiglobata*) can be recognised from afar, with its perfectly hemispherical, yellow cap the size of a coin balanced on a slender stipe, and dark gills.

The inkcap tribe is represented by the wonderfully shining white Snowy Inkcap (*Coprinopsis nivea*), which is a scaled-up version of the tiny white species I had raised on rabbit 'pearls', covered in white powdery cells, and destined to turn from white to black as it matured. One year I found its beautiful pale-pink relative (*C. pseudonivea*) in great profusion, and never saw it again, which is what fungi do to wind you up. A variety of small brown toadstools are especially there to test the taxonomic abilities of the enthusiast. Rarely, there is even the Dung Bird's Nest fungus (*Cyathus stercoreus*) vying with some larger orange 'discos' for attention. There are no Field Mushrooms on dung, even though tradition has it that they like fields with horses. What they like is the grassy spaces *between* the droppings. Even a single meadow can be a mix of several fungal habitats; fungi see the world in a discriminating way so that they pick and choose exactly where to appear.

In pursuit of a close encounter with a great rarity, Stuart and I went into the heart of the New Forest on a perfect autumn morning. We were looking for pony dung. The dew still painted up the spider's webs, linking one clump of heather to another with threads almost as delicate as mycelium. Corvids croaked a welcome. Scattered birch trees were surrounded by Amanitas and milkcaps, but tempting though these toadstools were, our search was for something more extraordinary. Several piles of fresh dung were not sufficiently mature. Some scuffed-out patches were probably too old; their fungal days were over. Then we saw what we were looking for. Emerging from the top of a horse dropping the size of a small potato were what looked like half a dozen small white coins. The Nail Fungus (*Poronia punctata*)! There is a particular thrill in seeing in the flesh something that for years you have only seen in books. Some part of you believes that it doesn't really exist – that it is something like a leprechaun, not to be taken too literally. But here it was, in the flesh, and just as odd as it is supposed to be. The white 'coin' was just the outermost part of the fungus; it was like the flat head of a longer nail, and the lower part of the nail was hammered into the dung. Of course, it was really the other way round: mycelium fed the fruit body, and a 'stem' grew upwards and outwards before opening out on top of the heap. On closer examination I saw that the white surface was dotted with black points, a dozen or more, which stood out clearly from the white background. These were the mouths of immersed flasks containing asci with brown spores, which would be expelled when ripe to spread the Nail across the forest. Extraordinarily, this very odd fungus is a relative of the Candlesnuff fungus that feeds on dead wood, a species familiar from every copse and forest. At some distant time an ancestral pioneer species 'jumped' from wood to dung. The versatility of fungi never ceases to astonish me.

The Nail Fungus is a very uncommon species now, and the New Forest is one of its few redoubts. At one time it was abundant. As long ago as 1753 it came to the attention of the great Linnaeus, who gave it the specific name we still employ. It was everywhere in the nineteenth century, when horses were used for all manner of tasks, from drawing carriages and barges to transporting commodities around cities. Disposing of tonnes of horse dung proved a major logistical problem. Trams, trains and petrol-powered vehicles helped to end that era and *Poronia* became less frequent. It did not respond well to agricultural chemicals like artificial fertilisers and pesticides, which fed into the grass that the horses ate, nor to the treatments developed to 'worm' the animals. The Nail Fungus began to go into full retreat across the whole of Europe. It survived only in places like the New Forest where there were still 'wild' ponies that fed upon natural vegetation in unimproved countryside. Fortunately, its very oddity attracted enough attention to give it protected status and it is now the subject of a Biodiversity Action Plan, and the New Forest population is monitored. Future mycologists should still be able to discover those Nails hidden among the heather on a bright September morning.

My most recent encounter with the Nail Fungus took place not on the wild slopes of the New Forest (Hampshire) but in a suburban garden in Henley-on-Thames (Oxfordshire). As I walked past the front of a Victorian house I noticed some horse manure on a flowerbed, and from deeply ingrained habit glanced to see if there were any mushrooms about. I was astonished to see a *Poronia* poking out from one piece of dung. I thought it might be the first record for the county, and was not unreasonably excited. After dithering for some time, I went up to the front door and rang the bell. I attempted to explain something about the Nail Fungus to a nice woman who answered the door, and I have to say she looked rather sceptical. Then I had a bright idea. 'I don't suppose that manure came from the New Forest?' I enquired. 'How did you know?' she responded, with obvious astonishment. She told me she had brought back a bag of pony manure to treat the roses after a visit to Hampshire. While I was happy to feel my expertise had impressed, I could not record this occurrence as a first Nail for the county. It was just the dung taking a holiday.

19.

Rotters

Lily, our Polish cleaner, brought the object to me in a waste paper basket. She had been working in a house along our street when she noticed an alien growth in the corner of one of the children's bedrooms. The owners had been on holiday with their family for several weeks, and the thing had grown since her last visit. The house was immaculate, so a lurid, living carbuncle more than a foot across erupting from near the top of a white-painted room was not something that she could have failed to notice. It had grown with dispatch since her last visit. It had a soft texture, but coherent; almost gelatinous, yet hanging together. It somehow boded evil intent, but it was hard to say why. Lying in the basket, it was reminiscent of a dead jellyfish. Much of the object was orange-brown and roughly corrugated, oozing a few water droplets, but surrounded by a white fringe, as a gown is by selvedge. Lily had been able to peel it off from the wall using a broomstick. It had offered little resistance and was readily dislodged, falling into her improvised receptacle. I recognised it at once: it was the Dry Rot Fungus, *Serpula lacrymans*. 'Lacrymans' means 'weeping' – referring to the water droplets exuded during rapid growth of the fruit body – but it could equally refer to the emotions that are stirred in householders on discovering they are hosting an insatiable fungus; 'odious, insidious, hideous, obnoxious, downright abominable', as the American mycologist David Arora described it.

Dry Rot Fungus eats the wood used in buildings, spreading by means of mycelial cords that seek out new sources of food at astonishing speed once they are well established, passing over and even through inedible objects in pursuit of uninfected wood. Unchecked, it continues its relentless progress until the affected building falls into ruins. When the pest is discovered there is no choice but to remove all the infected timber – with a wide safety zone around it to eliminate any that may have been infiltrated by the invader but not yet shown symptoms. As my neighbour discovered, this can cost several thousand pounds. The fungus often produces its fruit body well away from the wood that is being plundered, as it needs to find an appropriate place to release its spores directly into the air. Its hyphae can pass through the pores in brickwork, to ooze out into bedrooms, as in my neighbour's house, or even on to stored paraphernalia in attics, there to form the brown wrinkled surface from which the spores take flight. To add insult to wooden injury, it smells unpleasant and musty. The rusty stain of masses of spores often covers nearby surfaces, looking like spray paint.

Dry rot refers to the kind of attack made by several

different wood-rotting fungi, even though *Serpula lacrymans* is the most dreaded culprit. It is also something of a misnomer because to get started this fungus requires damp conifer wood, where its spores can successfully germinate – a completely dry wooden building will not be infected. A temperature of just above 20 degrees Celsius promotes optimal growth, but the fungus tolerates colder conditions with aplomb. Once established, its mycelium breaks down wood in such a way that it releases water molecules, so then it becomes like an internal combustion engine capable of manufacturing its own fuel. It is free to race ahead without further impediment. Its hyphae pillage extra nutrients from plaster or brickwork to help it grow – oil in the engine, if you like. It is implacable. Fortunately, modern regulations are designed to ensure dry buildings, so the Dry Rot Fungus cannot get going. The majority of infestations are associated with Edwardian and Victorian buildings; our neighbour had a flat roof that was prone to collect water, covering a large Edwardian dwelling, so the slightest leak might have allowed a passing spore to find suitably moist timber.

'Species jumping' has been much bruited since the appearance of COVID-19 and other malevolent viruses. A virus species on bats – who often get the blame – vaults on to a human in a 'live meat' market, usually in China, and then proceeds to cause global mayhem. For the plot of a horror story one might toy with the idea that *Serpula lacrymans* could take a similar jump on to humankind. Such a scenario with regard to *Cordyceps* has already been mentioned. The grisly movie would show the mycelium plunging into the bowels and up the spinal chord, fuelled by the riches of a high-protein diet. Victims would stagger around making suitably agonised cries while the white-coated scientist declared herself baffled. The climax of the life cycle might be the slow-motion eruption of the fungus fruit body from the side of the head. Such fantasies are worth entertaining if only to point out why they are impossible. *Serpula* is *not* free to jump around the animal kingdom in a way that is frequent in viruses. It is a dedicated vegetarian specialist. Its feeding mechanisms are obligatorily linked to an ability to degrade cellulose. Its mycelium is susceptible to certain 'prompts' that allow it to identify a specific food source and move towards it. Its spores can only germinate on certain kinds of wood, and under particular conditions of moisture and temperature. It has already travelled an evolutionary marathon alongside its hosts and cannot be diverted into a sudden sprint elsewhere. One measure of its exquisite adaptations is that it has a 'wild' close relative, *Serpula himantioides*, that does not cause much domestic chaos, but mostly lingers harmlessly in woodland on fallen trunks: it is another specialist that knows its own place, and does not feud with its more damaging relative. It is quite dramatic enough that Dry Rot Fungus can bring the house down.

Serpula lacrymans may not be native to the United Kingdom. It is, after all, never found in woods and parks in our islands, but specialises in causing havoc in interiors, an 'unnatural' habitat. Recent molecular evidence gleaned from collections around the world has shown that our destructive fungus may be identical to one found in natural habitats as a degrader of conifer wood in the Far East and the Himalayas. Another, North American variety is apparently not so determined to do damage to housing. Even if our movie proposal is impossible, fungal invasion can still happen if the fungus doesn't have to leap organism but simply trade location. Given a suitable habitat, a spore will eventually find its way there: crumbling timbers follow inexorably. The destructive species was given a boost by the Second World War, when bomb damage gifted the Dry Rot Fungus as much food as it wanted. Stately homes were abandoned in the aftermath, when His Lordship moved into a comfortable modern bungalow in the grounds so he no longer had to worry. Molecular studies have also proved that *Serpula* is more closely related to the boletes – including the Cep with which this book began – than to either gilled mushrooms or puffballs, while resembling none of these familiar fungi in any obvious way. What shape shifters fungi are!

Wood infected with dry rot is distinctive. Where it has been invaded by mycelium, it characteristically shrinks and cracks, often breaking up into little dice-sized cubes. Afflicted wood changes to a typically warm brown colour, and when it eventually loses coherence it can be crumbled into dust. Even if there is no physical evidence of the fungus responsible, cracked, brown wood can be readily spotted on walks through pinewoods, especially in forests that have been neglected, which allows fallen trunks the time to decay. The fungi responsible for breaking down wood in this fashion are the brown rot fungi (BRF) that I shall simply call brown rotters. Less than 10 per cent of fungal species that break down wood are brown rotters. This is a sketch of how they work. The structural components of wood include three dominant molecules: cellulose, hemicellulose and lignin.

They are what give wood its mechanical strength, engineer its water-transporting abilities, protect its internal chemistry and determine its rates of growth.

Of these, cellulose is the most abundant biopolymer on Earth, widely distributed in algae and higher plants; in wood it can make up to 50 per cent of the bulk. The structure of cellulose is important for its strengthening function, as it consists of chains of hundreds, or even thousands, of simple, conjoined glucose-like ('sugar') molecules – technically, it is a polysaccharide. It is wood's scaffolding and building material combined. Hemicellulose works alongside: a more complex molecule with a branched structure, and including a varied array of sugar-like molecules. Brown rotters dismantle both of these components of wood and utilise the sugars and energy released to build their own carbon compounds from this plunder. What the sun's photosynthetic generosity and the long-term growth of the tree joined together these fungi put asunder. A simplified view of this stratagem of decomposition is that the third woody component – lignin – remains behind, and is responsible for both the colour and substance of the emasculated wood that we notice on our woodland walks.*

* $(C + H + L) - (C + H) = L$. The chemistry is much more complicated than that simple representation. While fungal degradation is often mediated by special enzymes, the brown rotters employ another method to cut cellulose down to size. Fenton's Reaction produces highly reactive hydroxyl (OH) free radicals that degrade the unwieldy cellulose molecule in a highly efficient way. The fungus then builds its own carbon compounds from its plunder. Even the lignin is not entirely unaffected by the red rotting process, but survives in somewhat modified forms, the chemistry of which is very complex, and still under investigation.

In our Grim's Dyke Wood we leave the branches that have broken off our trees to rot away in their own time. Over a year or so we get to see many different saprotrophic fungi that make a living from breaking down wood, and have to remind ourselves that even when we can see no evidence of fruiting, the mycelium is working away inside the tissues of fallen branches, extracting what it needs, and that sooner or later we will be rewarded with mushrooms that allow us to finger the guilty party. We have only a couple of oak trees, but we recently spotted one moderately substantial fallen branch a few feet in length that was lying half concealed by brambles. When I grasped it, I was astonished at how little it weighed. I expected a cudgel and got a wand. Although it still retained some bark, the wood at one of its broken ends was easily visible. Quite unlike the solid oak that makes furniture and supports cottages, this was pale and delicate, a fibrous ghost of Hearts of Oak. Its substance had been sucked away, leaving a spectre of oakiness, a failed promise of robustness, a fragile simulacrum.

My branch had been processed by one of the white rot fungi ('white rotters' herein). The cellulose and hemicellulose of the original wood had been almost entirely consumed, but, in addition, the lignin had been bleached of its character and broken down into its component parts. This was as far as fungi can go to exploit the creative work carried out by years of photosynthesis in the canopy; it was almost the end point of recycling. I looked again at my featherweight branch. There was a white patch as large as a beermat on what must have been its underside when it was lying on the ground. At this point my hand lens was brought into play.

(I still call it a hand lens, following the example of my first biology teacher, though many people know it as a jeweller's loupe.)

The white patch was revealed as a delicate maze, a miniature white labyrinth with a hundred tiny walls. This was the spore-bearing surface of one of the white rotters, whose mycelium must have drained my oak branch of its strength and colour, leaving behind only a few wispy struts of white cellulose. The maze-like surface identified it as the Split Porecrust (*Schizopora paradoxa*), one of the commonest white rotters in English woodlands. It had no stem, nor did it bear any cap or bracket, it was just this thin patch adhering to the underside of the branch where it would have been hidden from the light among the leaf litter to shed its spores into the darkness. It is described in the textbooks as one of the resupinate fungi, and indeed it is supine in the sense that it is not elevated above the rotten branch to which it is attached, but if supine means lying flat on your back staring upwards, then this fungus was doing just the opposite – attached by its back and facing downwards. It is one of those fungi that people pass by without noticing, unless they start turning over rotting wood lying on the ground. Then it is likely to be found within ten minutes in the autumn or early winter. To examine it properly a microscope slide is easily made from a small piece of the tissue from a wall of the 'maze', and under high power it can be quickly determined that the Porecrust is a typical basidio with small, colourless spores. Tiny black mites graze upon these spores, like grotesque, spiky little cows, and once I spotted an equally diminutive pseudoscorpion on the same sample equipped with fearsome pincers that was clearly in pursuit of the 'cows'; so this inconspicuous upside-down fungus was evidently the basis of a Lilliputian ecosystem. Thus my one small oak branch was both recycled and made into a microhabitat of unsuspected diversity.

There are many more species of white rotters than brown rotters, but both kinds of rot are overwhelmingly the territory of the spore droppers, the basidios.* Hundreds of species have adopted this mode of saprotrophic life, almost as many as those that form mycorrhizal partnerships. They ensure that the cycling of natural materials pursues its leisurely course: what goes around comes around. The various species of rotters display the whole gamut of fungal form: they can be brackets, shelves or toadstools that may be soft and yielding, or crusty and hard; they can bear their spores in tubes, on spines or gills. Many of them face downwards as they grow, like the Split Porecrust, and pose particular challenges for identification, though few destroy wood so definitively. It is generally accepted that both kinds of rotters have originated several times during the evolution of the fungi, so it is a way of earning a living rather than a sign of a close evolutionary relationship. However, rot is also taxonomically significant, as no one genus includes species with both white and brown rotters. When I recognised the importance of these fungi in nature, I toyed with the idea of calling this book simply *Rot*, until it was pointed

---

* I must mention one asco that is very common in beech wood, the Brittle Cinder Fungus (*Kretzschmaria deusta*), which fruits as black, tar-like patches on the base of trees, and can be a pathogen.

out to me by a well-wisher that I could scarcely say I was 'busy writing *Rot* at the moment'.

Some rotters are very widespread. The white rotter Splitgill (*Schizophyllum commune*) is found all over the world. This fungus forms tiers of small, whitish, scurfy brackets on wood, and the common name refers to the fact that the pale-purplish gills are indeed neatly split along their edges, especially when dry. It is a remarkable fungus in many ways. It can be revived with moisture after being kept dry for more than a year (some reports say a decade or more). It has more sexes than any other organism, that is, 23,328, according to one researcher. This refers to different mycelial 'mating types' that can only combine with another, compatible mating type to produce viable fruit bodies. None of my books say it is edible, but I saw a bucket of dry Splitgill on sale in a street market at Luang Prabang in Laos, and I understood from local intelligence that it was a favourite in omelettes and much used in traditional medicine. *Schizophyllum* can be found on wood from the tropics to high latitudes. It has even been reported from whale bones! As so often with widespread species, there is a debate as to whether there are 'cryptic species' in different parts of the world, distinguishable at the genomic level. All I can say is that these little fungi look exactly the same wherever I have come across them. The Oyster Mushroom is another familiar white rotter that is almost as widespread, but, as I have said elsewhere, it is typical during the earlier stages of timber breakdown and hence not found in association with the kind of end-of-the-line wood I described for the Split Porecrust. It is one of the least fussy of cellulose feeders, however, and so of particular use in 'cleaning up' organic waste, not to mention food production from woody waste materials.

White rotters have at their disposal a greater chemical armoury than brown rotters. It is helpful to think of the enzymes they deploy as a kind of toolkit that can be used to dismantle large molecules into convenient and useful pieces. Different tools are used for different purposes, but most have the function of degrading complex chemicals by cutting the bonds that hold their structures together. Organic molecules often have structures that are portrayed as huge and frequently irregular climbing frames with atoms at their joints, which is a visual model used for convenience rather than a literal description of the molecule in question. Nonetheless, it is acceptable to think of enzymes as a set of secateurs laying into the target molecules, cutting and shaping. I imagine fungal hyphae as wielders of molecular instruments of degradation as if they were a kind of demolition squad retrieving sugar bricks from cellulose for further use, or capturing nutritious chemical elements that could be redeployed in making a fruit body. Fungal hyphae delve into, and joust with, complex organic molecules. Lignin is the most complex puzzle of all, a polymer far more multifarious than cellulose, dangling with benzene rings and subsidiary branches that only make sense to an organic chemist. There are different kinds of lignin, some of which are only now yielding their secrets. No matter: there is a white rotter to take them on and cut them down to size.

If fruiting fungi provide the most obvious display of rotters at work, hidden dramas are played out within the interior of ageing trees or prostrate logs long before a blatant show of brackets or mushrooms unveils the stars of decomposition. Mycelium is at work on the available wood, recruiting nutrients and growing as it does so, guzzling through a woody volume to take over as much as it can to further its own eventual fruition. Visualise three-dimensional territories dividing a tree trunk into separate realms, wherein one fungus species takes command, seeking to repel unwanted invaders. Questing mycelium can recognise its own kind, a friend, but can also detect a rival for its resources, an enemy. There will be confrontations, vying for position, fast-growing mycelium trying to outflank its rivals for territory, or slower-growing mycelium using a chemical arsenal to deter its speedier rival. Lynne Boddy, the University of Cardiff professor who has done so much to understand these confrontations, refers to the competitions playing out in dead wood as 'fungus wars'.

In Grim's Dyke Wood we have been obliged to fell ailing beech trees. One of these had a trunk that looked reasonably sound when the tree was standing, but the felled tree showed a hole at its centre, proving decay was already underway Even an apparently sound tree showed characteristic outlines on its cut surface. The cross-section of the trunk revealed thin black lines unrelated to the obvious tree rings marking its annual growth, and these divided the surface of the cut tree into perhaps half a dozen or more territories. If it were a map, they could have been coloured in with distinctive hues and named as different countries. Projected into three dimensions they would be cylinders of wood, delimited from their neighbours by thin sheets rather than lines. Each cylinder embraced one mycelial individual, its lines black, produced by the pigment melanin, and marking out the territory occupied by that one mycelium. They are the equivalent of a notice saying: 'Private. Keep Out. Trespassers will be prosecuted.' Such marked wood is familiar to wood turners, who refer to it as 'spalted' and value it for making interesting wooden bowls. It is a matter of delicate timing to find the desirable raw material before degradation of the wood has gone too far.

Lynne has set up experiments to understand how mycelium behaves in wood. It is a dynamic system. If a new food source (a wooden block) is made available, the mycelium from an established source will grow preferentially towards it and other parts of the mycelial system will begin to shrink. It is opportunistic behaviour, based on hyphal tips being sensitive to foods that will promote further expansion of the individual mycelium: more branching, more absorption of nutrients. Resources are moved via the mycelium network to the most profitable position at the front line. Further questing leads to preferential growth: the Dry Rot Fungus can pass through walls to reach new wood to destroy, in this case without a rival.

Under natural conditions, competition rules. Even different individuals of the *same* species fight for territory. If more than one species is involved in the experiment, there will be winners and losers. If conditions are changed, so might the species having the more successful outcome. Some are more tolerant of high or low temperatures, others more susceptible to drying out. Over time, one fungus will be replaced by a successor in an ecological duel. Some of the winners are commonly seen on fallen wood: the abundant Turkey

Tail bracket displaces the equally common Hairy Curtain Crust, but since the latter is usually among the first to colonise freshly fallen (or cut) branches, both species have ample opportunity to spread their spores. The Stinkhorn trumps the Whitelaced Shank (*Megacollybia platyphylla*), although both quest through leaf litter and twigs with similar-looking white, stringy fibres of mycelium. As more species are added to the competition, the possibilities for rivalry and interaction multiply exponentially. In a wood on a warm and humid autumn day the tranquil atmosphere will conceal all manner of frenetic interactions between dozens of different mycelia vying for space and nutrients. The quiet wood conceals deadly conflict! A standing dead beech might seem lifeless but in its interior a score of species will be trying to establish supremacy. Spores arriving on the breeze will germinate and may prosper briefly only to be ousted by a rival. Now that fungi can be identified from their DNA, samples taken from wood that includes growing hyphae can identify the actors in this hidden drama before they have a chance to reveal themselves.

Many more kinds lurk within the wood than would be expected, judging from the meagre number of species of brackets or toadstools that finally erupt from the trunk of the tree. Which fungus finally gets to release its spores must depend on a hundred battles fought unseen. Fungi even lurk in waiting for years for their moment to come, surviving as mycelium in nooks and crannies in living trees (even inside living plant cells) until the tree begins to age, when they will start to join the battle for supremacy in the woody boxing ring.

When there is a life-or-death competition there will be a premium on getting an edge over rivals. In the early stages of decay some nutrients – such as nitrogen – are in short supply. Mugging a nematode eelworm might be the remedy. I frequently see nematodes under the microscope when I am examining fungus samples: tiny (less than 2 mm long), slowly thrashing, transparent, tapering thread-like animals that are very abundant within woody tissue. Within the secret depths of decaying wood, the Oyster Mushroom has evolved a way of capturing, killing and consuming nematodes to help its network gain an advantage over its rivals. Some Oyster hyphae produce specialised hourglass-shaped outgrowths, and if a nematode brushes by one of these it first becomes stuck by a glue-like substance and within a short time is immobilised by a paralysing toxin. Then the helpless worm is penetrated by hyphae growing from the point of attachment and, as if by a lethal vacuum cleaner, the contents are removed to supply nourishment to the network. If that sounds grisly, other fungi have evolved loops that tighten rapidly if an eelworm passes through, then to be drained dry of the goodness it contains. I could add spores that stick in the gullets of the unfortunate worm only to germinate and dine upon their consumers. There are dozens of mycological monsters that have learned to take advantage of these tiny worms. Capture and consumption are just another ruse to nudge ahead in the 'fungus wars'.

By the time a sequence of rotters have been at work on a log for several years, it has lost much of its substance. The remains of what was once firm wood have become soft and spongy: a finger can be pushed into the mush without too much resistance. This has one advantage for fungi because such wood readily absorbs rainwater – even a short shower leaves behind a moist, crumbling cake through which mycelium can move with dispatch. Patches of ghostly fungi like white cobwebs decorate damp corners. Tiny white discos dust the lower surfaces. Some toadstools prefer such a late stage in the life of a log and are able to dine on the leftovers from the generations of different fungi that preceded them. Nothing is wasted. In dismal corners of woodland, dripping with damp, some of these toadstools shine bright as lamps: shields (*Pluteus*) can be white, yellow or red, as well as every shade of brown, and all eventually have pink gills that fall short of the stem. Many are fragile, as if the effort of making flesh out of very old degraded wood could not produce anything of real substance.

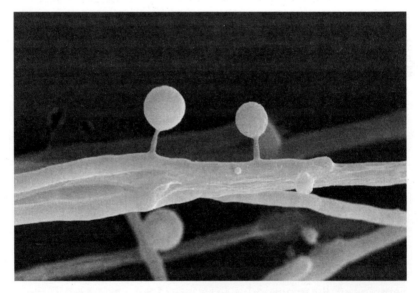

Electron microscope image of toxocysts on the mycelium of the Oyster Mushroom that target nematode worms. Courtesy Huen-Ping Hsueh.

What I believe to be the most beautiful mushroom of all grows from knotholes in dead or dying trees, often from well-rotted wood remaining in the interior of a standing relic. It is a rare fungus. Every mushroom lover will remember seeing it in the flesh for the first time. I knew the black and white photograph of it in John Ramsbottom's *Mushrooms and Toadstools* from my early days, and always yearned to find it. I failed to do so until I was in my middle age. It did not disappoint. In the Chilterns, several mushrooms were rising out of the remains of an ancient beech tree, which was long dead and much decayed, but still upright. They could not be missed in dimly illuminated summer woodland because they were shining white from afar; the largest was the size of my outstretched hand. The caps were opened into a wide parabola. Extraordinarily, the fungus had arisen out of a thick, cup-like volva, like the Death Cap – in fact, there was an as-yet unexpanded 'egg' nearby that was entirely covered by an off-white membrane, through which the mushroom would erupt, pushing upwards as the cap expanded. Unlike the Death Cap, there was no ring on the firm stipe: and the free gills were pink in colour (as was the spore print). This Silky Rosegill (*Volvariella bombycina*) was no poisonous temptress dressed in virginal white, it belonged to another group of fungi from the deadly Amanitas. What made it altogether exceptional is expressed in the 'silky' part of the name: the surface of the cap was decked completely in delicate, short, white hairs running down its surface, so perfect that it looked as if it must have been carefully groomed by some sprite of the woods. Not a hair was out of place. My close encounter with the perfect mushroom on beech was followed by one almost as beautiful on an oak, a tree that had been struck by lightning several years earlier. How could I possibly think of such a paragon as a rotter?

20.

Mind blowers

C arrying a mushroom basket in early autumn in the heather-clad uplands of the Peak District invites knowing looks from passers-by. 'Anything about?' they will enquire with a meaningful wink. In some places peaty soil is exposed where many walkers have worn paths crossing and recrossing the austere landscape. Stretches of purple moor grass undulate in the cool breeze. The habitat could not be more different from the sequestered woodlands of the south, and the fungi will surely include distinctive species. It rains a lot up here and the soil is acid. In the distance another searcher, his long locks only partly concealed by a woolly hat, moves slowly across the moor, displaying the bowed head of a confirmed mushroom spotter. We might be after the same species. This is where the Magic Mushroom (*Psilocybe semilanceata*) can be found in some numbers. It is one of those small fungi that are easily confused with many others of similar stature – and there is a bewildering variety of these perplexing toadstools, many of them with brownish caps, sprouting from the sides of the path.

You have to be something of a fanatic to relish sorting out such inconspicuous species. The magical one is also known as Liberty Cap, which is a better common name because it does indeed resemble the Phrygian cap worn by Marianne, the woman who is the French emblem of freedom (and not to be confused with the spikes on top of the Statue of Liberty in New York). There is a prominent nipple on top of the conical cap, the edges of which often converge rather than flare outwards; pale brown when moist, the cap dries almost white, while the gills are darker brown. The cap is propped above a relatively long and very slender stipe, which is often quite bendy. Liberty Caps may occur in troops if conditions are favourable. A small but diagnostic characteristic is a blue coloration at the bottom of the stipe. Nonetheless, it is easily confused with other small fungi by beginners. When I was a student I remember a friend in my college walking around with a slice of toast laden with small fruit bodies of the common Brown Mottlegill (*Panaeolus foenisecii*) that he had collected from the lawn that morning. He was, I thought, rather churlish when I pointed out his error.

Had I collected those moorland Liberty Caps, I would have been breaking the law. Here are the words of the 2005 Act: 'It is an offence to import, export, produce, supply, possess or possess with intent to supply magic mushrooms whatever form they are in, whether prepared or fresh.' That does not leave many loopholes. By merely putting some specimens in my basket I would be in possession of a Class A drug. How ironic if Liberty Caps led to loss of liberty! If

I am leading a group on a fungus foray and discover Magic Mushrooms, I am allowed to identify them, but not to pick one up and take it home. Were I to give one away, I would be a 'drug pusher'.

Mushrooms and toadstools cannot be told where to grow. The genus *Psilocybe* is not confined to moorland. There are several species that are far more potent than the Magic Mushroom, as they can have up to ten times more of the psychoactive compound psilocybin. These are Very Magic Mushrooms Indeed. I have met them in surprising places. The Blueleg Brownie (*Psilocybe cyanescens*) favours rather nutrient-rich habitats where there is not too much competition. Yet again, the fashion for bark dressing flowerbeds or around the boles of trees is encouraging it. From a distance it is a typical LBM (little brown mushroom), one of dozens, if not hundreds of small fungi with brown caps that usually demand much dedication to identify. It is more substantial than the Liberty Cap, often clustered, and remains brown on top, with gills of a similar colour; the cap opens out to become flat, often with a wavy margin. The blueing of the flesh of the stipe gives it away, as no other small brown mushroom does this to the same extent. I found great numbers of the Blueleg in the grounds of a private school when I was desultorily walking around their park. They were growing around ornamental conifers in places where needle duff had discouraged the grass, and the fruit bodies almost carpeted the ground. They left me with a dilemma: should I tell the head of the school? If the news leaked out, I could imagine the enthusiasm that might grip the more adventurous members of the senior school when they heard of their psychedelic guests. It could lend a new meaning to the phrase 'school trip'. I concluded that I would say nothing and leave the mushrooms to spread their spores in peace.

A few years later I was invited to survey the fungi of a private woodland belonging to an estate on the Berkshire Downs. A business had been set up there to encourage 'bonding' for wealthy industrialists, who spent an enormously expensive few days getting back to nature (in considerable comfort), staying in yurts and eating meat from rotating spits while their chauffeurs waited for them up the lane. The woodland was part of the experience, no doubt, but to make a wander through the trees more commodious a path had been laid out winding hither and thither under the canopy. This path had been constrained by timber beams, and the space between these filled with woodchip and similar materials, so that there was no danger of the wealthy rustics getting muddy. It also proved the perfect culture bed for the Blueleg Brownie. If there were hundreds at the school, there were thousands in the wood. They erupted in droves, their mycelium clearly visible among the shredded bark and woodchip that lined the way. I pointed the mushrooms out to a charming estate manager, carefully refraining from becoming a 'pusher' by picking one up and offering it for inspection. It was certainly entertaining to speculate what would happen if a bunch of 'captains of industry' consumed these strongly psychedelic mushrooms. Once again, it was decided that the wiser option was to say nothing.

I doubt whether it is a necessary precaution to put mushrooms on the same list that includes dangerously addictive drugs. The psychedelic craze of the late 1960s and 1970s led to much-hyped stories of people jumping off balconies and generally freaking out under the influence of psilocin (and psilocybin) originating from mushrooms, or LSD from pop-up laboratories. The descriptions of 'mind expansion' that accompany advocacy of these substances have a literary tradition going back to Aldous Huxley's 1954 *The Doors of Perception*, although Huxley was experimenting with mescaline (a derivative of the *peyote* cactus with similar effects to psilocybin) rather than anything fungal. The same cactus, together with *Psilocybe*, was implicated in a series of novels[*] by Carlos Castaneda, starting in 1968 with *The Teachings of Don Juan: A Yaqui Way of Knowledge*, relating the doings and sayings of a mystic shaman allegedly from Sonora, Mexico. The sayings included a generous dose of what Richard Dawkins has dubbed 'deepities', gnomic utterances impossible to parse about the meaning of life, new ways of cognition and the deficiencies of western rational thought. I confess that my young mind was attracted to such stuff, as were those of another million readers. The doings were more concerning – descriptions of Don Juan flying or hanging upside down from the ceiling. Don Juan was always bursting into derisive laughter and floating about the place.

---

[*] They were originally presented as anthropological reports, which may be why they achieved such traction, but it soon became clear that the imagination was at work more than the notebook. There are curious echoes of the work of Lobsang Rampa (aka Cyril Hoskin, b. Plymouth, UK) who adopted the persona of a Buddhist mage in his wildly successful book *The Third Eye* (1956). Even though he was revealed as a fraud, there remains a strong desire among many readers to believe in ancient mystical wisdom, whether it hails from Tibet or Mexico.

This did not bode well for the rational use of psychedelics. In 1966 Professor Timothy Leary had advised young people to 'turn on, tune in and drop out', and a sufficient number of them did just that, to increase concern about these consciousness-altering substances. Some researchers were discovering interesting facts about how they affected the brain, which did not include fostering an ability to fly, but their work was not looked upon with favour by granting bodies, and mushroom psychedelics were soon beyond the pale and eventually banned, except in military establishments as a way of disorientating the enemy.

This attitude has changed. In the twenty-first century the biochemistry and possible uses of psychedelic compounds have once again become the subject of research. Psilocybin can be employed under licence by university institutions studying the effects of the drug under controlled conditions. In Britain, Imperial College hosts the Centre for Psychedelic Research, staffed by a team of encouragingly young scientists, working in conjunction with clinical trials conducted at a dedicated medical unit. The head of the Imperial research team, Dr David Nutt, has a long track record of supporting the potential of psychedelic substances in psychotherapy, often in the face of opposition from those politicians who tended to lump psilocybin together with opioids and other addictive drugs. Studying the brain's reaction to psychedelic compounds is now aided by the latest technology. Three-dimensional images of the effects within the brain can be compiled from PET scans, while electroencephalograms monitor the electrical activity as dosage proceeds. The research touches upon fundamental questions about the meaning of consciousness, the tantalising will o'the wisp that has forever tortured philosophers and psychologists.

More immediately, links with a dedicated clinical unit allow a dispassionate assessment of the effectiveness of psychedelics in ameliorating the symptoms of distressing mental conditions. Long-term depression is very recalcitrant, and ruins the lives of thousands. Treatment with traditional antidepressants often serves to muffle the emotions rather than tackle the root of the problem. I recall a period when I suffered from a short bout of depression, and the pills I took made me feel as if my head was in a muslin bag; it did not hurt so much, but I was unable to think or see clearly. It was a relief to give up the medication. Reports of treatment with psychedelics include remarkable accounts of some patients feeling their 'black dog' lifting for the first time in years, but with their cognition still functioning. Properly conducted studies proved that this help was more general than anecdotal. People with severe depression have resorted to opioid drugs like heroin to numb their pain, which provides temporary relief, but leads to addiction and its catalogue of dire consequences. It appears that psychedelics are not addictive, which, if true, offers the possibility of longer-term treatment, perhaps in conjunction with more traditional psychotherapy. It does cast doubt on their classification with Class A drugs. The practical benefits of psilocybin and related psychoactive chemicals may move ahead of understanding *how* they work in the most complex organ of the human body. It is known that connective pathways are opened up (for example, between the two brain hemispheres) and this may link with the feelings of having seen the world afresh, colours more vividly and the senses being more exquisitely attuned that are so often reported with 'good trips'.

The Imperial College centre is one of several taking *Psilocybe* therapy seriously. In America, the equivalent team is run by Johns Hopkins University, and was started in 2000 when permission to resume serious research into psychedelics in the USA was finally allowed. Since then, tests have proved that even a few doses of psilocybin can be helpful in treating addictions to alcohol and tobacco, and may even be able to reduce the intense anxiety associated with post-traumatic stress disorder. The Johns Hopkins Center for Psychedelic and Consciousness Research was inaugurated in 2019 with $17 million found by private donors, but had to wait until 2021 to receive the first federal grant for 'magic mushroom' research awarded for fifty years. The overreaction going back to the hippy era might have come to an end at last, and psilocybin may eventually be taken off the register of dangerous drugs. I have to note that the website for Psychedelics Research and Psilocybin Therapy of the Johns Hopkins Psychiatry and Behavioral Sciences (to give the full grand title) features a lovely photograph at the top of its page showing a pair of delicate white mushrooms arising from wood. They are certainly bonnets (*Mycena*) and nothing to do with *Psilocybe* (Brownies). I am not aware of any mind-altering substances in the bonnets, although one or two would deal out a nasty stomach ache. One of the problems with being a field mycologist is that it is hard to avoid becoming something of a pedant.

21.

Feeders

This toadstool is rotten! An apparently sound example of a Blusher (*Amanita rubescens*) falls apart in my hands, and the inside of the stipe is little more than a heaving mass of maggots. They extend into the flesh of the cap, where the tunnels of the feeding larvae create a series of miniature catacombs. Where they have been at work the flesh of the fungus turns a pink colour – it 'blushes'. For these larvae the fungus is only interesting as a foodstuff. The maggots do not eat the gills of the Blusher, so they can continue to shed spores in their hundreds of thousands every hour; the outer shell of the stem retains enough strength to hold the toadstool upright even though its hyphae have turned it into a feast. Only when the fungus eventually collapses will the maggots have dealt a blow to sporulation. Then they will crawl off to pupate on the forest floor.

Mycologists do not take home maggoty specimens if they can avoid it, as it is not very pleasant to have a heaving basket. My family likes to remind me of an occasion when

I brought back a generous haul of Ceps, which are a particular favourite among the legion of flies, and after I left them for half an hour during the cleaning process a regiment of 'uninvited guests' were advancing purposefully across the table top in search of a new home. It did not do much good my pointing out to my unappreciative offspring that these white wriggling things were actually *made* out of delicious Ceps. There is an innate revulsion for maggots. I admit that it took me some time to appreciate that they were all part of the fungus story. After all, that one Blusher must have housed hundreds of maggots that would eventually turn into almost as many flies; and those flies would have made food for insectivores on a scale spanning spiders to birds. If I called to mind the woodland where the Blusher grew, there were dozens, if not hundreds, of similar fruit bodies, so it was possible to conjure up a vision of many thousands of tiny flies feeding into the ecology, anchoring the food chain. The flies did not seem to do the fungi much harm, and they contributed much to the biodiversity. They were heroes not horrors.

I decided that I should learn more about these insects. The lockdown during the COVID pandemic provided a chance to raise my own fungus-eating insects in the privacy of my home laboratory. Although I knew quite a lot about fungi, I was no entomologist and would need help with identifications. My colleagues in the Natural History Museum were happy to name any beetles I collected. I had guidance from *the* best experts: Max Barclay, Roger Booth and Michael Geiser. However, most of the insects whose larvae eat mushrooms are flies, and for that a skilled dipterist* is a sine qua non. I was lucky enough to contact Peter Chandler, who knows more about fungus flies than anyone else, and he was happy with the idea of my raising flies from named fungi then sending them to him for identification. Many of them should be the fungus gnats on which he was the authority. We might even make some new connections between host and fly.

My first attempts at raising flies were not successful. I soon learned that just putting a mushroom in a sealed jar and standing back to see what happened was usually disastrous. As the mushroom aged it decayed malodorously, and since a mushroom is 90 per cent water it eventually breaks down into a kind of soup in which any maggots simply drown before they have a chance to pupate. When this happened I felt like some kind of murderer. In nature, the products of the decaying mushroom would leach into the leaf litter and soil – my jar just turned into a small, smelly, greenish pond. The answer was coir – the fibrous part of the coconut husk – which has a remarkable ability to absorb water without turning into something soggy and nasty. Fly species that like to pupate in the soil are happy to use coir as a substitute. I tried again with a larger container, this time a third filled with coir. Another mushroom was selected and after a week or two had apparently rotted almost away, and the coir had absorbed the products of decay. Within another

---

* Dipterists study the vast range of insects (Diptera) with only two wings (as opposed to the four-winged species) that include flies of all shapes and sizes, mosquitos, gnats, midges and many more.

week the jar contained some small flies, flying about, or resting on the side. They were about the same size as mosquitoes. I was quite elated. If they had been free in the forest they would have set out to find a mate and, no doubt, another mushroom, using their precise chemical sensors to locate exactly the right species. Now they had to be put into the freezer to kill them so that I could send them off for identification.

After a few hours I took the now-icy container out of the freezer and under the low-power binocular microscope located the poor dead flies, mostly by the light catching on their pair of wings. It took a little practice to master the art of picking them up on the moistened tip of a very fine paintbrush. Then they could be transferred one by one to a tiny phial nearly full of alcohol (in lockdown I was forced to use Gordon's Gin). Once stoppered, they could safely be sent to Peter Chandler in the post. I refined my vessels for the experiments: a Kilner jar with the top disc removed and replaced by gauze and screwed tight to allow the jar to receive oxygen without danger of escaped flies. Some bracket fungi were not fleshy and therefore in less danger of rotting away, but these took much longer to yield their secrets, as the maggots took more time to mature. The coir was less important for these 'dry' fungi. Some encrusting fungi could not be separated from the wood on which they grew, so it was always possible that the larvae fed on mycelial wood as well as fruit body. My practical experience soon became an education.

Peter Chandler identified my first small phial as containing *Mycetophila fungorum* . . . well, you could not get more fungal than this because the scientific name of this fungus gnat is translated literally as 'mushroom lover of the mushrooms'. This little gnat was one of the least discriminating of its kind, relishing everything from boletes to False Death Caps on which to lay its eggs, and only avoiding tougher fungi. I was to become quite familiar with this small fly. Like all members of the family Mycetophilidae, it had elegant wings held aloft and long, dangling legs equipped with impressive spines, the details of which are the meat and drink of the skilled dipterist in determining which species is what. I soon learned that some fungus gnats had black spots on the wings (but not *M. fungorum*), which is an easy feature to see, as opposed to the details of the genitalia, which remain the arcane territory of the knowledgeable expert. *M. fungorum* was the first of many different flies from the same fungus gnat family.

As more and more species were added to the list from the fungi growing in our wood, my admiration for Peter's expertise grew exponentially. My first success from a bracket fungus hatched from what is probably the commonest bracket of all, the Turkey Tail. This somewhat larger fungus gnat, *Ditomyia fasciata*, belonging to a different family, had distinctive waves of black on its wings. Unlike the mushroom lover of mushrooms, this fly is a specialist for Turkey Tail, and turned up with other specialists for the same tough-textured fungus, to whit, flat-footed flies of the appropriately named genus *Polyporivora* (eater of polypores).

In a few weeks my list of flies whose larvae dined on fungi had grown to more than a dozen different species, with no sign of it coming to an end. From my student days studying practical genetics in the laboratory I was able to recognise that mainstay of inheritance experiments, the tiny fruit fly (perhaps more accurately called vinegar fly) *Drosophila*, with its compact abdomen and wings folded down on its back. One common species had glowing orange eyes. I noticed that fruit flies dominated a single sample if they were present, sometimes almost too many to count. They revelled in slightly soggy fungal specimens. In the end there were seven different kinds of these little flies, one of which, *Hirtodrosophila trivittata*, had only appeared in Britain in 2005 but was already widespread on its preferred host, the Oyster Mushroom. Presumably, it moved from fungus to fungus colonising new territory as it went. My first crane fly was a surprise, as it was so much larger than *Mycetophila*. It just sat, wings folded back, on top of the rather tough bracket from which it had emerged, seemingly in no hurry to do anything but rest. One crane fly species proved rather common, and clearly had larvae able to grow up on recalcitrant bracket fungi like the Lumpy Bracket (*Trametes gibbosa*), a fungus that is so tough and rubbery you cannot break it with your fists. I learned to recognise this fly species quickly as it rejoiced in the mouthful of a name *Achyrolimonia decemmaculata*, which helpfully points out the ten spots on its wings.

So, fly by fly, the list of species that needed fungi to feed their maggots grew ever longer. When the study came to an end, no less than seventy-seven different species had been reared in my upstairs laboratory. There was one solitary moth in addition. By now, I had begun to get a picture of the relationships between fungi and the flies that ate them.

There was a distinction between those that would only eat one species and those that were less choosy. The sample size was relatively small, so it was possible that some of the rarer species might have chosen more widely, but the same associations had been noticed by previous researchers and seem well-founded. There was a clear division between flies that consumed soft mushrooms and toadstools and those that preferred more challenging, tougher brackets and other fungi growing on wood. The latter were often not in so much of a hurry to eat their way to adulthood, and even came out during the winter months. As for being a source of food, I counted more than eighty fungus gnats emerging from one brittlegill (*Russula*) fruit body, and I lost count of the number of fruit flies from an Oyster Mushroom. That was plenty of lunch for an insectivore.

In 2022 Peter published his definitive work on British species of the fungus-reliant gnats, which now number an extraordinary 501. They are, in their way, paralleling the diverse kingdom that gives them nourishment as larvae. Entomologists do not usually raise flies. Their standard *modus operandi* is to wave fine sweep nets over vegetation on warm days. The flies captured on the wing are transferred to safekeeping by means of a pooter (although I have never heard it used as a verb: 'to poot'). Thence they go for microscopic examination of hairs on legs and other defining characteristics. For those gnats that had grown up in fungi there were still unknown links between the adult fly collected in the usual way and its foodstuff while a maggot. I concentrated particularly on raising flies from some less conspicuous fungi, including the basidios that could be found underneath rotting logs.

Bleeding Porecrust (*Physisporinus sanguinolentus*) was discovered attached to the underside of a rotting beech branch. The fungus gnat that emerged after the rearing protocol did not seem very different from many I had reared before. Peter Chandler had no such misconceptions. The gnat was *Mycetophila unipunctata* and its host had never been determined, because it was one of those species originally captured as a flying adult. It had been described and named by the pioneer German entomologist Johann Wilhelm Meigen (1764–1845). In fact, it had received its scientific name in 1818, three years after the Battle of Waterloo. The publication of Darwin's *On the Origin of Species by Natural Selection* was still forty-one years in the future. This little fly had to wait more than two centuries to have its life cycle completed! It was rather wonderful that such a discovery could be made from a fungus collected within walking distance from home and in the modest surroundings of my domestic laboratory. It is not going to make any headlines, but it is one small brick in the vast edifice of science. By the time our study was completed and published in 2021, four more larval hosts had been identified for the first time for named fungus gnats. That makes a total of five small bricks in that scientific edifice, almost enough to see from a short distance.

Close encounters with fungus beetles were part of a longer project over the five-year period of 2014–18, concentrating on finding distinctive adults rather than larvae. Bioblitzes in 2014 and 2015 included a team from the Natural History Museum in London rootling around in canopy and forest floor, which got the project off to a good start. By the end of the study period, 253 species had been identified, although only a fraction of these were associated with fungi. For a short while I became an obsessive coleopterist. The first thing a tyro discovers is that most beetles are *small*. After a few good-sized, brightly coloured species comes a long list of dark-coloured species a few millimetres long. Second, some beetles can be *fast*. A few of the bigger ones can be captured with tweezers in the field, but others have to come home as part of a sample, and be chased round under the microscope. It is quite extraordinary how small beetles can hide in a collecting tray. Flush them out, and in a trice they have vanished again behind a grain of soil. I developed a technique to catch these diminutive Olympic champions. Speeding beetles can be caught on a soft, damp brush and then quickly transferred to a shallow tray of water, where surface tension stops them making a quick getaway. Even so, some of them 'row' across the surface with their six legs and before you can say 'woodworm' have reached the edge and shot off. Successfully captured beetles are lifted from the water on the brush, popped into the sample bottle and given to the experts.

We caught more than fifty different beetles associated with fungi. Some were well known as fungus eaters; others were bigger, and probably chased and ate the small ones. This was voracious nature in miniature! The speediest of all were rove beetles, known in the trade as 'staphs' (Family Staphylinidae), which have miniature wing cases with perfectly functional wings folded away underneath. This leaves the rest of the abdomen flexible and versatile so that they can crawl into spaces where other beetles cannot go.

They also run away from a collector with panache. There are so many subtly different species that they are most challenging to identify, but Roger Booth at the Natural History Museum is the high priest in their identification. Almost eighty species of staphs were identified by Roger, and quite of few lived on fungi. One mushroom, the grey Whitelaced Shank, supported great numbers of minute *Gyrophaena affinis* on its gills, obviously feeding on spores, looking like animated black specks. Such tiny beetles were obviously direct fungus feeders. Larger rove beetles of the genus *Atheta* – but still only four millimetres long – may have been predators upon the grazers as well as fungus eaters themselves. A relatively monstrous staph distinguished by a mostly orange abdomen – *Lordithon lunulatus* – lurked inside the old hollow stipes of the fungus. This predator was equipped to outrun its prey. If I flushed one out it sped away like a photophobic racing car until it found somewhere out of sight. I finally persuaded it to scuttle into a dark sample tube. I assume its hunting skills didn't confine it to a fungal host, but *Lordithon* knew the most profitable places to hang out.

The most beautiful fungus fancier was *Triplax aenea*, which favoured Oyster Mushroom in our wood, and sported shining wing cases of gorgeous metallic blue contrasting with orange colours on the rest of the animal, including the antennae. Another beetle on the same fungus was almost as glamorous, with four big red spots on the wing cases. The scientific name tells you all you need to know about it – *Mycetophagus quadripustulatus*, the four-spotted mushroom eater. Both these beetles were about half a centimetre long. What with the larvae of fungus gnats, fruit flies and beetles, the competition for the succulent flesh of the Oyster Mushroom was intense, and mushroom aficionados can face disappointment to find a prime-looking Oyster already under multiple occupation. The soft flesh of Chicken of the Woods supported a brown beetle, *Hallomenus binotatus*, as well as the inevitable staphs, but when it was old and white later in the summer, another specialist, *Eledona agricola*, was perfectly happy in a corky matrix avoided by all other organisms, including fungus gnats. The versatility of beetles knew no bounds.

Beetles could even tackle relatively hard bracket fungi. One of the tough brackets is Common Mazegill (*Datronia mollis*) that grows in autumn on fallen trunks and branches of beech, and, as its common name suggests, features a labyrinthine under-surface where the spores are produced. The upper surface is black and solid. I was surprised to find the spore-bearing surface covered with numerous tiny staphs (*Agaricochara latissima*). There were larvae among them, which were pallid in colour and even smaller than their minute parents, so this was both a feeding and breeding ground. They were like diminutive, invertebrate sheep grazing the meadows of the maze, with spores taking the place of grass, and were surely obligatory fungus feeders – it was not surprising to find them on a variety of other brackets, but curiously not on agarics, as implied by their scientific name. Probably the commonest two fungi in our beech wood are the Turkey Tail and the Hairy Curtain Crust, both of which can be leathery even while still young, when they grow on stumps and fallen beech branches. To find the beetles hidden within these small brackets they have to be rather ruthlessly sliced with a sharp knife, then the slices shaken in a small pot with a tightly fitting lid. Almost every sample yields tiny beetles. They are not runners like the staphs. These brown, very compact-looking insects look dazed to be released from the security of their bracket home, and move slowly. They are not more than four millimetres long, with conspicuous antennae carrying knobs. Their identification is difficult, but six different species were recognised from our wood thanks to Roger Booth and Glenda Orledge, who has made a special study of these tiny beetles; five of the six belong to the genus *Cis*, which must hold the record for the shortest Latin name. They are rarely found away from the fungi on which they dine. One of them, *Cis bilamellatus*, is a stranger that arrived unbidden from Australasia (presumably in imported wood) and is now probably the commonest of its kind in many places, feeding on many different brackets – but it does seem to rub along with the natives. There are predators here, too. *Rhizophagus* is an overall paler brown, elongate beetle that lives in the same habitat. Despite its name, which means ‘ root eater’, it preys on the smaller beetles, even though its larvae probably eat mycelium.

These close encounters with flies and beetles made me realise that the fungus itself is an ecosystem: a single fruit body can be a city of insects, an interconnected hub of life. Without fungi our whole fauna would be impoverished, with hundreds of species lacking a livelihood. I must have looked at dozens of Turkey Tails without appreciating that these tough little brackets fed the fungus gnat *Ditomyia fasciata* and many others, and supported a miniature food chain even in the midst of winter. The understanding of nature requires concentration and observation more than anything else. Every one of the beetles associated with a fungal habitat has its own biography and all of these narratives combine to make the greater narrative of ecology. Science has moved into smaller and smaller compartments over the course of my lifetime, and while this allows insights from molecular evidence that would have seemed incredible to our scientific antecedents, it also means that there are fewer professional scientists who are able to stitch it all together. Synthesis is still more important in an age of specialisation. There is a conventional 'greenwash' in television treatments of the environment that hymns the interconnectedness of nature in a general, and often sentimentalised way, usually to the accompaniment of a string orchestra. What is missing is an acknowledgement that close inspection is required. If nature is like a symphony, the placing of every note must be understood. A fungus might be a good scale at which to start because its life is short – at least as a fruit body – where the timescale of a whole forest is written in centuries.

22.

Puzzles

S ometimes the most obvious questions are also the most difficult. They may seem so blatant that after a while they are simply ignored. Like a familiar blemish on a familiar face, they may not bear close examination for fear of causing offence. Or maybe just asking the question seems surprisingly naive, as though to reveal that if you don't know the answer it diminishes your stature. It is challenging to put your hands up and admit that an answer eludes you. Many people may not even recognise the question. Classical anthropologists were trained to drop their western perceptions when approaching a new tribe, to avoid applying their own values and never to prejudge. They had to *think* like a Trobriand Islander or Nootka Native American, to get on the inside of their subject of study, to understand their different rules. To approach the kingdom of fungi it may be necessary to abandon everything we know from animals and plants. Is it feasible to think like a fungus, to apply fungal logic, to climb aboard the mycelium for the ride? Even after decades of close encounters with fungi there are apparently simple questions for which I have no matching simple answers. To use conventional principles of natural selection is comparatively uncomplicated in understanding why truffles developed underground, or how fetid *gleba* benefits a stinkhorn; but other phenomena are elusive. I have already mentioned the mystery of luminescence, but there are more unsolved enigmas. For every thought about these outstanding questions, there is an objection – or perhaps I have not yet learned to think like a mushroom.

Colour. The caps of brittlegills and Amanitas and webcaps can be almost any colour and it is a mystery why. The cap of the Fly Agaric is shameless scarlet, but that of the Destroying Angel virginal white. The Death Cap is livid green, while the Orange Grisette (*A. crocea*) requires no description. Yellows, browns and greys decorate other woodland *Amanita* species to complete the palette – but there is no blue. Webcaps (*Cortinarius*) span the same range, with many bluish or violet species in addition, while the Bloodred Webcap (*C. sanguineus*) is the most enthusiastic deep red in the whole kingdom. As for the brittlegills, they sport a range of colours to match the full palette of a painter in oils, and even include black, as some species blacken as they age. Just to add to the profusion – or confusion – some brittlegill species can be more than one colour: the Rosy Brittlegill (usually called *Russula lepida*) is a lovely red coral colour in our woodland – sometimes with an extra splash of the same on the stipe. Another, pale-yellow *Russula* that grew at the same time under the same beech trees was a puzzle until I realised it was a non-rosy Rosy Brittlegill. It was described as a variety but is regarded as just a colour form. Many *Russula* species have cap colours that are a mix of green and purplish tones. Others are reliably coloured in the same shades at all times. Those brought up with orchids, birds and butterflies are conditioned to accord importance to colour. In animals it is part of the recognition system that helps perpetuate the species – something for natural selection to work on. I cannot see this in the fungi. The pigment is usually concentrated in the skin of the cap (in some webcaps it fully infuses the flesh). Red might be thought a warning colour, as it is in some insects, but that is implausible in fungi. Slugs chomp into red fungi with the same enthusiasm they give to brown ones or even green Death Caps. I have often observed that they start with grazing the gills, and I suspect (to anthropomorphise) that the fungus might not care, or might even welcome the attention as an aid to spreading its spores through the forest. It has been estimated that an ordinary gilled mushroom can release thirty thousand spores every second, but this is completely unrelated to the pigmentation of the cap – the brightest and the dullest drop their tiny propagules at the same rate. The same puzzles could be rehearsed with regard to the fungus's edibility for humans – the species that kill us are much appreciated by invertebrates. Flies swarm around the deadliest and the most delicious with equal vigour. Must we assume that the colours of fungi are accidents of metabolism – pigments produced as a by-product of biochemistry, perhaps, dumped into that part of the cap which lies at the outer edge of the developing fruit body? Early mycologists would have had no problem:

a plethora of colour was yet another demonstration of the generosity of the Almighty, painter and creator. This sits ill with what has been termed the 'adaptationist paradigm', where any hereditable feature deserves examination for its role in the life of the organism. Try as I might, I cannot construct a hypothesis to take on the beautiful dabs of colour that are splashed over the forest floor in due season.

Rarity. The majority of larger fungi are uncommon or rare. A glance through some of the more comprehensive identification handbooks shows how few fungi are described as common or very common. Some species are quite extraordinarily rare – and many of these are large enough not to be readily overlooked, rather than being one of the legion of small brown mushrooms it would be easy to pass by without noticing. The Umbrella Polypore (*Polyporus umbellatus*) presents a spectacular collection of dozens of little grey caps with pores beneath that form a natural bouquet at the base of beech or oak trees. Anyone who knew anything about fungi couldn't fail to stop in wonder if they found it, but there are very few UK records each year. It is genuinely rare, though it is so large it must release billions of spores when it fruits. Its fecundity is inversely proportional to its size. The shields (*Pluteus*) are pretty, pink-gilled toadstools that grow on wood, and one, the pale-brown Deer Shield (*P. cervinus*) is described as common in all the books. Others are rare, and the beautiful orange Flame Shield (*P. aurantiorugosus*) is one of the rarest of all, and also unlikely to be missed. It grows out of wood, like all shields, but I have seen it but once in my lifetime. The

Italian mycologist Marco Floriani told me of a whole toad-stool *genus* called *Musumecia* that is quite striking and likely to be spotted; it includes four species known only from one or two collections from Switzerland and northern Italy – and one species from China. This seems almost perversely elusive. After all, the whole purpose of making a fruit body is concerned with survival of the species. Maybe the fungus is commoner somewhere else – this could be the case with the extraordinary *Battarrea*, which is rare in Britain but quite frequent in desert regions (p. 109), yet it certainly does not apply to polypores and shields. 'Thinking like a mushroom', it becomes more plausible that a rare fungus could be para-doxically quite common – but endures as mycelium in soil and only rarely produces a fruit body. It is 'invisible'. This has been proved by DNA sampling from forest soils, where apparently rare mushrooms can be more prominent under-ground than they are above it (and vice versa); this applies more particularly to ectomycorrhizal species that can happily bide their time associated with the roots of their hosts until just the right conditions turn up. Even so, it hardly explains why there are hundreds of species of webcaps (dozens of them just associated with beech woods on chalk) and nearly all of them are rarely encountered. Even experienced mycologists are bewildered by their sheer variety. The brittlegills (*Russula*) are almost as prolific as webcaps. Nor can the 'invisibility explanation' be applied to saprotrophs. Many of these fungi are specialists. A large number of species growing only on fire sites are not really rare, because when a fire site turns up and the conditions are right they regularly put in an appearance. But some small dapperling toadstools (*Lepiota*) and many inkcaps that might appear by any path side turn up very rarely. There is nothing special about the site, but there must be something special about the mushroom. Selfishly, this is a good thing, because every year I see something I have never seen before. It keeps me on my toes. One year I found a very rare, small, but distinctive fungus for the first time on 'my patch' in Oxfordshire, only to learn that it had been found all over the south of England at the same time. This is baffling: I cannot explain why so many fungi are rare, nor why they may occasionally break their own rules.

To pick or not to pick. To return briefly to the topic of fungi as food, I like to eat mushrooms, and I have believed that modest consumption of wild food was a reward for a certain expertise. Our mushroom forays* were not to be confused with foraging, where the sole purpose is gathering species for the table. I have already described how depressing it is to find woodland trashed by foragers turning over every fruit body in pursuit of Ceps, but this is particularly because I want fungi to be appreciated for their beauty and their interest. Naturalists would be outraged to a woman if wild-flower meadows were partially picked and then trampled. I am fully in sympathy with the legislation that now protects our scraps of ancient forests from indiscriminate exploitation. The unanswered question is to what extent picking the

---

* I still like 'foray' to describe what we do, and have used it throughout. Sensitivity over possible confusion with 'forage' has led some mushroom groups to simply describe their activities as 'walks'.

fruit bodies affects the future of the species. Again, I find myself perplexed. This book began with a trip to Borgo Val di Taro, where the *porcini* festival celebrates the abundance of a few delicious species of *Boletus*. The collecting baskets are still full after hundreds of years. The local mycologists are not worried, and I found my own concerns about picking slipping away. If enough fungi survive to spread their spores the population is not threatened.

This is not the full story. The most wonderful treat for any mycologist, and almost any gastronome, is to discover a mossy bank covered with chanterelles. They erupt like bouquets of exotic, bright-yellow flowers from the ground, and they can be abundant. Yet the figures from Saarbrücken (p. 213) show that the numbers taken to market have greatly declined over recent decades. In the Netherlands, fungi have always been taken seriously, and a study published by the distinguished Dutch mycologist Eef Arnolds in 1991 showed that between 1972 and 1989 species of ectomycorrhizal fungi like chanterelles had drastically declined in controlled study woodland plots to about a third of what they used to be – while the number of fruit bodies per hectare had decreased even more dramatically. Atmospheric pollution (and particularly nitrate pollution) is fingered as the culprit, as even protected habitats have experienced comparable decline. Rain does not recognise fences. It is the same story that I have outlined in the grasslands in my local churchyards, and it is very worrying. Arnolds believes that fungi are the 'canary in the mine' in warning of widespread ecological damage. In a far less controlled way, I have noticed lovely mushrooms of no culinary interest disappearing from my local beech woodlands, particularly woodwax (*Hygrophorus*) species that were once common and are no longer to be seen.

This brings us back to the dilemma about picking. I believe that we can be fairly certain that this activity is *not* primarily responsible for a decline in numbers of edible species, though it is obviously readily visible compared with pollution and climate change. *Pfifferlinge* in particular are usually picked after they have had time to release a lot of their spores. There is an odd parallel with the blame attached to schoolboy egg collectors for the decline of common birds in the mid twentieth century. No doubt that played a part, but not compared with the growth of chemical farming and loss of habitat. Only when a bird becomes very rare does the price of the eggs to fanatical collectors rise, and then every egg is important. The benign conditions that succour *porcini* in northern Italy must have remained relatively unchanged. I am still uncertain about picking, and have settled for the compromise that I will only collect species for the table that are still common, and assume the uncommon ones need every spore they can shed.

Mystery origins. Species have origins. Some evolve because of geographical separation from an ancestral stock; they may occupy different continents, or are found to either side of an oceanic or mountain barrier. Others are the result of genetic mutations that confer some advantage upon them that encourages their spread to new areas, where they might suddenly appear as opportunists in a competitive world. With thousands of species of larger fungi known in Europe, it is inevitable that thousands of matching speciation events must have taken place in the past – but where are they happening now? It is relatively common for a 'new' species to appear in Britain, but when the detective work has been done they are discovered to have migrated from elsewhere, often thanks to human agency. The most striking example is probably the Starfish Fungus that was well known in the Antipodes before its appearance in England. On bark-dressed flowerbeds the brilliant-capped Redlead Roundhead (*Leratiomyces ceres*) is now very common. In my annual talk at the Harcourt Arboretum at Nuneham Courtenay these richly red toadstools become more numerous with each passing year. Twenty years ago I realised that the name that had been applied in the United Kingdom to this fungus was mistaken, and that it was an Australian native that had gone the other way from the 'ten pound poms'. Many of the microfungi that have caused havoc with our native trees have come in from elsewhere in the world, and sweep through the habitat unchallenged. These case histories are understandable, if sometimes regrettable: strangers find a niche that allows them a foothold in an alien land.

The mystery relates to the hundreds of *native* species of mushrooms and toadstools of field and forest, many of them rarely encountered. Mycorrhizal fungi include many species that favour the same kind of tree; on our own patch we have cause to wonder at the variety of brittlegills and webcaps that we can find under our familiar beech trees. The growing conditions are apparently similar, even if the weather alters from season to season. These different species must live together in some kind of dynamic equilibrium, with the more uncommon species only occasionally having a 'good year' for fruiting. This poses the question of why, how and when they speciated – and should there not be evidence of the appearance of new species, just as there are for new strains of bacteria? I have one possible example among the saprotrophic jelly fungi. Bruce Ing is the veteran expert on slime moulds, a wonderful group of organisms that are not moulds (nor any type of fungus) but can indeed be slimy at an early stage in their growth. In his spare time, he followed the story of one true fungus, the Pale Stagshorn (*Calocera pallidospathulata*), a jelly basidio which grows in lines out of dead sticks, and finishes up looking like a series of tiny, semi-transparent spoons or table tennis bats – it is easy to recognise. It was first found in 1969 in a coniferous plantation between Pickering and Scarborough, but it was not named as a new species until 1974 by Derek Reid, the expert mycologist who worked at the Royal Botanic Gardens, Kew (where he generously put up with some of my early mistakes). By 1978 it had been collected from twenty-seven sites and had reached Cheshire and Lancashire. The early occurrences seemed to be confined to conifer wood. In two more years it had spread to Wales, and by 1989 it had reached southern England in the New Forest. It managed to outcompete a small, orange jelly, *Calocera cornea*, which is generally more spike-like, and easily distinguishable. The Pale Stagshorn had reached Norway a year earlier. By this point the species had also consented to grow happily on broadleaved wood. When I led fungus forays in the early 1990s, it nearly always turned up somewhere: clearly, it was a successful invader. I wagged my finger at my small band of fungus enthusiasts as I told the tale of a new interloper. I had hoped that this might be my flagship example of speciation in action, but Bruce Ing reported seeing a similar fungus in Mexico – so invoking once again the principle that evolution always happens somewhere else. Yorkshire would just be a staging post in the story of the Pale Stagshorn. It would be fair to say that it is quite as difficult to import a species to Mexico from Yorkshire as it would be to move one from Yorkshire to Mexico – particularly if their identity is still unproven. But my example of speciation in action is not bombproof. The origins of the thousands of species of mushrooms and toadstools that we are cataloguing have defied attempts to trace them to speciation events in historical time. They are like spooks that appear unannounced from a past that is invisible; they are enigmas. We know from hundreds of molecular studies that species of mushrooms and toadstools are related in hierarchies no different from those of other organisms, which proves that evolution has indeed happened – but apparently not in front of our eyes.

As a postscript, it seems from my recent experience that the Pale Stagshorn is no longer as common a find as it was a decade ago. I feel sure that the little jelly is out there, it is just that I do not meet up with it as often as I used to. Maybe it is jostling into place among the hundreds of other sapro-trophs that dine on wood, whatever the initial advantages that helped it spread so widely from a small copse in Yorkshire. This makes just another puzzle to add to the enigma.

23.

Perfetto!

In a lifetime of forays there have been a few days when everything meshes. It may have been raining to encourage the shyer mushrooms to make an appearance, but then the sun is warm and the sky is clear, and the light has that peculiarly limpid quality that is special to autumn. The dampness is in no way oppressive; it is creative. The woodland smells of moss and fallen leaves – a perfume that is associated with new fruit bodies pushing out of the ground in their transient perfection. Dewdrops still hang on the spiders' webs, their patient spinners lurking and plump before the winter closes in. It is difficult to avoid damaging their delicate traps as the undergrowth is breached. There is a frisson of anticipation; it is going to be one of those days when the unexpected can be expected: maybe a spectacularly coloured cup fungus, or even a species never seen before.

If there is an unusual find, the more knowledgeable forayers point out important features of gills or stipes to the beginners; if it were not so joyful it might be overwhelming.

All known colours paint the forest floor, from subtle brown to blatant scarlet. On this perfect day toadstools do not have to be sought out, for they are on all sides, some sprouting in clusters from fallen trunks, others tucked under their tree of choice, or so minute they grow from a single, fallen leaf, like the white Beechleaf Bonnet (*Mycena capillaris*). On this day knowledge becomes pure pleasure, not a matter of status; to share knowledge is itself a gift. Maybe some small, rare mushrooms will be collected for microscopic examination, but for the moment discovery is all. Webcaps, brittlegills, dapperlings, fibrecaps, boletes, puffballs and bonnets all vie for attention underfoot; fallen branches are covered in Oysters or Porcelain Fungus. Even high branches boast bracket fungi. Those who carry a hand lens inspect the white patches on the undersides of logs. If decay can be exuberant, this day is its carnival. If every fungus species played a different note this afternoon would be a symphony. The days of high summer when this same stretch of woodland lacks a single mushroom are now impossibly remote: this, for a mushroom lover, is how it is meant to be.

Was there ever such a perfect foray? I recently discovered my old leather-covered notebook for 2010, and came to a page labelled 'Perfetto!', which should settle the question. The date was Wednesday 6 October, and the country was Italy, where this book began, but on the high, eastern subalpine side of the country above the town of Cuneo. That incomparable day was part of an Overseas Foray of the British Mycological Society, organised with the help of a hospitable local group of enthusiasts (headed by charming Yolande and Giovanni). In our group was a couple of distinguished elderly Chinese professors and young Mr Wu, a research student, along for the ride. He was having a wonderful time in the wicked West. Enthusiastic amateurs like myself and a couple of professional mycologists comprised the British contingent. There were similarities to Borgo Val di Taro in the mushroom festival held in the nearby small town of Rossano. The former mayor, Gianfranco Armando, knew everyone, and dashed about the stalls shaking hands, fixing and dealing. His way of communicating with the English was to speak Italian very loudly and very slowly, accompanied by vigorous hand gestures. My own Italian is derived entirely from Bruno Cetto's six volumes of *I Funghi dal Vero*, so I was able to talk about fungus gills and taste and abundance with some aplomb, but I could not ask for the lavatory or pass the time of day. It did not seem to matter. Goodwill was ubiquitous. I found that if I smiled at a stallholder and cried, 'Bellissimo', pointing at his or her fungi, it worked under all circumstances. *Porcini* were on sale, though not in the sheer abundance I was later to see in Borgo.

Hereabouts, the fungus fanciers particularly appreciated Hen of the Woods, a large, grey, pore-bearing fungus that grows in stacks of thin tiers at the base of old oak trees. When it is young and soft it is quite delicious, but when it is old and leathery only the fungus gnats appreciate it. A big clump was priced at 75 euros. It is rather uncommon in Britain and best left to spread its spores. There was, of course, a fungus display in the old town hall, following the format of identified species laid out on plates. Many familiar fruit bodies were on show, but the enviable range of lovely woodwaxes in this part of Italy seem to be becoming rarer in southern England. The common Blackening Brittlegill on display prompted one of the Chinese professors to mention a lethal lookalike (*Russula subnigricans*) that has been discovered in the Far East, which carries a previously unknown and deadly toxin that does horrible things to the blood and kidneys. I was reminded of my own confusion in Australia when I almost mistook the Ghost Fungus for the Oyster Mushroom. Fungi can play dangerous games of deception. Near Cuneo, we were to see a relative of the Ghost Fungus, the Jack o'Lantern, clustered at the base of a dead tree, but since it was coloured bright orange nobody was going to have it for supper.

Wednesday 6 October was an ideally warm and brilliant day for an excursion into the wooded foothills. We suspected that Gianfranco's influence had been at work to get us along the Via del Boleti, Venasca, into the private farm of Luigi Falco. Off the road, an old stone building was graced by fig trees; a vine-covered pergola lay at the other side of the yard. The owner greeted our disparate party with perfect good humour, in that particular Italian way where charm is unfeigned and genuinely concerned that everyone should have the best of all best possible times. Luigi farmed sweet chestnut trees in the groves above his house, but was well aware of 'organic' principles. These trees yield the chestnuts that seem so impossibly large and plump compared to those that grow in England, and the same that find their way to old-fashioned braziers in London streets around Christmas. These chestnut trees were mature, but not ancient. Ancient trees not only have girth, but acquire a curious spiralled pattern on the bark (some can be seen in Kensington Gardens near the Serpentine). Gentle terracing has modified the moderate slopes. Underneath the trees the scrub has been removed: this must be how many of our English woodlands were before the inroads of impenetrable brambles and nettles. The undergrowth has been burned in small piles, creating bald patches rich in charcoal. One of the farm labourers was at work when we arrived, bent over an old wooden tool with many tines, raking and clearing, in a process older than the trees themselves.

Fungi abounded. My notebook says: 'Every step revealed another species.' I cannot list them, but the sheer fungal profusion left us almost overwhelmed. Mushrooms and toad-stools of all kinds grew along the tracksides and underneath the trees. Cut stumps were bedecked with them. We were all familiar with chanterelles, but here were other species of *Cantharellus* that few of us had seen before. All the *Amanita* species of our own woodlands, and then others we did not readily recognise. Boletes on every side – our bolete expert rattled off names while we tried to remember them, but five minutes later that set of synapses in the brain had overloaded, to be replaced by milkcaps of a dozen kinds. The afternoon sun pointed up the cap colours, all as fresh as those in watercolours from the standard reference works – all too often the 'real thing' does not quite live up to its portrayal, but this afternoon bounteous reality topped artifice. It was enchanting, and the enchantment turned science into something almost ecstatic. Even that most difficult of all toadstool genera, the webcaps, obliged with species that we could recognise in the field, like *Cortinarius humicola* with curved-back scales along its stipe, and the inedible *C. purpurascens* that tries so hard to imitate the edible Wood Blewit. Sixteen species of brittlegills kept the *Russula* people happy. There were even three different kinds of a fungus that I hardly ever see in the south of England – so-called stipitate hydnoids, toughish fungi that have spines under the cap where mushrooms have gills. If I found a single one in Oxfordshire it would be worth a small celebration. The fire sites had a host of quite different species that loved charcoal and mosses, including ascos both brilliant scarlet and brown, and the Firesite Funnel black as the old coals it sat on. I could add to my list of fungal mysteries the question why so many fire site toadstools are nearly black, as if they do not wish to be spotted. I did not recognise the many kinds of coral fungi, or have time to look at the little brown mushrooms (LBMs). Even the common-or-garden earthball pulled a new trick, with *Scleroderma polyrhizum* turning into something like a stranded starfish as it matured to reveal its dark spore mass to the world.

All the while the sunshine caught flashes of light as insects flitted across the sunbeams. These fungus gnats and flies were all part of the vibrant woodland, and though they might imply the end of the mushrooms, they were welcome as guests to the biological feast. I am sure that the leaf litter swarmed with ground beetles. One of our number found among the moss a yellow and black salamander that would feed upon the beetles and any grubs it could find. Doubtless there would be small mammals like shrews waiting until the sun set – though we never spotted one. This was one interconnected system. Perfetto!

A species list is usually just a dull catalogue. By the time it is compiled the magic has evaporated. I do not know how many fungal species there were in Luigi's wood, but they must have totalled more than two hundred, even without the LBMs. Much has been written about biodiversity, but the fungi often seem to get relegated to a footnote. The biodiversity of Luigi's perfect wood was practically *all* fungi – and that is without adding the many more microscopic species that we walked past without noticing. Why, even the insects have a whole order of minute fungi (Laboubeniales – 'beetle hangers') that depend on them as hosts. When a species list becomes part of a measure of total biodiversity it also becomes animated into something of living importance. A good list can record the first appearance of invaders or the last of an ecologically sensitive soul. Lists contribute to our understanding of the effects of global climate change, or levels of pollution. There is nothing more annoying than fellow scientists comparing the hard work of compiling and storing lists on databases to stamp collecting. Skilled people who compile lists are the foot soldiers in a battle to keep our planet diverse. This book has visited just a few fungi for close encounters – ones that are interesting to me, or that illustrate something of the extraordinary versatility of the neglected kingdom. I opted for close examination rather than a panoramic overview. I have not even mentioned many extraordinary (or even ordinary) fungi because no book should rival the length of *A Suitable Boy*.

At the end of our afternoon on the chestnut slopes, a glowing sun dipping behind the hills dimmed our chances of finding anything. We returned to the farm where a simple supper of mushroom pastries made from chestnut flour was waiting for us under the pergola, with local wine to wash it down. There were figs as well – not the bloated purple variety, but little green ones from a nearby tree. No figs were ever more delicious. No fungal afternoon was ever more productive. Ottimo!

Acknowledgements

This book was never going to be written. Fungi had been my lifelong hobby rather than my profession, and I felt inhibited about writing about the kingdom when many others had been there before me. My editor, Arabella Pike, and my old friends (and agents) Heather and David Godwin persuaded me that my own take on my favourite living organisms might be worthwhile. I am so grateful to them for their confidence that this book could be successfully conceived and completed. As ever, I could not have written it without support and help from my wife, Jackie, who has joined me in countless forays over the years, handled the logistics of our field trips with exceptional aplomb, and scanned page proofs with acuity.

Many people have helped along the way. Marco Floriani was our generous host in Italy, and introduced us to new species. Professor Gareth Griffith put me in touch with Torben Fogh, who kindly led us to Strangler fungi in the Lake District and provided the photograph. My sister-in-law Caroline Lawrence generously hosted us in the Australian rainforest on several occasions, and showed us luminous brackets. Many of the Close Encounters were in the company of members of the Oxfordshire Fungus Survey, my long time foraying companions. Dr Aljos Farjon invited me on to the survey of Blenheim High Park. Dr Martyn Aynsworth and Alick Henrici from Kew Gardens have supplied me with identifications of tricky species over many years. Their expertise was invaluable. I thank Professor Lynne Boddy for wise advice on matters of mycorrhiza and wood rotting. Dr Sarah Watkinson helped me with the basics of the chemical armoury of the fungal kind. Without the incomparable expertise of Peter Chandler there would have been no chapter on fungus gnats. My former colleagues at the Natural History Museum identified the many beetles associated with fungi. I thank especially Roger Booth, Max Barclay and Michael Geiser. Mike Richardson shared his lifetime experience with dung fungi, and Derek Shafer identified the appropriate inkcaps. My old friend Stuart Skeates kindly read through the manuscript and spotted errors. I need hardly add that any errors that remain are entirely my responsibility.

Photographic figures came from many sources, and I could not include as many illustrations as I would have liked. All are thanked. Linda Seward provided several pictures from our local area in Oxfordshire. Geraldine Gates and Joseph Neilson supplied pictures of fungi from 'down under'. Paul Kenrick kindly allowed me to use his sketch of Prototaxites, and Huen-ping Hsueh the oyster mushroom worm killers. Other photographs were generously supplied by Andrew Padmore, Penny Cullington, Rob Francis, Stuart Skeates, Aljos Farjon and Derek Schafer. All other photographs were taken by Jackie Fortey over several years among the fruit bodies.

Index

Ainsworth, Martyn, 231, 233, 235
Angel's Bonnet (*Mycena
arcangeliana*), 242
Aniseed Funnel (*Clitocybe odora*),
57–8, 62
anthropomorphism, 94–7, 108
Antrodia albida, 45–6
Arched Earthstar (*Geastrum f
ornicatum*)., 131–2, 134
Armando, Gianfranco, 315, 316
Arnolds, Eef, 308
Arora, David, 115, 264
Artusi, Pellegrino, 10
Ascobolus hawaiiensis, 256
Ascofrance website, 181*
Ascomycetes ('ascos'), 31–5, *33*,
166*, 175, 180, *189*, 244, 271*,
318; 'discos', 31, 32, 178–82, 183,
194–5, 200, 255–7, 259, 278;
'pyrenos', 32, 185–8, 187*, 190–2,
196–7; reproductive structures,
31–4, 69, 98–9, 100 *see also* truffles

Australia, 64–70, 74–6, 101–2, 116,
117, 156–7, 310, 316

badgers, 100–1
Barclay, Max, 290
Bark Bonnet (*Phloeomana speirea*),
198, 242–3
Basidiomycetes ('basidios'), *31*, 31–3,
40, 46, 67, 117–20, 125, 270–2,
295–6; and 'anamorph' phase,
192*, 192–3; Clavarioids ('corals'),
22, 30–1, 220, 222, 224, 318; jelly
fungi, 183–5, 311–12; phalloids,
59, 80, 83, 87, 109–14, 117–18,
149–57, 158; and truffles, 101,
107, 108
Basque country, 53
bats, 66, 229, 231, 265
Beech Barkspot (*Diatrype disciformis*),
187
beech trees, 5, 17, 81–2, 105–6, 209,
233, 248, 251, 305, 308–9; bark
of, 39, 187; rotting/decay of dead

wood, 42, 187, 279–80, 299–300;
and toxic fungi, 13, 56–7, 245–6;
webcaps associated with, 306,
310 *see also* Grim's Dyke Wood
(author's beech woodland,
Chiltern Hills)

Beech Woodwart (*Hypoxylon fragiforme*), 187

Beechleaf Bonnet (*Mycena capillaris*),
314

Beechwood Sickener (*Russula
nobilis*), 85

Beefsteak Fungus (*Fistulina hepatica*),
236–8

beetles, 42, 45, 152, 196, 250, 290,
296–300, 319

Berkeley, Miles J., 141, 152

Berkshire Downs, 284

biodiversity, 66, 137, 221, 224, 225–6,
308, 319

Birch Polypore (aka Razor Strop
Fungus) (*Fomitopsis betulina*), 232–3

bird's nest fungi, 134–5, 259

Bitter Bolete (*Tylopilus felleus*), 9, 11

Black Morel (*Morchella elata*), 174–5

Black Truffle (*Tuber melanosporum*),
12, 101, 102, 103, 105

Blackening Brittlegill (*Russula nigricans*), 82, 84, 85, 163, 240, 241

Blackening Waxcap (*Hygrocybe
conica*), 219, 225

Blackfoot Polypore (*Cerioporus
varius*), 233

Bleeding Porecrust (*Physisporinus
sanguinolentus*), 296

Blenheim High Park, 228–33, 235–46

Blistered Cup (*Peziza vesiculosa*), 179

Bloodred Webcap (*Cortinarius
sanguineus*), 89, 303

Blueleg Brownie (*Psilocybe
cyanescens*), 283–4

Blusher (*Amanita rubescens*), 289–90

Blyford Church (Suffolk), 110–11

boar, wild (*sanglier*), 102

Boddy, Lynne, 274

Boertmann, David, 220

Bolete Eater (*Hypomyces chrysospermus*), 165

Boletus, 7–11, 14–17, 21–2, 30, 108,
267, 317; in Britain, 8, 9, 10,
14–15, 82, 83, 84, 164–7, 209,
211–12, 245–6; mycorrhizal relationship with trees, 5, 16–17,
35–6, 83–4, 91, 97, 209; structural
distinction from *Agaricus*, 6–7,
21–2, 83 *see also* porcini

Bolton, James, 140

Booth, Roger, 290, 298, 300

Box Crust (*Peniophora proxima*), 129

Box Hill (Surrey), 126

brackets/polypores, 22, 30, 67, 166,
232–5, 236–9, 305; insects feeding
on, 293, 294, 295, 299–300;
rotters, 40–2, 44, 74–5, 232–5,
236–9, 271, 272, 273–4, 275–6

Bresadola, Giacomo, 141

Brighton, 196–7

Britain: *Amanita* species in, 87–8;
ancient oaks in, 228–45; boletes
in, 8, 9, 10, 14–15, 82, 83, 84,
164–7, 209, 211–12, 245–6; fungi
migrated from elsewhere, 67*,
67–8, 116–17, 193–6, 310; grassland fungi in, 216–27; as
important redoubt for waxcaps,
223–7; knights (*Tricholoma*) in, 88;
luminous fungi in, 76, 78; native
truffles, 105–8; parasitic fungi in,

160–71; phalloid fungi in, 152, 154–5, 156; Sandy Stiltball in, 110–12, 113–14; Shaggy Inkcap in, 115–16; surviving open woodland in, 126–9, 228–33; webcaps in, 89–90, 306, 310

British Puffballs and Earthstars (Royal Botanic Gardens, 1995), 131

Brittle Cinder Fungus (*Kretzschmaria deusta*), 271*

Bronze Bolete (*Boletus aereus*), 7–8

Brown Birch Bolete (*Leccinum scabrum*), 82

Brown Mottlegill (*Panaeolus foenisecii*), 282

Buchwaldoboletus lignicola, 165–6

Buller, Arthur Henry Reginald, 31

burdock (*Arctium*), 199–200, 202

Burgundy Bonnet (*Mycena haematopus*), 242

Burnham Beeches, 16

Cabbage Parachute (*Gymnopus brassicolens*), 60

Caesar's Mushroom (*Amanita caesarea*), 12, 13

Calocera cornea, 311

Candlesnuff Fungus (*Xylaria hypoxylon*), 31, 260–1

Cantharellus melanoxeros, 213

Castaneda, Carlos, 285

caterpillars, 68–70, 72

Cauliflower Fungus (*Sparassis crispa*), 241

Cenococcum geophilum, 98–9

Cetto, Bruno, 315

Chandler, Peter, 291, 292–3, 295, 296

Chanterelle (*Cantharellus cibarius*), 77, 212–13, 308, 309, 317

Chaucer, Geoffrey, 229

CHEGD ('chegged') species., 221–7

Chicken of the Woods (Sulphur Polypore) (*Laetiporus sulphureus*), 40–2, 44, 299

Chiltern Hills, 16, 111–12, 126–9, 172–3, 193, 193–4, 247–9, 279 *see also* also Grim's Dyke Wood (author's beech woodland, Chiltern Hills)

China, 71–3, 153, 156–7, 185, 265, 306, 316

Claudius (Roman emperor), 12

Cloud Ear Fungus (*Auricularia cornea*), 185

Clouded Funnel (*Clitocybe nebularis*), 27, 159–60, 161–2

Club Foot Funnel (*Ampulloclitocybe clavipes*), 147

Clustered Brittlestem (*Britzelmayria multipedata*), 243

Cockley Cley church (Norfolk), 132

Collared Earthstar (*Geastrum triplex*), 127–8

Collins, Alfred, 105–6

Collins Guide to British Fungi (1961/63), 144, 161, 240

Colonsay (Scottish island), 223

colour of fungi, 84–5, 303–5

Common Bird's Nest (*Crucibulum laeve*), 134–5

Common Bonnet (*Mycena galericulata*), 44

Common Mazegill (*Podofomes mollis*) (*Datronia mollis*), 46–7, 299

Common Puffball (*Lycoperdon perlatum*), 119–20, 122–3

Common Stinkhorn (*Phallus impudicus*), 149–52

Common Tarcrust (*Diatrype stigma*), 187

Cooke, M.C., 52–3

Coprinellus pusillulus, 254

Coprinopsis pseudonivea, 259

Coprinopsis radiata, 254

coprophilous (dung-loving) fungi, 179, 249–51, 253–5, 256–62; *Ascobolus*, 255–7; Spore Shooter (*Pilobolus*), 251–3, 255, 256

Coral Tooth Fungus (*Hericium coralloides*), 67

Cordyceps gunnii, 69–70, 72

Corpse Lily (*Rafflesia*), 157–8

Cortinarius armillatus, 89

Cortinarius bergeroni, 89–90

Cortinarius elegantissimus, 89–90

Cortinarius humicola, 317–18

Cortinarius purpurascens, 318

Cortinarius violaceus, 89

coumarin, 58–9

COVID-19 pandemic, 247, 255, 265, 290

Cowpat Gem (*Cheilymenia granulata*), 255

Crimped Gill (*Plicaturopsis crispa*), 42–3

Croatia, 104

crust fungi, 22, 30–1, 40, 42, 44, 200

Cucumber Cap (*Macrocystidia cucumis*), 59–60

Cultivated (supermarket) mushroom (*Agaricus bisporus*), 6–7, 20–1, 26, 49–50, 114, 205–7

Curry Milkcap (*Lactarius camphoratus*), 59

Czech Republic, 15

Czechoslovakia, 246

Dark Bolete (*Boletus aereus*), 209

Dawkins, Richard, 285

Death Cap (*Amanita phalloides*), 12–13, 87, 167, 239, 303, 304

Deceiver (*Laccaria laccata*), 98

deer, 100, 230–1, 248–9, 254, 258

Deer Shield (*Pluteus cervinus*), 305

Denmark, 202

Desert Mushroom (*Agaricus deserticola*), 114–15, 117, 118

Desert Shaggy Mane (*Podaxis pistillaris*), 115–19

Destroying Angel (*Amanita virosa*), 87, 303

Devil's Bolete (*Rubroboletus satanas*), 245–6

Devil's Fingers or Octopus Stinkhorn (*Clathrus archeri*), 116–17, 155–6, 158

Dewdrop Bonnet (*Hemimycena tortuosa*), 198–9

Dissoderma pearsonii, 170–1

Dog Stinkhorn (*Mutinus caninus*), 153

Drechmeria gunnii, 70, 71

dry rot, 263–7, 275

Dry Rot Fungus (*Serpula lacrymans*), 263–7, 275

dung, 179, 247–62

Dung Bird's Nest fungus (*Cyathus stercoreus*), 259

Dung Inkcap (*Coprinopsis stercorea*), 253–4

Dung Roundhead (*Protostropharia semiglobata*), 259

Dyer's Mazegill (*Phaeolus schweinitzii*), 166

Earthy Powdercap (*Cystoderma amianthinum*), 168, 170–1
ecological succession theory, 251
ecology/environmental issues, 301; climate change/global warming, 13, 43, 51, 103, 214–15, 227, 319; pollution, 43, 87, 148, 223, 225–7, 308, 319; Protected Geographical Indication (PGI) status, 11; 'rewilding', 218, 251; Sites of Special Scientific Interest (SSSI), 16, 212
edible fungi, 205–16; caution over eating brittlegills, 85; chanterelles (*Pfifferlinge*), 77, 212–13, 308, 309, 317; confusion over False Morels, 176–8; culinary uses of phalloids, 153, 156–7; Cultivated (supermarket) mushroom, 6–7, 20–1, 26, 49–50, 114, 205–7; eating of Beefsteak Fungus, 237–8; Fairy Ring (or Champignon), 27–8, 60; Field Mushrooms, 21, 30, 49–50, 62, 147, 207–8, 217, 259; Hen of the Woods, 315; Horse Mushroom (*Agaricus arvensis*), 62; Jelly Ear, 184–5; milkcaps, 15, 59, 85–7, 88, 97, 107, 163*, 240, 260; Millers, 53–5; morels (*Morchella*), 31, 32, 172–6, 176; mushroom-porcini distinction, 6–7, 21–2, 83; *ovolo*, 12–13; Oyster Mushrooms, 75, 77, 80, 206–7, 272–3, 277, 278, 294, 295, 298–9, 316; Parasol Mushrooms, 23, 60, 208–9; Portobello Mushrooms, 206–7; preference for baby Ceps, 4, 209–10; Rooting Shank, 143–5, 243; in rotting/

decaying wood, 40–2; Shiitake (*Lentinula edodes*), 207; St George's Mushroom (*Calocybe gambosa*), 51–3, 55, 62; to pick or not to pick question, 307–9; young Giant Puffball, 121–2 *see also Boletus; porcini*
Ellis, Martin and Pam, 188
Epping Forest, 16, 233
evolutionary science, 117–20, 141, 142–3, 158, 160, 166–7, 266, 271, 296; 'adaptationist paradigm', 305; convergent evolution, 76; and hierarchical view of fungal complexity, 175; mystery origins of fungi species, 309–12; 'parallel evolution' in fungi, 116, 177–8; processes of natural selection, 71, 79, 119, 125, 157, 195–6, 303, 304; and truffles, 101, 102, 108
Eyelash Cup (*Scutellinia scutellata*), 182

Fairy Ring (or Champignon) (*Marasmius oreades*), 27–8, 60
fairy rings, 26–8, 52, 60, 81, 87, 159–60, 161, 162–3, 170, 208, 243
Falco, Luigi, 316–20
False Death Cap (*Amanita citrina*), 55–7, 87, 147, 239, 241, 293
False Morel (*Gyromitra esculenta*), 176–8
False Truffle (*Elaphomyces muricatus*), 99–101
Farjon, Aljos, 230–2
Fenugreek Stalkball (*Phleogena faginea*), 58–9

Field, Katie, 97

Field Bird's Nest (*Cyathus olla*), 134

Field Mushroom (*Agaricus campestris*), 21, 30, 49–50, 62, 147, 207–8, 217, 259

Fiery Milkcap (*Lactarius pyrogalus*), 86

Finland, 87, 177

Firesite Funnel, 318

First World War, 77

Flame Shield (*Plutcus aurantiorugosus*), 305

flies: as distributors of spores, 150–1, 152, 153, 156, 157, 158, 250; drawn to stinkhorns, 80, 150–1, 152, 153, 155, 156; eating of fungi, 50, 289–95, 298–9; fungus gnats, 210, 291, 292–4, 295–6, 298–9, 300, 315, 318; maggots, 50, 187, 209, 210, 250, 289–90, 291, 294; and poisonous fungi, 304; as pollination agents, 157–8; and truffles, 106

Flirt (*Russula vesca*), 146

Floriani, Marco, 11, 305–6

Fly Agaric (*Amanita muscaria*), 57, 82, 87, 98, 140, 239, 303

Fogh, Torben, 169–71

Fool's Funnel (*Clitocybe rivulosa*), 27–8

Forestry Commission, 212

forests/woodland: Australian rainforest, 64–70, 74–6, 101–2; in Borgo Val di Taro, 5–6, 16–17; in Britain, 14–16, 27, 67, 69, 106, 126–9, 211–12, 228–33, 235–46, 259–62, 307–8; of Oregon, 24–5; protected by SSSI status, 16, 212;

'wood wide web' in, 95–7, 98 *see also* also Grim's Dyke Wood (author's beech woodland, Chiltern Hills)

fossils, 32–5

Fragrant Funnel (*Clitocybe fragrans*), 58

France, 10, 85, 101, 102, 110, 141, 173, 195, 212

Fries, Elias Magnus, 61, 98, 139, 140–2, 254

Fungae Europeae (multi-volume series), 203

fungi, structures of: asci, 31–2, 69, 100, 177–8, 186, 187*, 190–4, 244, 255–8, 260–1, 271, 318; basidium, 30–1, 33, 40, 46, 67, 117, 119, 124, 156, 192–3, 199; cleft cup (*volva*), 12, 88, 109, 141, 161, 175*, 240, 279–80; *gleba*, 119, 124, 150–1, 153, 157, 303; *hyphae*, 17, 23, 25–6, 33, 44, 92, 100, 118–19, 163–4, 237, 265, 273, 276, 277 *see also* mycelium

fungi genera: Amanita, 12–13, 55–6, 87–8, 97, 167–8, 175*, 239–40, 303, 317; Antrodia, 45–8; Ascobolus, 255–7; 'bonnets' (*Mycena*), 44, 57, 60, 67, 83, 198–9, 242–4; brittlegills (*Russula*), 59, 82, 84–5, 88, 97, 98, 163, 172, 240, 295, 303–4, 306, 310, 316, 318; brittlestems (*Psathyrella*), 83, 243; *Cantharellus*, 77, 212–13, 308, 309, 317; *Ceriporiopsis*, 202; *Clathrus*, 18–19, 154–6, 158; *Cordyceps*, 69–73, 265; cup fungi (*Peziza*), 31, 32, 179; dapperlings (*Lepiota*), 60, 243,

306–7; *Dermoloma*, 222; *Dissoderma* (formerly *Squamanita*), 167–71; Ear fungi (*Otidea*), 179–80; Earth Tongues (*Geoglossum*), 222; earthballs (*Scleroderma*), 100, 117–18, 123–6, 164–5, 318; earthstars (*Geastrum*), 117–18, 127–33, 134; *Favolaschia*, 67; fibrecaps (*Inocybe*), 62, 90–1, 97; funnels (*Clitocybe*), 27–8, 57–8, 62, 81, 83, 147, 159–60, 161–3, 243, 318; *Ganoderma*, 22; *Glonium*, 99; *Hapalopilus*, 203–4; inkcaps (*Coprinopsis*), 22, *31*, 83, 115–16, 254, 259, 307; knights (*Tricholoma*), 41, 51, 63, 88, 97, 243; milkcaps (*Lactarius*, *Lactifluus*), 15, 59, 85–7, 88, 97, 107, 163*, 240, 260; morels (*Morchella*), 31, 32, 172–6; *Musumecia*, 306; *Omphalotus*, 74–7, 79–80; pinkgills (*Entoloma*), 55, 67, 217–18, 220–1, 222; *Psilocybe*, 281–8; shields (*Pluteus*), 278, 305, 306; Spore Shooter (*Pilobolus*), 251–4, 255, 256; *Sporormiella*, 257–8; stinkhorn (*Phallus*), 59, 80, 83, 113, 117–18, 149–54, 155–6, 158, 276, 303; *Thelobolus*, 256–7; toughshanks (*Gymnopus*), 83, 243; waxcaps (*Hygrocybe*), 61, 146, 170, 218–20, 221–7; webcaps (*Cortinarius*), 88–90, 97, 98, 303, 306, 310, 317–18; woodwax (*Hygrophorus*), 308–9, 315–16
fungus hunting/foraging, 2–3, 5, 14–16, 209–15, 307*, 307–8, 313–20

fungus identification in the field: development of quick recognition, 242–3; experts' use of taste for, 85; illustrated guides, 19–20, 20*, 131, 133, 139–40, 143–4, 160, 161, *189*, 190–1, 240, 279; 'lookalikes' confusing the unwary, 9, 54–6, 75–7, 85, 87; Moser's handbook, 11; protocol for, 28; smells used for, 28, 49, 50–1, 52, 56–60, 61–3, 85, 88, 89; subtleties of, 8; tasting of milk, 86–7
Fungus Survey of Oxfordshire, 231

Geastrum britannicum, 132–3
Geiser, Michael, 290
geographical distribution of fungi, 87–8, 98, 109–17, 122, 158, 266–7, 309–12; migration, 67*, 67–8, 116–17, 193–6, 310
geological time, 32–6, 158
Geranium Brittlegill (*Russula fellea*), 85
Ghost Fungus (*Omphalotus nidiformis*), 74–6, 79–80, 316
Ghost Moth, 69–70, 73
Giant Puffball (*Calvatia gigantea*), 120–2, 159
Golden Waxcap (*Hygrocybe chlorophana*), 170, 219
grassland fungi, 216–21; in waxcap grassland, 221–7
graveyards/churchyards, 41, 110–11, 120, 130, 132, 216–19, 220, 224–7, 234–5, 308
Greys Court (Oxfordshire manor house), 199–202, 216, 238
Griffiths, Gareth, 169

Grim's Dyke Wood (author's beech woodland, Chiltern Hills): ash trees in, 193; in autumn, 54, 81–3; *Clitopilus cystidiatus* found in, 54–5; feeders in, 299–300; hazels in, 107–8, 187; mycorrhizal fungi in, 85, 91–2, 94, 99–101, 310; Oyster Mushrooms in, 75; 'pyrenos' in, 187; rotting logs / wood in, 37–48, 269–71, 274–5, 295–6, 299–300

Haeckel, Ernst, 188
Hairsfoor Inkcap (*Coprinopis lagopus*), 31
Hairy Curtain Crust (*Stereum hirsutum*), 42, 276, 299–300
Hambleden (Buckinghamshire), 112
Hapalopilus eupatorii, 200–4
Harcourt Arboretum, Oxford University (Nuneham Courtenay), 124, 135, 310
Hare's Ear (*Otidea onotica*), 180
Hawaii, 116, 117, 256
Hawksworth, David, 19
Hedgehog Mushroom (*Hydnum repandum*), 213–14
hemp agrimony (*Eupatoria*), 203, 204
Hen of the Woods (*Grifola frondosa*), 315
Henley-on-Thames (Oxfordshire), 106, 111–12, 225, 238, 261–2
Henrici, Alick, 55
Hobart, Caroline, 106–7, 108
Holden, Elizabeth, 146
Honey Fungus (*Armillaria mellea*), 78–9
Honey Fungus (*Armillaria ostoyae*), 24–5

Horn of Plenty (*Craterellus cornucopioides*), 214
Horse Mushroom (*Agaricus arvensis*), 62
Hoskin, Cyril (Lobsang Rampa), 285*
huntsman spiders, 66
Huxley, Aldous, *The Doors of Perception* (1954), 285
Hygrocybe aurantiosplendens, 220
Hygrocybe reidii, 61
Hypoxylon fusca, 187

Imperial College London, 286, 288
Ing, Bruce, 311, 312
Ingold, Terence, 30
insects, 222, 319; anthills, 126, 248, 250; beetles associated with fungi, 196, 296–300; carpenter ants, 70–1; declining numbers in Britain, 226; as distributors of spores, 79–80, 150–1, 152, 153, 156, 157, 158, 250; eating of fungi by, 50, 289–301; eggs laid on fruit bodies, 50; as prey of fungal parasites, 68–73 *see also* flies
Isle of Wight, 13, 154, 213, 227
Italy, 76, 141, 154, 305–6, 314–20; Borgo Val di Taro (Emilia-Romagna), 1–10, 11–12, 16–17, 210, 231–2, 308; truffles in, 101, 102, 103–5
Ivory Waxcap (*Cuphophyllus virgineus*), 219, 225

Jack o'Lantern (*Omphalotus illudens*), 76–7, 316
James, Peter, 179

Japanese knotweed, 202–3, 204
Jelly Ear (*Auricularia auricula-judae*), 184–5
jelly fungi, 183–5, 311–12
Johns Hopkins University, 288
Junius, Hadrianus, 152–3

Karst, Judith, 96–7
Karsten, Petter Adolf, 203, 204
Kenrick, Paul, 35
Kensington Gardens, 317
Kew Gardens, 54–5, 111–12, 132, 201, 230, 231, 311
Kibby, Geoffrey, 20*, 89–90, 90*, 136
Kissinger, Henry, 157

Laboubeniales ('beetle hangers'), 319
Lactarius torminosus, 86–7
Laessoe, Thomas, 20*, 136
Lake District, 169–71, 223
Lange, J.E., 144, 175*
Laos, 272
The Last of Us (television series), 71
Lawrence, Caroline, 66–7, 68, 75–6
Leary, Timothy, 286
Legon, Nick, 201
Lemon Disco (*Bisporella citrina*), 181
Lentinellus cochleatus, 58
lichen, 36, 178–9
Lilac Bonnet (*Mycena pura*), 57
Lilac Pinkgill (*Entoloma porphyrophaeum*), 220–1
Linnaeus, Carl, 117, 139, 140–1, 147, 261
Livid Pinkgill (*Entoloma sinuatum*), 55
Lovecraft, H.P., 78, 154

luminous fungi, 74–80, 303
Lumpy Bracket (*Trametes gibbosa*), 294

Magic Mushroom (Liberty Cap) (*Psilocybe semilanceata*), 281–3
Maharajah's Well (Stoke Row, Oxfordshire), 221
Mahler, Neil, 133–4
Marren, Peter, 245–6
Maui, Hawaiian island of, 116, 117
Meadow Coral (*Clavulinopsis corniculata*), 220
medicine, traditional, 72–3, 153, 156–7, 272
Meigen, Johann Wilhelm, 296
Meitennen, O., 203
Melanogaster ambiguus, 107–8
Mexico, 312
mice, 44, 45
microfungi, 19, 23, 31–2, 91, 194–5, 195*, 196–7, 249–62, 310
Miller (*Clitopilus cystidiatus*), 54–5
Miller (*Clitopilus prunulus*), 53–4
molecular/DNA sequencing, 8, 19, 29, 116, 118, 144–5, 178, 203, 241, 276; and concept of a fungus *individual*, 24; of Dry Rot Fungus, 267; of earthballs, 125; of earthstars, 132; of forest soils, 306; of morels, 177–8; of nutrient-poor grassland, 222; of parasitic fungi, 168–9; of roots, 244; of truffles, 99, 108; of webcaps, 90†, 90
Money, Nicholas, 21, 30
Moody, Lilian, 105–6
Moser, Meinhard, 11, 167
moths, 69–70, 72, 73, 197, 294

mushrooms (*Agaricus*): Agaricaceae family, 20–1; derivation of word 'agaric', 21; distinction from porcini (*Boletus*), 6–7, 21, 83; distinction from toadstools, 20–1; little brown mushrooms (LBMs), 88, 91, 318, 319; psychedelic, 281–8 *see also* edible fungi
mutualism, 23, 33, 92, 100
mycelium, 6, 16–17, 22–8, 82, 100, 118–19, 148, 170, 243; of the anamorph, 192; of brown rotters, 236–8; of CHEGD species, 222; of coprophilous fungi, 250, 252, 260–1; cultivated, 206; and DNA identification techniques, 24, 241, 244, 306; *ecto*mycorrhiza, 91–3, 94; of funnels, 159–60; *gleba*, 119, 124, 150–1, 153, 157, 303; luminous, 77–80; and mushroom picking technique, 14, 23; of parasitic fungi, 69, 70, 162–3, 165; of *Psilocybe* fungi, 284; in rotting/decaying wood, 38, 39–40, 44, 46, 96, 143, 264, 265, 266, 267–79; *sclerotia*, 99; species associated with oak roots, 244–5; of stinkhorn, 151, 152
Mycena leptocephala, 60
mycology: author's 'new species', 200–4; Blenheim survey, 231–3, 235–45; British Mycological Society, 245–6, 314–20; British webcap expertise, 89–90; compiling/storing of species lists, 319; hierarchical views of fungal complexity, 175*, 175; history of science of, 139–41; Kew Gardens' mycological repository, 111–12,

132; Moser as twentieth-century leader, 11; mysteries/puzzles, 34–6, 79–80, 171, 302–12; nineteenth-century pioneers, 8, 29; and 'wood wide web', 95–7; work of Tulasne brothers, 29, 189, 189–91, 193 *see also* taxonomy/naming/classification
mycorrhizal fungi (collaborators): and Blenheim survey, 235, 236, 239, 244–5; boletes, 5, 16–17, 35–6, 83–4, 91, 97, 209; complex biochemistry of, 92–3; *ecto*mycorrhiza, 91–3, 94, 99–101, 108, 244–5, 306, 308; in Grim's Dyke Wood, 85, 91–2, 94, 99–101; mutually beneficial partnerships, 23, 83, 91, 92; mycorrhizal process, 94–7; and parasitic fungi, 163–4; puffball pretenders, 124–6; species favouring same kind of tree, 83–4, 310–11; survival strategies, 97–9; types of, 83–91; in waxcap grassland, 222 *see also* truffles

Nail Fungus (*Poronia punctata*), 260–2
Nascia, Caro, 10
National Trust, 193–4, 199, 223, 238
Natural England, 212
Natural History Museum, London, 18, 137, 141, 179, 246, 290, 298
nematodes, 277, *278*
Neottiella rutilans, 33
Netherlands, 133, 152–3, 193, 223–4, 230, 308
Nettle Rash (*Leptosphaeria acuta*), 187

INDEX

New Forest, 14–15, 16, 27, 67, 69, 211–12, 240, 259–62, 311

New Zealand, 116–17, 156

Newfoundland, 36, 212, 232

nitrogen, 60, 92–3, 121, 159, 179, 218, 222, 225–6, 250, 259, 277, 308

Norfolk, 132, 133, 152, 193

Norway, 201–2, 311

Nutt, David, 286

Oak Goblet (*Ciboria batschiana*), 244

Oak Mazegill (*Daedalea quercina*), 238–9

Oak Polypore (*Buglossoporus quercinus*), 232–5, 239

oak trees, 59, 76, 87, 230, 251, 269–71, 305, 315; ancient oaks, 228–45; Blenheim survey, 231–3, 235–45; boletes under, 8, 84, 209; 'stag's horns' in, 229, 230; and truffles, 102, 104, 108

Ochre Brittlegill (*Russula ochroleuca*), 85

Omphalotus olearius, 76

Ophiocordyceps sinensis, 72–3

Orange Grisette (*Amanita crocea*), 303

Orange Peel Fungus (*Aleuria aurantia*), 180, 181

orchids, 224, 248

Orledge, Glenda, 300

Oudemans, Cornelius Anton Jan Abraham, 144

Oyster Mushroom (*Pleurotus ostreatus*), 75, 77, 80, 206–7, 272–3, 277, 278, 294, 295, 298–9, 316

Pale Stagshorn (*Calocera pallidospathulata*), 311–12

Parasitic Bolete (*Pseudoboletus parasiticus*), 165

parasitic fungi, 68–73, 160–7, 184; stranglers, 167–71

Parasol Mushroom (*Macrolepiota procera*), 23, 60, 208–9

Parasola misera, 254

Parrot Waxcap (*Gliophorus psittacinus*), 170, 219, 225

pathogens, 69, 110, 172, 193–7, 235, 271*

Peak District, 281

Pearson, A.A., 246

Pepper Pot (*Myriostoma coliforme*), 133–4

Persoon, Christian Henrik, 141, 177

Pestle Puffballs (*Handkea excipuliformis*), 224–5

Petersen, Jens, 20*, 136

Peziza domiciliana, 179

phalloids, 59, 80, 83, 87, 109–14, 117–18, 149–57, 158

Phallus indusiatus, 156–7

Phillips, Roger, 20*, 131, 133, 144

Piggyback Rosegill (*Volvariella surrecta*), 160–3

pin mould (Mucorales), 23, 253–4

Pine Bolete (*Boletus pinophilus*), 8

Pink Oakleaf Bonnet (*Mycena smithiana*), 243–4

Pink Waxcap / Ballerina (*Porpolomopsis calyptriformis*), 146, 221

Platoni, Flaminio, 9–10

Pliny the Elder, 210

poisonous fungi, 18, 20, 55, 57, 89, 125–6, 304; Death Cap (*Amanita phalloides*), 12–13, 87, 167, 239, 303, 304; Destroying Angel (*Amanita virosa*), 87, 303; Devil's Bolete (*Rubroboletus satanas*), 245–6; the False Morel, 176–8; Fly Agaric (*Amanita muscaria*), 57, 82, 87, 98, 140, 239, 303; Fool's Funnel (*Clitocybe rivulosa*), 27–8; Ghost Fungus (*Omphalotus nidiformis*), 74–6, 79–80, 316; Jack o'Lantern (*Omphalotus illudens*), 76–7, 316; *Russula subnigricans*, 316

Poland, 15, 177

porcini, 2–12, 14–17, 125, 308, 315; ancient preference for, 9–10, 17, 210; *Boletus edulis* (Cep/Cèpe), 7, 9, 10–11, 14–15, 83; gastronomic preference for baby Ceps, 4, 209–10; mycorrhizal relationship with trees, 5, 16–17, 35–6, 83–4, 97, 209; as Penny Buns in Britain, 10, 83, 209, 210; structural distinction from *Agaricus*, 6–7, 21–2, 83; survival/abundance of, 4–6, 9–10, 16–17, 210–11

Potter, Beatrix, 29

Powdercap Strangler (*Dissoderma paradoxum*), 168–71

Powdery Piggyback (*Asterophora lycoperdioides*), 163–4

Prototaxites (Devonian fossil), 34–6, 35

psilocybin, 281–8

puffballs, 22, 30, 58–9, 81, 83, 117–23, 141, 159, 224–5, 243; and bird's nest fungi, 134–5; and

earthballs, 100, 117–18, 123–6, 164–5, 318; and earthstars (*Geastrum*), 117–18, 127–33, 134; fruit bodies of, 118–19, 121, 123, 127–33; Grey or Brown Puffballs (*Bovista*), 122; and the Pepper Pot, 133–4; puffball pretenders, 123–6; and Sandy Stiltball, 109–14, 117, 306

Pyrenopeziza arctii, 200

Quélet, Lucien, 141

rabbits, 27, 218, 248–50, 254, 255–7, 258, 259

Rackham, Arthur, 229

Rackham, Oliver, 229

Ramsbottom, John, 77, 105, 109, 154–5, 160–1, 173, 246, 279

Ranuccio I (Farnese duke of Parma), 9–10

Rayed Earthstar (*Geastrum quadrifidum*), 131, 132

Red Cage Fungus (*Clathrus ruber*), 18–19, 154–5

Redlead Roundhead (*Leratiomyces ceres*), 310

Reid, Derek, 311

reproduction: 'anamorph' phase, 189, 191–3; in autumn, 81–3; of Beefsteak Fungus, 237–8; Boletus-Agaric distinction, 6–7, 21–2, 83; central spore 'factory' (*gleba*), 119, 124, 150–1, 153, 157, 303; construction of fruit bodies, 23; of coprophilous fungi, 250, 251–4, 255–8, 260–1; development of fruit bodies, 26; division between ascos and basidios,

29–33; of Earthstars, 127–31; flies as distributors of spores, 150–1, 152, 153, 156, 158, 250; fruit body of *Cenococcum*, 98–9; 'fruit body' term, 22; germination and growth, 25–6, 29–30; low feritility rate, 25, 121, 148; of morels, 176; mouth in fruit body (*ostiole*), 119, 127, 188, 257; number of spores, 25, 26, 120–1, 239, 304, 305; opening of fruit body cap, 26; of parasitic fungi, 162, 163–4; poroid fruit bodies, 200–2; raising of fruit body cup, 177–8; release of ascospores, 180; secotioid fungi, 114–15; small mammals carrying spores, 44; spore release, 25, 26, 30–2, 117–21, 124, 127–8, 133, 134–5, 148, 180, 183–4, 186, 188, 304, 305; of truffles, 101–2 *see also* Ascomycetes ('ascos'); Basidiomycetes ('basidios')

Revett, Jonathon, 132

Rhynie Chert (Scottish silica deposit), 32–3

Richardson, Mike, 249, 251

Roberts, Peter, 20*

Rooting Bolete (*Caloboletus radicans*), 84

Rooting Shank (*Hymenopellis radicata*), 143–5, 243

Rossano mushroom festival, 315

Rosy Brittlegill (*Russula lepida*), 303–4

rotters, 45–8, 263–7, 269–79; brackets/polypores, 40–2, 44, 74–5, 232–5, 236–9, 271, 272, 273–4, 275–6; brown rotters (BRF), 46–8, 236–9, 267–9, 271, 273; chemistry of, 268*, 268; in Grim's Dyke Wood, 37–48, 269–71, 274–5; white rotters (white rot fungi), 269–71, 272–3, 277, 278 *see also* saprotrophic fungi (recyclers)

rotting/decaying wood, 38–48, 74–8, 83, 179, 181, 185–7, 198, 202, 207, 234–5, 242, 267–79; and basidios, 40, 46, 67, 120, 270–2, 295–6; beech trees, 42, 187, 279–80, 299–300; dry rot, 263–7, 275; mycelium in, 38, 39–40, 44, 46, 96, 143, 267–79; and saprotrophic fungi, 40, 111, 269–79, 312, 314

Russula subnigricans, 316

Ryvarden, Leif, 201–2, 203

Saarbrücken, 213, 308

Sagan, Carl, 240

Sand Stinkhorn (*Phallus hadriani*), 152–3

Sandalwood Waxcap (*Cuphophyllus russocoriaceus*), 219–20

Sandy Stiltball (*Battarrea phalloides*), 109–14, 117, 306

saprotrophic fungi (recyclers), 22–3, 25, 27, 83, 129, 157, 159–60, 179, 181; and Blenheim survey, 235–6, 243; cultivated, 207; and fire sites, 173, 306–7; *Glonium*, 99; jelly fungi, 184–5, 311–12; in rotting/decaying wood, 40, 111, 269–79, 312, 314 *see also* rotters

Sardinia, 55, 103

Savernake Forest, 106

Scarlet Caterpillar Club (*Cordyceps militaris*), 69

Scarlet Elf Cup (*Sarcoscypha austriaca*), 181–2, 185

Scarlet Waxcap (*Hygrocybe coccinea*), 219, 225

Schaeffer, Jacob, 141

Schizothecium tetrasporum, 257

Scleroderma citrinum, 124

Scleroderma polyrhizum, 318

Scotland, 87–8, 206, 211, 212, 223

Scurfy Twiglet (*Tubaria furfuracea*), 82

Second World War, 77–8, 267

Serpula himantioides, 266

Shaggy Inkcap (*Coprinus comatus*), 115–16

Sheldrake, Merlin, 24

Shiitake (*Lentinula edodes*), 207

Shiplake Church (Oxfordshire), 129–33

Silky Piggyback (*Asterophora. parasitica*), 164, 167

Silky Rosegill (*Volvariella bombycina*), 279–80

Simard, Suzanne, 95

slime moulds, 311

slugs, 14, 214, 304

smells/odours/scents, 8, 51–61, 62–3, 80; author's anosmia, 61–3; chemistry of scent molecules, 50, 58, 60; disgusting/offensive, 59–60, 80, 149–51, 152, 153, 154–5, 158; human experience of, 49–51; as prompt for insects, 50; of truffles, 49, 101–2, 104–5, 107–8; used for fungus identification, 28, 49, 50–1, 52, 56–60, 61–3, 85, 88, 89

Smoky Spindle (*Clavaria fumosa*), 220

Snakeskin Grisette (*Amanita ceciliae*), 240

Snowy Inkcap (*Coprinopsis nivea*), 259

Soapy Knight (*Tricholoma saponaceum*), 61, 88

Sotterley Hall (Suffolk), 234–5

South Africa, 117

South Downs (Sussex), 173, 196–7

Sowerby, James, 77

Spain, 102

'species jumping' notions, 265–6

Spiny Puffball (*Lycoperdon echinatum*), 123

Spiral Tarcrust (*Eutypa spinosa*), 185–6

Split Porecrust (*Schizopora paradoxa*), 270–1

Splitgill (*Schizophyllum commune*), 272

Spooner, Brian, 20*

Spotted Blewit (*Lepista panaeolus*), 27

Squamanita schreieri, 167–8

squirrels, grey, 101

St George's Mushroom (*Calocybe gambosa*), 51–3, 55, 62

Stapelia (succulent plant), 158

Starfish Fungus (*Aseroe rubra*), 157, 310

Stinking Brittlegill (*Russula foetens*), 59

Stinking Dapperling, (*Lepiota cristata*), 60

stipitate hydnoids, 318

Striated Bird's Nest (*Cyathus striatus*), 134, 135

Striated Earthstar (*Geastrum striatum*), 128

Stump Puffball (*Apioperdon pyriforme*), 120, 243

Suffolk, 59, 110–11, 113, 125, 164–6, 184, 234–5

Sulphur Knight (*Tricholoma sulphureum*), 41, 51, 63, 88

Sumatra, 157–8

Summer Bolete (*Boletus reticulatus*), 8

Summer Truffle (*Tuber aestivum*), 105–7

Sweet Woodruff (herb), 58

Switzerland, 43, 306

Tanguy, Yves, 190

Tasmania, 69, 156

taxonomy/naming/classification: and 'anamorph' phase, 192; Ascomycete group, 31–4; Basidiomycete group, 30–3; as changing with advances in knowledge, 47, 70, 117–18, 139, 142–5, 146–7, 194–5, 202–3, 310; common names, 10–11, 32, 112, 145–7, 155, 184–5; compiling/storing of species lists, 319; confusion over brittlegills, 85; disappearing names, 147; division between ascos and basidios, 30–3; first fungi to be described, 152–3; Gasteromycetes ('stomach fungi'), 117–18; genus as evolutionary entity, 142–3; hierarchies, 312; history of mycology as science, 139–41; Latin or Greek roots, 21, 86, 88, 108, 138–9, 143–5, 149, 166, 238; Linnean binomial system, 139, 140–1, 145, 147, 261; and mushroom-toadstool distinction, 20–1; number of species, 19, 20, 29, 136–7, 147–8, 204; restriction on changing of names, 185; role of Fries, 139, 140–2; rotters as significant, 271–2; scientific names for species, 11, 137–9, 140–5, 185;

stabilising of common names, 146–7; tool of molecular/DNA sequencing, 29, 70, 90†, 90, 99, 108, 116, 118, 125, 132, 144–5, 168–9, 178, 203, 276; traditional English names, 10, 11, 145–7; vast importance of, 137; of webcaps (*Cortinarius*), 89, 98

Tennyson, Alfred, 96

Thailand, 156

toadstools: distinction from mushrooms, 20–1; some as toxic, 18, 20

Toothed Crust (*Basidioradulum radula*), 40, 44

Tortelli, Mario, 89–90, 90*

Tragedy of the Commons, 73

Trametes suaveolens, 58

trees: alder, 87; and anthropomorphic notions, 94–7, 108; ash dieback, 172, 193–6; birch, 59, 82, 84, 86–7, 124–5, 232, 233, 239, 251, 260; box trees (*Buxus sempervirens*), 126–9; cedar, 130; cherry, 37–48; chestnut, 5, 17, 35–6, 316–20; conifer, 59, 60, 87, 98, 135, 230, 265, 266, 311; Dutch elm disease, 110, 196–7; eucalypts, 64, 65; hawthorn, 251; hazel (*Corylus*), 86, 102, 105, 107–8, 187; larch, 84; mycorrhiza as essential for healthy growth, 91; pine, 8, 84, 166, 177; threat from Honey Fungus, 78–9; traditional method of ageing, 231; willow, 36, 87, 181, 232, 251; wych elm, 197; yew, 41–2, 112 *see also* beech trees; forests/woodland; oak trees; rotting/decaying wood; wood

Tremella mesenterica, 184
Trichoderma delicatula, 189
The Truffle Hunters (film, 2020),
    103–4
truffles, 99–108; species of, 12,
    99–101, 102, 103, 104–8; truffle
    hounds/pigs, 49, 103, 105, 106
Tulasne brothers, 29, 189, 189–91,
    193
Tulosesus pellucidus, 254
Turkey Tail (Trametes versicolor), 237,
    275–6, 293, 299–301

Umbrella Polypore (Polyporus umbel-
    latus), 134, 305
United States, 24–5, 76, 77, 112–16,
    117, 176
Uppsala, University of, 140

Ventnor Botanical Garden, 13
Vittadini, Carlo, 141

Wakefield, E.M., 143–4, 160
Wales, 311
Warlock's Butter (Exidia nigricans),
    184
Weather Earthstar (Geastrum
    corollinum), 128, 129
White Saddle (Helvella crispa), 175,
    176
White Spindle (Clavaria fragilis), 220
White Truffle of Italy (Tuber
    magnatum), 101, 104–5

Whitelaced Shank (Megacollybia
    platyphylla), 276, 298
Windsor Great Park, 228, 231, 233
Winter Agaric (Flammulina velutipes),
    183
winter fungi, 183–8, 198–200
Witches' Butter (Exidia glandulosa),
    184
Wohlleben, Peter, 95
wood: cellulose/sugars in, 38–9,
    44–5, 207, 236, 266, 267–8, 268*,
    269–70, 272–3; cherry, 38, 39–41,
    42–8; commercial uses of, 37,
    126–7; glowing/shining, 75, 77–8;
    structural components of, 267–8,
    269, 273 see also rotting/decaying
    wood
Wood Blewit (Lepista nuda), 318
Woodward, Thomas, 113

Xerula pudens, 144

Yeats, W.B., 91
Yellow Brain (Tremella mesenterica),
    184
Yellow Morel (Morchella esculenta),
    172–3, 174
Yorkshire, 311, 312

Zombie Ant Fungus (Ophiocordyceps
    unilateralis), 70–1
Zoned Rosette (Podoscypha multizo-
    nata), 241